The Garden in Autumn and Winter

The Garden in Autumn and Winter

Raymond Foster

DAVID & CHARLES
Newton Abbot   London   North Pomfret (Vt)

All photographs by Michael Warren

British Library Cataloguing in Publication Data

Foster, Raymond
   The garden in autumn and winter.
   1. Gardens – Great Britain   2. Autumn
   gardening   3. Winter gardening
·   I. Title
   635.9′53   SB406

   ISBN 0–7153–8416–3

Filmset in Monophoto Times New Roman
by Latimer Trend & Company Ltd, Plymouth
and printed in Great Britain
by Butler & Tanner Ltd, Frome and London
for David & Charles (Publishers) Limited
Brunel House   Newton Abbot   Devon

Published in the United States of America
by David & Charles Inc
North Pomfret   Vermont 05053   USA

Contents

1
Planning and Planting

Planning a garden with autumn and winter in mind can, in its simplest form, involve little more than the thoughtful inclusion of a winter-flowering jasmine or an evergreen bush; more interestingly, in gardens of all sizes it can include a living framework that will be both beautiful and functional throughout the year – the basic skeleton to which the floral trappings of spring and summer can be added. Such a framework will be real and tangible, creating a solid bastion of foliage and flower in spring and summer, a brief show of brilliance in autumn, and a continuing source of interest, colour, fragrance and shelter in winter.

In a large garden, if the site is particularly exposed, this framework needs to be substantial enough to provide positive permanent shelter against the worst of the elements. In small gardens, though it may not be practicable to provide a shelter-belt as such, the autumn and winter theme can still be very much an intrinsic part of the design, unsuspected during the growing season, becoming obvious only when the last of the summer flowers have faded.

A well-planned garden, whether the planner has winter in mind or not, always takes due account of its surroundings. Quite often, a neighbouring eyesore needs to be camouflaged; conversely, a particularly beautiful view might be not only retained but also accented by planting trees and shrubs carefully chosen to frame the vista and lead the eye in the desired direction. Whether a new garden is to be large or small, a plan, however roughly drawn, is always useful in the initial stages. The local topography and aspect are of particular significance: firstly, because adequate protection should be provided where necessary when the site is open to prevailing winter winds; secondly, in taking account of sun and shade, the lack of sunlight limits the range of plants which can be used; and thirdly, the required visual effect must be achieved.

If appropriate, the planting plan should show the approximate extent of complete winter shadow in the garden so that suitable plants can be chosen and their sites allocated. In plots which offer a choice of north- and south-facing aspects, as seen from the house, plants which are at their best in sunlight will find an ideal site at some distance to the north, clear of the maximum winter shadow. Shrubs with brightly coloured bark, and other plants of particular interest in the winter, such as heathers, always look most attractive when illuminated by the sun, however weak its rays, and need to remain unshadowed if they are to do well. On the other hand, colourful vistas can often be seen just as well through a thin tracery of deciduous twigs, without the view being spoiled. In this way, provided they are sited in full sunlight, coppiced plants which are not particularly interesting in summer, such as the scarlet willow or the red-barked dogwood, can be so placed that they are screened by summer- or spring-flowering deciduous shrubs which allow them to be seen clearly only when they are at their best. Heaths and heathers, which have continuous year-round beauty, should occupy a sunny site which remains fully in view at all seasons.

Vistas are normally designed to be seen from the everyday viewpoint of the house, and if nobody walks down the garden during the winter months there is little point in arranging special effects which can only be seen from within the garden itself. So there should always be an uncluttered field of view towards areas of year-round interest which need full sunlight – such as a bank of heathers – whilst a group of deciduous ornamental shrubs or tall-stemmed herbaceous plants, either transparent or cut back for the winter, is often best sited as a screen to add to the summer effect of coppiced plants included mainly for the colour of their bark after leaf-fall.

Thoughtful planning and planting can go a long way towards keeping winter's rigours at bay. Severe frost damage to plants occurs

Plants grown chiefly for the colour of their bark should be sited beyond the area of maximum winter shade (a), or where they are able to reach the sunshine (b)

chiefly in spring, usually when a very sudden drop in temperature causes water inside the plant cells to freeze and rupture the cell walls; many plants can however tolerate slow freezing. Damage may also be caused by too rapid a thaw, when internal water cannot be absorbed quickly enough by the plant tissues, and the cells become waterlogged so that parts of the plant are unable to breathe – this condition often occurs on east-facing sites which tend to be warmed too quickly on cold mornings by the rising sun.

Little can be done to prevent damage by overall blanket frosts experienced during really severe winters. Long freezes can result in the deaths of many normally hardy plants – conifers such as some of the cypresses; evergreens such as eucalyptus, pyracantha, even mahonia and laurel; and many herbaceous subjects. Protracted spells of heavy air frost can be fatal, but many evergreens are killed during the winter not by the air temperature but by the inability of their roots to absorb moisture from frozen soil. A protective mantle of ground-covering plants, and on bare ground deep-mulching with leaf mould or garden compost, normally prevents the soil freezing.

The radiation frosts that occur in Britain more frequently than the Arctic type of blanket frost are usually of short duration and easier to take precautions against. They normally occur at night following a clear, sunny day during which the soil has been warmed by the sun while the atmosphere has remained comparatively cool. As the sun sets, soil and vegetation rapidly lose heat into the air, which rises, forcing cooler air to take its place. An overhead layer of cloud will act as a barrier to prevent the warm air rising, and a similar effect can be achieved with a canopy of tree branches – even thin, deciduous twigs – acting as a blanket and holding the warmed layer of air sufficiently to prevent severe frost. In this way, valuable protection can be given to winter-flowering, shade-tolerant shrubs such as some of the earliest rhododendrons which flower in January and February, or the camellias which are often in bloom intermittently at any time between autumn and spring.

Cold air, if no warmer than the atmosphere above it, tends to sink and run downhill like water, chilling all in its path, so that gardens situated in a hollow of whatever size are often inescapably frost-bound – sometimes subjected to a deep layer of frosty air that limits one's choice of plants to the hardiest kinds, and to those which break into growth comparatively late in the spring. Gardens sited on a slope escape much frost of this type, and can often be designed so as to assist the smooth downhill flow of cold air by avoiding the creation of unnecessary frost pockets, taking care not to allow obstructions such as walls or hedges, or continuous clumps running across the slope, for these can easily act as reservoirs of freezing air and threaten damage to the plants growing above them. A local frost-hollow can sometimes be remedied by opening a gap in a wall or hedge, allowing the cold air to drain freely away.

A gradual, uniform drop in temperature as winter approaches does least damage to plant life, even if it falls well below freezing point; the worst damage in the autumn often occurs when a spell of unusually mild weather is followed by a sudden, severe chill. When an abrupt change of this type is expected overnight, it is sometimes useful to provide temporary shelter for those plants most at risk. Polythene, hessian, or even newspaper may be used, tied loosely over shrubs, in particular the winter flowerers already carrying buds or bloom. Particularly tender subjects, especially deciduous plants not normally expected to survive cold-temperate winters outdoors, can be given semi-permanent winter shelter with frames made of stakes and wire netting, using sacking, straw or bracken to trap an insulating pocket of air. Semi-hardy trees can sometimes be lagged with sacking, jacketing them from the base of the stem into the lower branches so that, even if the top branches are killed over winter, the crotch of the crown will survive as a base upon which to rebuild the framework.

Appropriate siting can go a long way towards protecting a plant over winter. Plants of Mediterranean type, such as the winter-flowering *Iris unguicularis*, give best results if the summer is hot and dry and the winter cool with a modicum of rain and, whilst the climate cannot be altered, these conditions can be simulated in the open garden. In Britain, for instance, the plants can be given a site near a south-facing wall which collects and retains as much warmth as possible, and the soil should be similar to that of their natural habitat – gritty, preferably with a little lime, not too rich in humus, and very well drained so that it is unlikely to freeze. And to ensure a frost-free soil for the roots of shrubs and bulbs, these areas can be blanketed with low-growing, shallow-rooted plants which either remain evergreen or retain their dead leaves over winter. For instance the creeping knotgrass, *Polygonum affine*, which looks very attractive at this season with its thick mat of bronzy leaves, can act as an insurance both against mechanical damage by frost and the harmful desiccating effect of frozen roots on evergreens.

Gardens wide open to prevailing winds are very often shielded by a shelter-belt of thickly foliaged evergreens; but this type of protection can cause more trouble than it prevents, for solid,

The effect on air currents of a solid evergreen barrier some 3m (10ft) high. The convolutions represent an area of turbulence where damage is liable to occur in the garden, while the truly sheltered zone is comparatively small

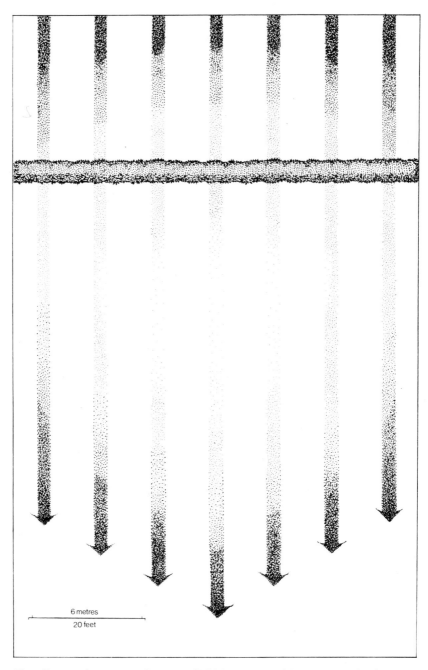

6 metres

20 feet

The effect on air currents of a 3m (10ft) high, partly deciduous screen that is 50 per cent permeable to the wind. Filtering shrubs strategically placed at the point where the wind starts to regain its speed will extend the sheltered area

impenetrable barriers frequently result in severe turbulence of the air currents to their lee. As the wind approaches a solid barrier it rises, leaving a comparatively sheltered zone in front of the obstruction – a useful pocket of undisturbed air that may extend as far back as twice or even three times the height of the barrier. But on the leeward side a semi-vacuum is formed by the overhead current, causing a powerful draught as the air is drawn upwards; this strikes the main flow and is forced back in an erratic circle, resulting in considerable turbulence over an area that may extend to nearly ten times the height of the barrier. The narrower the belt in proportion to its height, the greater the turbulence is liable to be. At each end of the shelter-belt and immediately above it there will be something like a 10 per cent increase in wind speed as the currents are deflected and funnelled, and this too can cause quite unforeseen results in the garden – or, indeed, in neighbouring gardens.

The ideal windbreak should act as a filter that slows down the wind speed without causing undue turbulence, and to do this it needs to be solid over only about 50 per cent of its surface. If a shelter-belt is doing its job efficiently as a filter, its beneficial effect can be felt at a distance equivalent to about thirty times the height of the belt. The maximum degree of shelter will occur at a distance to the lee about three times the height of the filter, at which point the wind speed will be only about one-quarter of its unfiltered speed.

In small gardens open to the wind, a balanced mixture of deciduous and evergreen shrubs will usually do the best job of protection, and in large gardens a series of baffles, or groups of tall shrubs in a coherent design planned with shelter in mind, is far more efficient than the solid screen of Leyland cypress which has often been the choice in the past. Initial planting for shelter is rather a long-term project; but it is possible to convert an existing solid barrier to a filtering screen and, in coastal or other windy districts, the resultant improvement in the quality of shelter will be impressive. Thinning an existing belt of Leyland cypress by removing alternate trees has the unfortunate effect of funnelling the wind, resulting in an increase in wind speed, plus an unknown degree of turbulence. Such belts can be thinned unevenly, however, and the remaining stems made to form the basis of mixed groups. A few of the conifers, if well developed, can be stem-pruned to a height of 1.5–2m (5–6ft), and deciduous shrubs and small evergreens introduced around them. Others can be topped, and kept trimmed to a height comparable with the other shrubs, and in balance with the designed groups.

If the garden is large enough to stand the root competition of such greedy trees, some of the willows can be used as rapidly grown deciduous filters. And the various types of scarlet and yellow-barked willows, though marginally less colourful for being freely grown as shrubs and standard trees rather than coppiced bushes, will still be very ornamental, and rank amongst the most beautiful of trees in winter when the sun shines through their twigs.

Shapely small deciduous trees with distinctive crown silhouettes which, though devoid of leaves or flowers, really add to the winter garden scene, include several of the hybrid cherries such as the amazingly perpendicular 'Lombardy poplar cherry', *Prunus* Amanogawa, which may eventually reach a height of some 8m (26ft); the contrastingly weeping *P.* Kiku-shidare Sakura, which seldom exceeds 3m (10ft), goes well with it and looks especially fine with a drift of winter aconites beneath its skirts; and the upright fan-shaped cherries, such as the vigorous *P.* Kanzan, which grows to a height of 9m (30ft) or so, or the smaller and more delicately proportioned *P.* Asano or *P.* Ito-kukuri, which grow to around 4m (13ft).

Besides *P.* Amanogawa, deciduous trees which have crowns slender enough to give pyramidal silhouettes in the winter include some of the maples, particularly *Acer macrophyllum* Seattle Sentinel, *A. rubrum* Scanlon, and *A. saccharum* Temple's Upright, all of which grow to a height in the region of 7–10m (23–33ft). Other remarkably upright deciduous trees include the Dawyck beech and its much smaller coloured summer-leaf varieties *Fagus sylvatica* Purple Dawyck and Golden Dawyck, neither of which should greatly exceed 10m (33ft); the upright common laburnum, *Laburnum anagyroides* Erect, at about 7m (23ft) tall; and the hybrid mountain ash or rowan trees *Sorbus* Embley and *S.* Ethel's Gold, which should attain a height of 6–7m (20–23ft).

Small deciduous trees with particularly rounded silhouettes to provide an ornamental filtering screen in the winter might include the hawthorns, in particular *Crataegus laevigata* Paul's Scarlet, *C. coccinioides*, *C. intricata*, *C.* × *lavallei* and *C. tomentosa*, all of which attain around 3–5m (10–16ft); the crabapple hybrids *Malus* Katherine and *M.* Wintergold, at about 4.5m (15ft); the dark-leaved cherry-plums *Prunus cerasifera* Nigra and Pissardii, the apricot-plum *P. simonii*, and the hybrid flowering cherry *P.* Snowgoose, all about 5m (16ft) high.

Deciduous trees with strongly weeping silhouettes include Young's weeping birch, *Betula pendula* Youngii, eventually about 8m (26ft) tall; the weeping Scotch laburnum, *Laburnum alpinum*

Pendulum, which is usually only about 2.5m (8ft) tall; the weeping mulberry *Morus alba* Pendula at about 3m (10ft); the flowering crabapples *Malus* Echtermeyer, *M*. Elise Rathke, *M*. Exzellenz Thiel, and *M*. Red Jade, all 3–4m (10–13ft) high; several flowering-cherry hybrids, besides the popular *Prunus* Kiku-shidare Sakura already mentioned, including *P*. Cheal's Weeping Cherry and *P*. Hilling's Weeping Cherry, at about 3m (10ft) high, and *P*. Pink Shell and *P*. Shidare Yoshino at about 4.5m (15ft); the rather untidy weeping willow-leaved pear, *Pyrus salicifolia* Pendula, at a height of about 4m (13ft); and the weeping goat-willow, *Salix caprea* Kilmarnock at 3m (10ft).

Grouped with evergreen trees and shrubs, berry-bearers and winter flowerers, symmetrical little trees such as these can be used as living sculpture in the garden to mould shapes both beautiful and useful. The most symmetrical deciduous crowns are often rather too dense to see through clearly, and when trees are being chosen as a summer screen to the forefront of a winter vista of coloured bark, the more loosely branched kinds are needed. Many of the rowans and whitebeams, most of the maples, the willows, some of the prunus family, laburnum, rhus, cotinus and the birches are ideal.

An effective shelter-belt can be ornamental as well as functional, and a series of staggered groups – quite as efficient in terms of filtering the force of the wind – will have none of the artificial appearance of a regular belt, and if required to double as a camouflaging screen will do so far less obtrusively. Internal clumps of tall plants will affect the wind flow in the same way as a main shelter-belt, and this is particularly true at the side of a house where a nearby building, fence, or line of tall plants can cause an increase in wind speed by creating a funnelling effect. Solid barriers in a wind funnel such as this are certain to cause turbulence, but a series of filtering screens of varied height and composition baffle the force of the wind most effectively. Diverse groups of this type not only add to the garden scene, they also increase greatly the range of plants that can be grown successfully on an otherwise difficult site, and are themselves able to provide continuing beauty of leaf, flower, berry and stem.

2
Autumn and Winter Flowers

Many of the late summer-flowering shrubs remain in bloom well into autumn, and a mild season encourages several autumn flowerers to continue supplying colour, often until the New Year. One such is the magnificent climbing magnolia, *Magnolia grandiflora*, its enormous ivory flowers spectacular in the autumn, even though they tend to appear only one or two at a time. In their homelands of the southern USA they open in June and reach their peak during high summer, but in Britain they are often at their best for September or even later. In its late-flowering habit this evergreen shrub contrasts surprisingly with the many deciduous spring-flowering magnolias, some of which, like the Himalayan pink tulip tree *M. campbellii*, qualify as winter flowerers by virtue of the earliness of their season. Notable among summer-flowering shrubs, the South American eucryphias, with their conspicuous yellow-stamened white flowers, sometimes also maintain their display for the autumn, especially the evergreen hybrids *Eucryphia × nymansensis* Nymansay and the double-flowered Irish cultivar Mount Usher, both of which may be seen in full flower in Ireland during September, and in Scotland too when the weather remains mild. Their beautiful deciduous parent *E. glutinosa* flowers earlier as a rule, but during mild seasons this too continues into autumn, and when the weather changes abruptly carries its numerous flowers almost until the first autumn tints appear in the foliage.

One or two subjects which typically flower in spring produce a supplementary crop in autumn, such as the normally May and June flowering *Laburnum anagyroides* Autumnale, which usually manages to display a second flush of golden-rain flowers in September. Others simply provide an extra-long flowering season, for example the many varieties of *Potentilla fruticosa* and other species and hybrids of the shrubby cinquefoil, which may still be flowering in December. One of the most attractive of these is *Potentilla* Elizabeth, with its sage-green dome of soft foliage well covered from spring at least until early autumn with flowers of a warm canary-yellow. A good planting companion for Elizabeth, its brilliant blue flowers contributing a classical blend of colours, is the shrubby plumbago, *Ceratostigma willmottianum*, which also remains in flower until autumn, though its first buds seldom open before midsummer. Other habitually long-flowering small shrubs include the hypericums or shrubby St John's worts, especially perhaps the hybrid *Hypericum* Hidcote, which is often still covered in October with its comparatively enormous blooms of glossy buttercup-yellow. Similarly coloured flowers adorn the autumn cassia, *Cassia corymbosa* – a large shrub suitable only for mild areas, or to provide a cascade of clear bright yellow in the conservatory from late summer at least until the first spell of cold weather.

Among medium-sized shrubs, hibiscuses sometimes flower late, the many clones of the shrubby mallow *Hibiscus syriacus* – known in America as the rose of Sharon – providing colour until October unless frost intervenes. The more tender *H. sinosyriacus* is normally autumn flowering; given a sheltered niche, its white and purple flowers sometimes persist until the first leaves begin to fall. In a similar category, the Asian *Clerodendrum trichotomum* – which incidentally can be grown to good effect as a small standard tree instead of an upright shrub – could also qualify as an autumn flowerer, though it is featured (see pp188–9) as an autumn-berrying subject. Its sweetly scented white flowers, each set in a contrasting red calyx, appear fairly late in the summer, then change into the fascinating blue berries.

Many modern hybrid roses produce belated flowers in autumn, often giving a somewhat blemished display until Christmas or so, the flowers thus outlasting the leaves by a month or more. Only a few wild or shrub roses behave like this. Among those that do tend to flower late, *Rosa moschata*, the musk rose, is seldom seen today, although as a parent of many hybrids it once provided a favourite garden feature with its vigorous, drooping growth and dark-green glossy leaves. The large clusters of heavily musk-scented creamy-white flowers appear late in summer and persist well into autumn. *Rosa nitida*, which makes excellent ground cover and displays vivid autumn foliage tints of crimson-orange and purple (see p98), also produces its large pink flowers fairly late in the summer. They frequently last until the leaves are on the point of turning colour, when showy scarlet hips take over the display.

A few shrubs retain their dried flowers attractively through the autumn and into winter – for example, some of the hydrangeas. Quite apart from the truly late-flowering *Hydrangea strigosa* (see p54), several of the common hortensia varieties keep their dead but still colourful flowerheads until late winter, the pinks, reds or blues often darkening or fading to a uniform shade of greenish purple. Those rather less formal shrubs of the woodland garden type, *Hydrangea serrata* Bluebird and Grayswood, both retain their more subtle colours until early winter, especially if they have a partially shaded site. The largest-flowering hydrangeas, such as *H. paniculata* Grandiflora, prefer a more open, sunny site where they create a particularly impressive display in early autumn. But their large, soft flowerheads tend to break up with the onset of winter's rough weather, so you lose both their attraction as dried flowers and the potential frost protection they might have given to over-wintering buds, as happens with the sturdier species with more persistent florets.

During the British October, whilst the late Michaelmas daisies are still at their best, the tardiest agapanthus also remain in flower and provide a glorious blend of colours when associated with the late-flowering yellow kniphofias. Some species of the blue African lily are habitually late to flower, such as the broad-leaved *Agapanthus caulescens*, whose deep-blue flowers open in September.

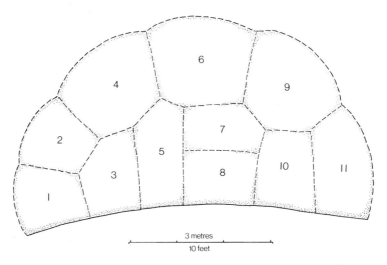

3 metres

10 feet

A mixed border planned to carry colour into the autumn, with the accent on yellow and blue:

1 *Ceratostigma willmottianum;*
2 *Coronilla glauca;*
3 *Perovskia atriplicifolia;*
4 *Hypericum* Hidcote;
5 *Elsholtzia stauntonii;*
6 *Mahonia* Charity;
7 *Kniphofia,* a late yellow variety;
8 *Aster spectabilis;*
9 *Hypericum forrestii;*
10 *Agapanthus,* hardy hybrids;
11 *Caryopteris × clandonensis* Arthur Simmonds

But the wide range of agapanthus hybrids contains the hardiest plants which produce the best show of flowers, often lasting until late October, and survive temperate winters outdoors if given a generous mulch of leaf mould before the worst frosts.

Amongst the truly winter-flowering plants some, like the witch hazels, are perfectly hardy and produce blossom whatever the weather. Others, like the winter-flowering iris which is native to parts of North Africa within the zone of Mediterranean influence, rely on a warm summer to ripen their subterranean growth, and will only give their best performance in a mild winter. When planted in Britain, *Iris unguicularis* really needs a sheltered position beneath a south-facing wall to ensure both winter protection and summer warmth (see pp52–4).

Native to temperate deciduous woodlands, and often flowering during winter and early spring as if to take advantage of the absence of overhead shade, the hellebores are quite hardy, and appreciate a cool, shady spot and a sticky, limy soil – as do many other winter-flowering woodland plants, such as snowdrops, aconites and *Daphne mezereum.* To simulate the heavy annual leaf-fall of their natural habitat, mulching after flowering is finished with leaf mould or well-rotted manure is a good practice. The rosy-purple *Helleborus atrorubens* and the pure white Christmas rose or black hellebore, *H. niger* – with its beautiful forms *angustifolius, maximus*, the tall and very early flowering *altifolius*, and Potter's Wheel which has the largest flowers tinted pinkish-purple on the petal reverse – flower more or less from Christmas until early spring, and revel in these woodland conditions. The comparatively tall Lenten rose, *H. orientalis*, a well-known and much-hybridised garden plant with flowers ranging from white with tints of green through shades of pink to wine-purple, is usually slightly later than the Christmas rose to flower, normally opening in January and producing a succession of bloom over a three-month period. The Lenten rose varieties tend to be easier to please than the Christmas rose itself: any type of soil will suit them, and their site need not necessarily be shady, though a sloping bed facing direct sunshine or the reflected heat of a south-facing wall may prove too warm and dry for them. Other winter-flowering hellebores include *H. lividus corsicus*, with glaucous, spiny evergreen foliage and large clusters of greenish-yellow flowers; the similar and closely related hybrid *H. × sternii*; and *H. abchasicus* which has large pink flowers speckled with purple, opening late in the winter and lasting into spring. The British natives too are winter-flowering, such as *H. foetidus*, the

Native to temperate deciduous woodlands, the hellebores take advantage of the absence of overhead shade by producing their flowers during the winter. They are easy to please and will grow in most soils

stinking hellebore, which occurs naturally in chalky soils and has dark evergreen leaves deeply cut almost like those of a fern. Its green flowers, stained with purple, open in late winter and last into spring. The smaller *H. viridis*, the green hellebore, usually opens its nodding green flowers in February. A rare wild plant of shady British beechwoods, it too prefers a calcareous soil, and does well in chalk.

Another category of winter flowerers produces often sweetly scented but inconspicuous flowers, typified by the wintersweet, *Chimonanthus praecox*, a sprawling deciduous plant. It may readily be trained as a wall climber and can act as nurse for some other climbing plant, perhaps a tender evergreen, or a summer-flowering species, or one with beautiful but scentless winter flowers – two team members combined for mutual protection and support, making the most both of senses and seasons. A small thicket patch or an outhouse wall covered with wintersweet will perfume a whole garden on a still winter's day, and just one cut sprig included in a floral arrangement is enough to scent a room. The variety with brighter yellow flowers, *C. p.* Luteus, is more colourful, and should be used when visual effect is wanted. Both forms of wintersweet usually bloom abundantly, but occasionally a good crop of buds fails to flower – usually due to the depredations of birds. Damage is likely to be less severe when the plant is grown as suggested, with an intermingling climber. Wintersweet tends to become bushy and densely twiggy if left unpruned indefinitely. Before this happens the plants should be thinned out and pruned back in spring, just before the leaves appear, and be given a mulch of leaf mould, garden compost or well-rotted manure.

The deciduous *Petasites japonicus* and its larger and even more impressive variety *P. j. giganteus*, with their enormous, bright-green, umbrella-like leaves on long stalks – which some people are reputed to eat like rhubarb – produce flowers in the winter. The bunches of white daisy-like blooms appear out of the bare stream-side mud during late February and early March, soon to be followed by the new year's leaves. A very invasive plant in moist soils, spread-ing rapidly by means of underground rhizomes, it is best suited to the lakeside or the more spacious type of wild garden. A rather similar wild British plant, *P. hybridus*, known as butterbur or bog rhubarb, flowers later, during early spring. The winter heliotrope, *P. fragrans*, runs coltsfoot-like over the ground to form a carpet a few inches deep, and produces its sweetly vanilla-scented white flowers in February before the leaves appear. Like its larger cousins it is strictly a subject for the wild garden, but is often grown for its fragrance as an indoor pot-plant. Plants of this genus show a re-markably irregular distribution of the sexes. The female plant of the British butterbur seems to be limited to a comparatively small area of north-west England although the male is a common streamside plant, familiar over most of the country. Both the foreign species, and especially the winter heliotrope, have become naturalised in several parts of Britain and elsewhere, yet they seem to be rep-resented entirely by male plants. They compensate for the absence of young seedlings by their ability to reproduce vegetatively and to spread invasively underground.

Amongst the showiest of autumn, winter and early spring flowering shrubs are the camellias and rhododendrons, many of them completely hardy and well adapted to life in sheltered gardens where the soil is moist, acid and rich in humus. Many camellias open a few buds in November, while odd flowers appear sporadically throughout the winter as a foretaste of the main display to come early in the spring. But though both rhododendron and camellia plants and their foliage are often completely hardy and weather-resistant, the flowers are susceptible to damage by heavy frost. Where camellias are concerned, those varieties which shed damaged flowers quickly are more convenient than those which retain their unsightly, frost-browned blooms and need to be dead-headed regularly (see ppl 12–13).

In contrast with the camellias, the early-flowering rhododendrons each mount a concerted display, commencing in January with *Rhododendron mucronulatum*, *R. dauricum* and *R. parvifolium*, all with mauve or magenta flowers, followed at the end of February and early March by the garden hybrid *R*. Praecox in light lilac-pink. Another garden hybrid, *R*. Nobleanum, with rosy-red or sometimes pink or white flowers, is an exception to the generic rule, and sometimes blooms as early as November. Of the truly winter-flowering rhododendrons, perhaps *R. mucronulatum* is the most valuable for garden use, although the small leaves become deciduous if the temperature drops much below freezing. It produces flowers by the hundred, opening miraculously from withered and apparently lifeless brown buds. When the leaves fall and only the unpromising, shrivelled buds are left, the plant is sometimes assumed to have died, early in the winter during spells of severe weather; but by the second week in January the buds are swollen and showing colour, and a week later the whole bush is covered with luminous-sheened magenta in a display that lasts a further three weeks. A sharp frost could spoil the flowers, but precautions can be taken: plants growing in the open can be swathed in newspaper the evening before a heavy frost is expected, or as an alternative, *R. mucronulatum* lends itself readily to culture in a shallow tub – either concrete, wood or plastic is suitable – so that it can be moved around as required for protection and floral display. Its upright habit of growth – it sometimes attains 2m (6ft) or more in height while barely 40cm (16in) wide – is ideally adapted to this, and as a garden resident the bush is suitable for places where there is little ground space but unlimited height, as beneath tall trees.

Woodland shelter helps to reduce the effects of cold wind and severe frost, and is especially appreciated by the tree-like *R. arboreum* from the Himalayan and Indian mountain forests. This species has enormous evergreen leaves – an impressive feature in themselves, with their contrastingly pale tawny-brown undersurfaces. Its numerous densely packed, well-rounded heads of bell-like flowers open in January and last successively well into spring, with several named varieties ranging in flower colour from pure white through shades of pink to scarlet. They appear freely in the early stages, and are liable to be nipped in the opening bud unless their site is well sheltered beneath a light canopy of overhead branches. Another large evergreen shrub suitable for a woodland garden is *R. sutchuenense*, a late-winter flowerer with enormous drooping, glossy-green leaves and waxy bell-like flowers in a pale shade of lilac, speckled with darker purple.

The named rhododendron hybrids are often said to be hardier than the wild species, but this is chiefly because most of the earliest are spring rather than winter flowering. Cultivars such as Tessa in rosy-purple, Bric-á-brac in white and Cilpinense in pink-spotted white (valuable for its habit of flowering while still very young), all open in March. One of the best-known names among the winter flowerers is Christmas Cheer, with frilly pink-budded flowers; but outdoors this hybrid seldom blooms in time for Christmas, and it needs a mild winter to produce good flowers during February.

Hardy shrubs which flower reliably during the winter include the well-known laurustinus, *Viburnum tinus*, always attractive whatever the weather, and excellent as an evergreen hedge; the winter-flowering bush honeysuckles *Lonicera fragrantissima, L. standishii* and the hybrid *L. × purpusii,* all of which bear fragrant cream-coloured flowers prolific enough to cover the upright branches, usually bare of leaves at this season unless the early winter months have been particularly mild; *Skimmia japonica,* with leathery dark evergreen leaves, which actually bears its fragrant white flowers early in spring, though the bushes appear to be in flower during the winter with their clustered red buds; and *Daphne mezereum,* which produces spikes of scented purple flowers from February into early spring, and does best in a shady site shielded from the cold wind. Another is the sweet box or Christmas box, *Sarcococca confusa,* which stands clipping and can be grown as a low evergreen hedge. Its small, sweetly scented white flowers, from the end of January onwards, are followed in succession by the others of its genus – *S. hookerana*, its geographical variety *digyna*, the aptly named Purple Stem, the dwarf *S. humilis*, all with attractive evergreen foliage and fragrant though inconspicuous flowers. *Abelio-* *phyllum distichum,* already covered with tiny purple buds as it loses its leaves in the autumn, blossoms in February, its sweetly scented flowers shaped like those of a forsythia but creamy-white, tinged with a pale brownish-pink. The forsythias themselves are all spring-flowering, although the earliest of these, *Forsythia giraldiana* from China, sometimes produces its pale yellow flowers before the end of February. It is a large shrub with sparse but

graceful stems arching to a height of some 2.5m (8ft). The Korean
F. ovata opens its amber-yellow flowers in early March. Following
the true winter-flowering shrubs closely, these two forsythias associate well with them.

Trees of the genus *Prunus* are mainly spring-flowerers, with a
few precocious species and their varieties coming out in winter.
The best known and among the most reliable are the so-called
autumn cherries, *Prunus subhirtella* Autumnalis with single or semi-
double white flowers, and *P. s.* Autumnalis Rosea with semi-
double flowers of pale pink. In late January or early February,
Father David's peach, *P. davidiana*, comes into bloom as a handsome, upright little tree, with a white-flowered form, Alba, and a
pink one, Rubra. These are followed by an early variety of the
Fuji cherry, *P. incisa* Praecox, a delicate sprinkling of pink-budded
white blossom along its bare branches. Next comes the Manchurian
apricot, *P. mandshurica*, with buds opening dark pink, paling to a
faint blush as the petals expand; then the Chinese peach, *P.
kansuensis*, with gracefully slender, wide-spreading branches and
blossom of palest shell-pink; and last Conradina's cherry, *P.
conradinae*, a small spreading tree with very pale pink flowers. Its
semi-double variety Semiplena and the darker pink form Malifolia,
open their buds a little later. All these are fragrant, but one of the
most strongly scented of the winter-flowering *Prunus* trees is the
Japanese apricot, *P. mume*, with single pink flowers which spread a
powerful fragrance of hyacinths through the garden. It is an attractive, shrubby little tree in winter, even without blossom, with a
loosely spreading habit and slender green twigs. Its double-flowered
garden varieties include Beni-shi-don, which has strongly fragrant,
conspicuous flowers of a rich magenta-carmine; its semi-double
forms include Alboplena with white flowers, and Alphandii with
pink. The Japanese apricot is not as weather-resistant as most of the
genus; it is hardy in southern England at least, but really needs the
protection of a sheltering wall anywhere else. Given this, Beni-shi-
don in particular can prove one of the best small winter-flowering
trees.

Such soft-petalled blossoms are, however, always vulnerable to
the weather; and their displays, though spectacular, are at risk in
any but the mildest of temperate climates. Ranking amongst the
hardiest of all winter flowerers are the enchanting witch hazels,
their long, hard, ribbon-like petals unaffected by the deepest frosts,
and able to waft a faint but pleasant perfume through the garden
on cold, still winter days.

The selection of autumn and winter flowering plants that follows is arranged according to approximate flower colour. It begins, in fact, with the witch hazels.

Yellow

Hamamelis mollis, Chinese witch hazel   Unless trained as a small tree, this species – the witch hazel most often seen in British gardens – develops into a large shrub with many slightly arching stems and spreading branches, forming a fan-shaped silhouette, usually 3m (10ft) and seldom more than 6m (20ft) tall, with large softly downy hazel-like leaves that have rich yellow autumn tints. The flowers, deliciously fragrant and amongst the largest of the witch hazels, open on the bare twigs from Christmas onwards and often last until spring. Beautiful from a distance, intriguing at close quarters, their rich golden-yellow petals are often tinged with red at the base, the filaments and anthers a deep puce-purple. The variety Coombe Wood has slightly larger flowers and the bush is more spreading and noticeably more vigorous than the typical species. The variety Brevipetala has shorter petals, which range in colour from a deep golden-yellow to a light orange, the flowers as a

Hamamelis mollis Pallida. The pale lemon yellow flowers of this witch hazel stand out well on a dull winter's day

rule opening rather later than those of the type. Both these varieties
retain their dead and withered leaves, which cling to the twigs often
until the flowers appear. Goldcrest is a particularly late-flowering
variety with comparatively strongly fragrant flowers of a much
darker shade of golden-yellow, tinged overall with pink – an effect
caused by red pigmentation on the petal reverse, which shows
faintly through the petals and makes the opening buds appear
orange. By contrast, Pallida has pale flowers, but nevertheless their
clear lemon-yellow stands out conspicuously on a dull winter's day
especially when seen against a dark background, for they are comparatively long-petalled and produced in copious clusters on the
bare branches.

H. japonica, Japanese witch hazel A smaller shrub than the
Chinese species, rarely exceeding 4m (13ft) and averaging around
2.5m (8ft) in height, with sweetly but not strongly scented lemon-
yellow flowers which usually appear in late December and last
until February. They too are attractive when seen at close quarters,
brightened with contrasting purple anthers and a tinge of red at the
base of the petals, and beautiful also from a distance but not as a rule
so striking as those of the Chinese witch hazel. The Japanese witch
hazel and its varieties sometimes produce a second flush of flowers
as the leaves open in the spring. The variety Arborea is taller and

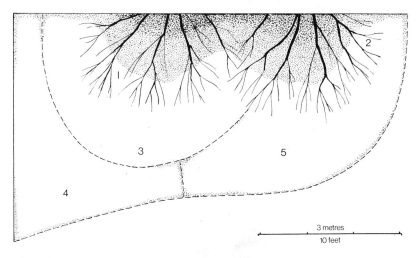

The colour of witch-hazel flowers is intensified by contrasting ground-covering
plants in the foreground:
1 *Hamamelis × intermedia* Jelena;   4 *Erica herbacea* Springwood White;
2 *Hamamelis mollis* Pallida;   5 *Erica herbacea* Vivellii
3 *Erica herbacea* Springwood Pink;

more vigorous than the type. It is gaunt and sparsely twigged with irregularly wide-spreading branches, often clothed in early winter with dead leaves which remain on the twigs after the yellow tints of autumn have faded – a tendency which contributes to its gaunt, ungroomed appearance. This variety produces numerous large clusters of small golden-yellow flowers with deep purple stamens. The yellow petals of the variety Flavo-purpurascens are strongly flushed with purple at their base, lending an overall tinge of reddish-bronze when seen from a distance. The distinctive variety Zuccariniana is usually the last of the witch hazels to bloom, waiting until early spring before opening its pale lemon-yellow petals. The flowers have a strangely crumpled appearance, particularly noticeable before they are fully opened, and when viewed at close quarters they are seen to be tinged green inside the sepals where the other Japanese witch hazel varieties are purple.

H. × intermedia A hybrid between the two common witch hazel species, which sometimes arises spontaneously as a self-sown seedling when both are grown close together. Somewhat variable in habit and characteristics, it normally makes a sizeable, spreading shrub of fairly vigorous growth, with large but poorly scented winter flowers of a light golden-yellow, stained in varying degrees with purple, and usually with purple sepals. There are several garden cultivars of this hybrid one of the best of which is Jelena, with petals of a coppery-bronze, the colour varying slightly from year to year and often appearing orange from a distance. Alternative names are Copper Beauty and Orange Beauty. Jelena is one of the most colourful of the witch hazels in autumn foliage too (see p92), and sometimes betrays its hybrid origin by producing a second crop of densely clustered pure yellow flowers before the leaves open in the spring. Allgold is a variety with clusters of deep yellow flowers, Carmine Red has rather pale bronzy-red ones, Ruby Glow's are very bright coppery-red, and Moonlight has particularly fragrant flowers of a pale sulphur-yellow.

H. vernalis, Ozark witch hazel A suckering shrub from the southern USA, usually between 2m (6ft) and 2.5m (8ft) tall, grown more for its vivid autumn colours (see p99) than for its flowers. These are a rather dull yellow, sometimes tinted with bronze or red, and produced between December and February. Less conspicuous than those of the other species their scent, though faint, is pleasant enough at close quarters on sunny winter days.

The variety of Ozark witch hazel best suited for British gardens is Sandra, cultivated chiefly for its vivid autumn foliage tints.

H. virginiana, American witch hazel   A small tree or large shrub around 4m (13ft) tall, and the source of medicinal witch hazel. An autumn flowerer, the bright lemon-yellow petals open in September and last until early November, fading before the leaves fall. Though fragrant and quite attractive they often escape notice, being masked by the leaves.

Sycopsis sinensis   An evergreen Chinese relative of the witch hazels with somewhat similar yellow flowers. These lack true petals, but are composed of clusters of orangy-yellow stamens and reddish-yellow anthers, surrounded by contrasting dark brown scales. They open in February and last until early spring among the pointed, glossy, leathery leaves. A fairly large, spreading shrub which, like the witch hazels, can be trained to make a small standard tree.

Azara microphylla   A large graceful South American evergreen shrub, in northern climes best grown on a south-facing wall. It has slender, easily trained semi-pendant shoots; and the heavily vanilla-scented yellow flowers open in February and last well into spring, clustered amongst dark, glossy finely divided leaves.

A. integrifolia   A tall South American evergreen shrub, like *A. microphylla* suitable for training against a warm wall. It has glossy green leaves and clusters of chrome-yellow, purple-sepalled flowers, conspicuous during late winter and early spring.

A. petiolaris   This Chilean shrub is probably the least hardy of the three, and really needs the protection of a sunny wall where it will reach about 3m (10ft) – only half the height of the others. The comparatively large evergreen leaves are dark glossy green above and pale beneath, and the small, fragrant, creamy-yellow flowers are produced in February and last until early spring.

Mahonia aquifolium, Oregon grape   A very useful North American evergreen shade-bearing shrub which will thrive in quite poor, dry soil (see p115). The bright mustardy-yellow flowers are carried in long clusters near ground level during winter and very early spring.

M. japonica   This handsome and hardy Japanese shrub has dark glossy-green holly-like leaves, and fragrant pale primrose-yellow flowers in long narrow clusters, whorled and often drooping in a spreading rosette, each flowering spray some 30cm (1ft) in length. In mild seasons they open as early as November, but are usually at their best during February and March.

M. bealei   A Chinese shrub similar to *M. japonica*, but with shorter and more stiffly erect lemon-yellow flower clusters, appearing as a rule during early spring rather than winter.

M. lomariifolia   As its specific name implies, this Chinese shrub has foliage reminiscent of a fern in its symmetrical arrangement, the stiff and spiny but graceful evergreen leaves divided into numerous small leathery leaflets. The flowers, a deep rich yellow, usually appear in November, crowded into erect, tightly packed clusters about 30cm (1ft) long. It is a fairly tender plant which appreciates a warm spot in the garden.

M. **Charity**   One of the best mahonias for flowering performance in the British Isles. The fragrant, rich lemon-yellow flowers often display throughout autumn and winter from October to April arranged in tightly packed, erect clusters crowning symmetrical whorls of evergreen foliage consisting of long compound leaves with bright-green holly-like leaflets. A magnificent shrub for planting beneath tall trees, and a valuable architectural feature in garden design. (For further information on the mahonias, see p114.)

Hypericum forrestii   One of the deciduous St John's worts, this neatly compact Chinese shrub, usually about 30cm (1ft) tall, is covered profusely with rich golden-yellow flowers, opening late in the summer and lasting well into autumn.

H. **Hidcote**   A very handsome hybrid hypericum which often retains its leaves during mild winters. It makes a neat dome reaching around 1.5m (5ft) high, broadening eventually to as much as 2m (6ft) across, profusely covered from midsummer until mid-autumn with broadly cupped flowers in a rich shade of buttercup-yellow – probably the largest and showiest flowers of the genus.

H. augustinii   A small, densely foliaged Chinese shrub with leathery deciduous leaves on arching shoots, tipped in the autumn with clusters of golden-yellow 5cm (2in) flowers.

Jasminum nudiflorum, winter jasmine   Perhaps the best known of all winter-flowering plants, this Chinese sprawler can become an untidy tangle of twigs if neglected. Unless used as ground cover at the base of small trees – in which case the flowering shoots can be clipped over after they wither – it needs thoughtful pruning and training in the early spring, after flowering is over, to ensure a good display of the cheerful yellow flowers which can wreathe the naked green twigs from autumn until February. When trained on a wall, this hardy tolerant shrub will reach a height of some 4.5m (15ft).

Coronilla glauca, crown vetch   This southern European bushy shrub of the pea family needs a warm, sunny spot to enable it to thrive. Clusters of bright yellow broom-like flowers are carried above the small blue-bloomed leaves, mainly in spring, though they continue to be produced intermittently throughout summer, autumn and winter. It appreciates conditions as similar as possible to the Mediterranean environment, with a dryish soil and a site which collects reflected warmth from the sun – for instance, the foot of a south-facing wall.

Cornus mas, Cornelian cherry   This large and spreading southern European deciduous shrub, which can be trained if preferred in the form of a small standard tree, bears countless little starry yellow flowers covering the naked twigs in late February.

C. officinalis   Rather like an early-flowering Cornelian cherry but distinguished by its peeling bark, this dogwood species from Japan and Korea similarly makes a large spreading shrub or a small tree, and produces profuse clusters of tiny yellow flowers on the naked branches in early February.

Clematis tangutica   An autumn-flowering clematis species native to China, valued for its very pretty rich yellow lantern-like flowers nodding on long stalks, followed in quick succession by feathery silver seedheads, so that both early seedheads and late flowers are on display at the same time. The display lasts until the first frosts cut back both flowers and foliage. With its finely divided bluish-green leaves, and reliably late-flowering habit, this is one of the best clematis species, suitable for any soil or situation and making an ideal backdrop up to 4.5m (15ft) high, to curtain a wire-netting fence or wall.

Salix aegyptiaca   A large shrub or small tree native to Russia, with densely downy grey twigs, made conspicuous in February and early March with numerous large bright yellow male catkins. Several willow species produce catkins in various shades of buff and yellow during late winter or very early spring.

Buddleia × ***lewisiana*** **Margaret Pike**   This vigorous evergreen shrub is rather tender, but able to grow in the UK if given a sheltered, sunny nook where, during the winter months, it produces soft yellow flowers arising in long, dense clusters from the tips of white woolly wand-like stems. A hybrid between two tropical buddleia species which are definitely tender and need conservatory protection, Margaret Pike will lose its leaves and fail to flower well if subjected to exposed conditions during winter.

Rhododendron lutescens   A fairly tall Chinese woodland rhododendron which, when grown in Britain and comparable climates, needs the shelter of taller surrounding trees, and possibly a light branch-cover high overhead to give some frost protection for the rather sparse but attractive flowers. Typically these are a pale primrose-yellow, but the clone Exbury is an improvement on the type, with brighter lemon-yellow flowers. They are produced from February successively until the spring, when they blend strikingly with the young drooping evergreen leaves, newly opened with a tinge of bronzy-red.

Chimonanthus praecox, wintersweet   An easily grown deciduous Chinese shrub which produces its sweetly fragrant flowers on bare light brown branches in the middle of winter. The pale yellow waxy flowers, centred with a purple stain, though pretty when seen at close quarters are not very conspicuous and, as a wall shrub, wintersweet is at its best when acting as a nurse to another, perhaps less hardy, climbing plant, supplementing evergreen foliage or a scentless flowering display with its winter fragrance. It will reach some 2m (6ft) if planted against a sunny wall, a site which allows the new woody growth to ripen thoroughly during late summer and give the flower buds a chance to develop properly. It is often regarded as being shy to flower, and lack of summer warmth is frequently responsible for this, but sometimes the buds form well in the autumn, only to be eaten by birds. Young plants in any case tend not to bear well for their first few years. When grown against a wall, established plants should have unwanted long growths cut back after flowering to keep them compact. The form known as Luteus has larger and more conspicuous sweetly scented waxy flowers which appear somewhat later than those of the type, a clear lemon-yellow without purple staining, hanging like rows of bells along the bare twigs. As with the typical species, it takes several years for *C. p.* Luteus to become well established and commence flowering profusely each year, but visually it is a definite improvement on the type. Any unshaded, well-drained patch of soil will support wintersweet, and it does well on chalky sites.

Corylus avellana, hazel   A British woodland and hedgerow coppicing shrub, well known for its pale yellow lamb's-tail catkins which usually appear in February. Useful as a background screen, and arguably at its best planted outside the garden and allowed to overhang the boundary wall, hazel is rather coarse for many planting schemes. Its yellow-leaved variety Aurea makes an attractive addition to a group of shrubs, however, and the so-called corkscrew hazel, *C. a.* Contorta, has curiosity value and bears good crops of catkins.

Helleborus orientalis, Lenten rose   The true Lenten rose from Greece and Turkey is distinct from the usual range of garden plants sold under that name. The large flowers are cream-coloured when they first open in January, maturing by February to primrose-yellow tinged with green, and lasting well into spring. Plants form sizeable clumps of large, leathery leaves, usually about 45cm ($1\frac{1}{2}$ft) high, and thrive in most types of soil preferably, but not necessarily, in the shade.

H. lividus corsicus   A spiny Corsican evergreen hellebore with large grey-green leaves, attaining about 60cm (2ft) in height, bearing large clusters of greenish-yellow flowers which open in February and last well into spring. It is best sited in a shady spot amongst tall shrubs, or given a place beneath a north-facing wall, where it will thrive in any good garden soil.

The Lenten rose, *Helleborus orientalis*, is a much hybridised garden plant with winter flowers ranging in colour from white and green to pink and purple. The true species has large, drooping flowers of a pale, green-tinged yellow

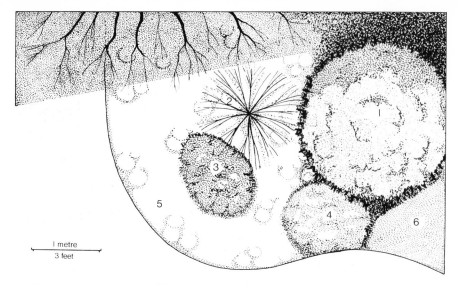

For a sunny corner backed by deep shade, a subtle display of purple, grey and green:

1 *Garrya elliptica* James Roof;
2 *Leycesteria formosa*;
3 *Hebe* Autumn Glory;
4 *Santolina chamaecyparissus*;
5 *Bergenia delavayi*;
6 *Iris unguicularis*

Green

Garrya elliptica   This large, leathery leaved, evergreen shrub, native to the western states of America, is able to thrive in all types of soil on sunny or shaded sites; it withstands sea-gales and industrial pollution, though appreciative of protection from icy mainland winds. Individual plants may be either male or female. The female is at its most attractive during late summer and early autumn, when festooned with clusters of purple-brown seed pods; the male plant bears numerous long pendulous greyish-green catkins during the winter, often covering the bush completely and making an eye-catching display in January and February. The catkins are particularly numerous and well developed on the vigorous male clones James Roof and Pat Ballard.

Correa backhousiana   A somewhat tender Tasmanian shrub with attractive evergreen foliage. The small leaves are dark green above with a felting of pale buff on the reverse, the sprays decorated during the winter with clusters of lime-green bells corresponding closely in flowering season and similar in colour to the male catkins of *Garrya elliptica* above. Cold areas are not suitable for growing this shrub outdoors and, in the northern USA and in northern and eastern Britain, it and other members of its genus are best in an unheated greenhouse, flowering abundantly there from autumn to spring.

The male catkins of *Garrya elliptica* make an eye-catching display during January and February

Helleborus viridis, green hellebore   A rare wild flower which flourishes in the shade of British beechwoods and prefers a calcareous soil. Quite widely cultivated in gardens by virtue of its interesting, nodding green flowers which appear in February, coinciding with the newly opening leaves.

H. foetidus, stinking hellebore   A wild British plant of chalk soils and shady beechwoods in southern England, usually growing to twice the height of the green hellebore at about 60cm (2ft). The finely divided, dark, evergreen leaves on shrubby stems last throughout the winter months, before fading to grow afresh in the spring – a pleasant foil for the large clusters of nodding green, purple-stained flowers, borne from late winter to early spring.

H. × nigricors   A hybrid between *H. niger*, the Christmas rose, and the Corsican *H. lividus corsicus*, this vigorous hellebore opens its flowers before Christmas and continues the display until spring. Six or more large blooms of creamy-white tinged with green are clustered on strong stems up to 45cm ($1\frac{1}{2}$ft) tall, not nodding like many hellebores, but fully visible and outward-facing, very conspicuous in the winter's gloom when viewed against a dark background or a north-facing wall. As with others of the genus, the clumps take a few years to become well established, but are then completely hardy and easy to please.

White

Buddleia auriculata   A somewhat tender deciduous South African shrub, very suitable for training against a wall, where it can be combined for winter protection with other, perhaps hardier, wall subjects. It produces its strongly fragrant flowers during the winter months, each individual flower creamy-white with a yellow throat, arranged in long cylindrical clusters, persisting until the white-felted leaves appear in the spring.

Clematis cirrhosa balearica, fern-leaved clematis   It takes three years for the first flowers to form on a young plant of this evergreen climber, but when they do appear they open as early as January,

A rare, wild flower of British beechwoods, the stinking hellebore *Helleborus foetidus*, produces its green flowers in February

and are in full bloom during February, as bell-flowers creamy-white or pale yellow on the outside, faintly streaked inside with crimson or purple. The flowers and the finely divided, bronze-tinted leaves are hardy, but the roots need some protection against deep frost, with either a temporary mulch or a large stone to cover them. If allowed to grow freely on a pillar, most of the flowers prefer to face north, and a completely north-facing wall or trellis makes a good site for this native of the Balearic Islands. (For early autumn-flowering clematises, see p162.)

Osmanthus yunnanensis   A large evergreen Chinese shrub with huge dark-green leaves, fairly quick growing and suitable for training into a small standard tree. Numerous small, fragrant, creamy-white flowers are produced in February, not particularly conspicuous but pleasing at close quarters, and a welcome addition to the overall fragrance of the winter garden.

Lonicera fragrantissima, bush honeysuckle   This deciduous Chinese shrub produces masses of very fragrant creamy-white flowers arranged in pairs, crowded along the bare twigs from late winter until spring, contrasting beautifully with the pale golden-brown of the bark. It flowers all the better when trained against a warm wall, where it will reach a height of some 2m (6ft).

L. × purpusii   A vigorous semi-evergreen hybrid honeysuckle which has *L. fragrantissima* as one of its parents. Its fragrant creamy-white flowers occur over a long period during winter and early spring; Winter Beauty is a particularly free-flowering clone.

Loropetalum chinense   A 2m (6ft) Chinese evergreen shrub, rarely seen in gardens, closely related to the witch hazels, and bearing similarly shaped but pure-white flowers in February and March. The leaves are shed during the winter in cold localities and this shrub, though fairly hardy, is best sited in a sheltered woodland type of garden where the soil is moist, acid and rich in humus.

Osmaronia cerasiformis, Oso berry   A suckering Californian shrub which tends to form a thicket of erect 2m (6ft) stems. Easily grown and suitable for a wild, woodland type of garden where it displays large purple berries amongst dark greyish-green deciduous leaves during summer, and pendulous clusters of fragrant white flowers on the bare twigs in February and March.

The Oso berry, *Osmaronia cerasiformis*, bears its fragrant white flowers in February and March

Buddleia asiatica A large East Indian evergreen shrub which can successfully be grown as a small standard tree, but which is somewhat tender, suitable only for the mildest areas. The narrowly pointed leaves are contrastingly white on their undersides, the foliage partially hiding the drooping clusters of sweetly scented white flowers which appear during winter.

Prunus davidiana **Alba** The white variety of Father David's flowering peach – otherwise a hardy little Chinese tree – really needs a sheltered spot in the garden to give the flowers some protection during January and February, when the upright leafless twigs are closely garlanded by comparatively large single white blossoms.

P. cerasifera, myrobalan or cherry-plum A native of eastern Europe and western Asia, this well-known small spreading tree becomes covered with little white flowers during February and early March. Myrobalan is perhaps even better known in some of

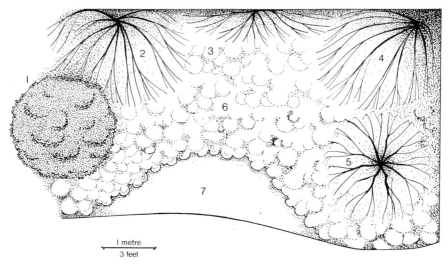

For the sunny corner of a wall, a collection of unusual shrubs to carry a succession of flowers from mid-winter to spring:

1 *Correa backhousiana*;
2 *Forsythia giraldiana*;
3 *Abeliophyllum distichum*;
4 *Forsythia suspensa* Nymans;
5 *Stachyurus praecox*;
6 *Bergenia cordifolia minor*;
7 *Anemone blanda atrocoerulea*

its pink-flowered, dark-twigged and purple-leaved varieties. All of them perform equally well as hedge plants, and can make an attractive screen, dense though deciduous.

***P. subhirtella* Autumnalis,** autumn cherry   This beautiful little tree is a variety of the Japanese spring cherry, with clusters of tiny single or semi-double white flowers, occasionally flushed very faintly with pink, on display intermittently between autumn and spring.

Osmanthus armatus A large Chinese evergreen shrub with dense foliage, thick and prickly like enormous holly leaves. It makes a splendid peep-proof screen able to grow in any reasonable soil in sun or shade, handsome all the year round, and particularly attractive in the autumn when covered with small but sweetly scented white flowers.

O. heterophyllus This large Japanese evergreen shrub has small, spiny, dark, glossy green leaves, so it is sometimes mistaken for a holly. Like hollies it makes a splendid densely foliaged screen or slow-growing clipped hedge. Alternatively, it can be trained to make an unusual small standard tree, closely covered in the autumn with tiny, sweetly scented white bell-like flowers. There are several varieties of the species, some of which have variegated leaves.

Sarcococca confusa, sweet box or Christmas box   A small Chinese evergreen shrub which spreads densely in any reasonable garden soil, and forms a waist-high thicket in sun or shade. Handsomely foliaged with long, slender-pointed glossy-green leaves, it is starred in late winter with small cream-anthered white flowers, inconspicuous but remarkable for their powerful fragrance.

S. hookerana   A small Himalayan shrub of spreading, thicket-forming habit, with erect green stems bearing narrow, glossy evergreen leaves and fragrant white winter flowers. The wild Chinese form *S. h. digyna* is said to be hardier, and the cultivated variety known as Purple Stem is more attractive for garden use, with hairy young stems and leaf stalks tinted purple.

S. humilis   A dwarf, densely branched Chinese shrub, which suckers profusely and makes extensive knee-high clumps of glossy dark evergreen leaves – excellent as a weed-excluding ground-cover plant. The flowers are sweetly scented, white with contrasting pink anthers, attractive when studied closely but inconspicuous from a distance.

Sarcococca humilis, a dwarf, suckering shrub which bears its sweetly scented white flowers amongst evergreen foliage during the late winter

S. ruscifolia chinensis   A small Chinese evergreen shrub which makes a waist-high thicket of glossy dark-green leaves, with numerous, very fragrant, tiny white flowers in late winter.

Pink and White

Abeliophyllum distichum   Rather like a forsythia in general appearance, this deciduous Korean shrub produces creamy-white flowers, faintly flushed with an overall pinkish tinge, wreathed along thin bare stems and yellowish-brown twigs. The flowers open successively over several weeks, and are profuse during spells of mild weather in January and February. They give off a faint but delightful scent, and are very useful for indoor flower arrangements, each little bell-flower attractive in detail, with yellow stamens and a brown calyx and stalk. The flowers themselves are frost-resistant, but the plant as a whole gives of its best when sited against or near a wall that faces south or west, allowing the sun's heat to ripen the wood thoroughly during late summer. Otherwise, it makes an excellent subject for training on a wire or trellis, and succeeds in any reasonably good garden soil. Prune, if necessary, immediately after flowering, when the branches can be cut back hard without harm.

Hydrangea paniculata   This large and vigorous Asian hydrangea, and its extra-large flowered variety Grandiflora, produce their huge flowerheads in late summer. Creamy-white at first, they continue to give a good display in the early autumn as they mature to a warm pinkish hue. The flowerheads however are fragile and tend to break up during stormy weather. Both types last longest if allocated a sheltered sunny spot, where they are sturdy and tall enough at 3m (10ft) to be trained as unusual small standard trees.

Viburnum foetens   A medium-sized Himalayan shrub which begins to open its profuse, rounded clusters of flowers, pink in the bud but pure white when fully opened, carried at the tips of thick and fairly loosely spreading twigs in October before the leaves fall, the display persisting throughout the winter until spring, with a main flush soon after Christmas. The species appreciates a modicum of overhead shade, or a north-facing site, with deep, moist soil.

V. farreri (syn. *V. fragrans*)   A large Chinese shrub with stiffly erect main branches beneath a domed outline, highly acclaimed for its numerous clusters of sweetly scented flowers. Pink in the bud opening white, they appear as the leaves are being shed in November and remain on display throughout winter until the young foliage opens with a bronzy tinge in the spring. The naturally occurring variety *V. f. candidissimum* produces flowers which are pure white both in bud and petal, particularly attractive in spring when displayed against a background of dark green opening leaves. Some seedlings and varieties of *V. farreri* flower rather sparsely; when propagating always make use of the most free-flowering specimens.

V. tinus, laurustinus   This well-known shrub is one of the most reliable winter flowerers, tolerant of shade and able to grow in most soils and situations, except very cold areas. A fairly large, densely bushy evergreen from southern Europe, laurustinus may readily be trained into a useful informal hedge which can be clipped in the spring after flowering is over. There are several cultivated varieties varying in colour of flower and foliage, amongst them Eve Price, with pink-tinged flowers; Purpureum, with purple young leaves; and Variegatum, reputedly less hardy than the type, with creamy-yellow blotched leaves. Typically, laurustinus produces dense, flat heads of pink-budded and often faintly pink-tinged white flowers, displayed against glossy dark green oval leaves, in a generous succession throughout winter from autumn until spring.

V. × bodnantense   A large and vigorous deciduous hybrid viburnum, with stiffly upright shoots bearing a magnificent display of fragrant, frost-resistant flowers, white-petalled delicately flushed with pink, lasting from October until Christmas. A cultivated variety of this hybrid, Dawn, is particularly vigorous and hardy, and produces clusters of richly fragrant pink and white flowers which persist from autumn right through the winter. Another cultivar is Deben, which also bears sweetly scented flowers, pink in the bud and opening pure white, displayed in succession during mild spells throughout the winter.

V. × burkwoodii   A medium-sized evergreen viburnum with rounded, glossy leaves, dark green above, backed with grey, which provide a striking setting for the numerous clusters of fragrant flowers, pink in the bud but white when fully open, on display from January until late in the spring.

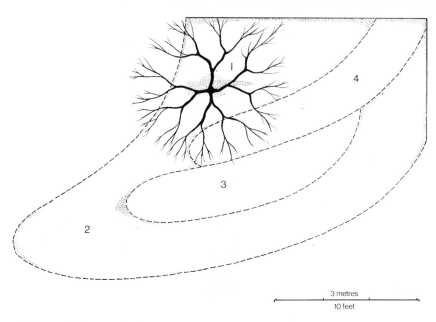

Pink peach blossom in the winter, over a carpet of purple crocuses:
1 *Prunus davidiana* Rubra;   3 *Crocus tomasinianus* Whitewell Purple;
2 *Crocus tomasinianus*;   4 *Crocus sieberi*

***Rhododendron* Christmas Cheer** When grown in the open garden, this old and very hardy hybrid rhododendron seems to have been named over-optimistically, for the flowers usually appear in early March; but it used to be housed or cloched in autumn, forcing the flowers to open in time for Christmas. Pink in the bud, they open white, clustered profusely on a neatly rounded dome of evergreen foliage.

***Prunus incisa* Praecox** A late winter-flowering variety of the Japanese Fuji cherry, its buds are pale pink, the fully opened flowers pure white. February Pink is another early flowering variety of the Fuji, producing masses of pale-pink flowers in February.

P. kansuensis A small Chinese peach-like tree with long, graceful branches, well laden in January and February with pink-tinged white flowers.

***P. conradinae*,** Conradina's cherry This small Chinese tree and its semi-double variety, Semiplena, both produce sweetly scented white or pale-pink flowers massed along the slender, spreading, bare branches during February, blooming often until the spring.

The pink autumn cherry, *Prunus subhirtella* Autumnalis Rosea, displays its blossom at any time between autumn and spring

P. davidiana, Father David's peach   The typical form of this small almond-like tree from China is consistently one of the earliest of the genus to come into flower, the stiffly erect branches laden as early as January with pale-pink or white flowers which last until March. The variety Rubra has darker pink flowers.

***P. subhirtella* Autumnalis Rosea,** pink autumn cherry   At any time between autumn and spring the neatly fanned branches of this shapely little tree can carry a sprinkling of semi-double flowers in a pale shade of pink, though the display is liable to be curtailed by spells of severe weather.

P. **Fudanzakura**   This earliest of the hybrid Japanese flowering cherries is liable to bear its single blossoms at any time between autumn and spring. They are always pink in the bud, sometimes opening to white, but usually retaining a tinge of the palest pink, and are delicately displayed on a neatly rounded crown of branches.

P. mandshurica, Manchurian apricot   A small Oriental tree which produces large single pale-pink flowers, darker pink in the bud, opening during February and March.

P. mume **Pendula,** weeping Japanese apricot   A small, gracefully pendulous apricot tree which bears its drooping, semi-double blossoms of pale pink from late February onwards.

P. dulcis **Praecox,** early almond   This precocious form of the common southern European almond displays its large, single, pale-pink flowers about a fortnight earlier than the typical species, and has often opened its buds before the end of February.

P. pseudocerasus **Cantabrigiensis,** Cambridge cherry   This uncommon little tree produces its fragrant pink flowers in mid February.

Pieris japonica **Christmas Cheer**   This Japanese shrub excels in woodland-garden conditions, needs a moist, acid soil, but is one of the hardiest of its genus. The dark, glossy evergreen leaves display a bright coppery tint as they expand on the young shoots, and the whole bush becomes covered with drooping clusters of flowers like red-stalked lilies of the valley, stained at the petal tips with pink. Opening during the winter months and remaining on display for the spring, the flowers are more likely to appear in February than in time for Christmas. Newly established young plants flower well, and thrive in the partial shade of taller shrubs and trees.

Rhododendron praevernum   A large Chinese rhododendron species with handsome evergreen foliage and huge clusters of bell-shaped flowers which often appear during February and last until spring. Each flower is pale pink, marked inside the bell with a central blotch of crimson-purple.

Lonicera setifera An unusual medium-sized deciduous shrub-honeysuckle from China. The delightfully fragrant trumpet-shaped pink and white flowers are closely clustered on bare but hairy stems during winter and early spring.

Abelia × grandiflora A small hybrid shrub with gracefully arching branches and dark, glossy foliage which remains evergreen except in the coldest winters. The clusters of slender trumpet-shaped flowers, pale pink and white with contrasting purple-red sepals, open during the summer and are on display successively at least until September, the persistent, colourful sepals often remaining until the first frosts.

Pink

Rhododendron sutchuenense A substantial woodland rhododendron from China, with strikingly handsome evergreen foliage, the drooping leaves measuring up to 30cm (1ft) long. Its magnificent bell flowers range in colour from palest pink to rosy-lilac spotted and blotched with purple, appearing during February and March.

R. arboreum The original tree rhododendron from the Himalayan forests, this handsome evergreen needs a mild district, or at least a very sheltered site, to do well. A striking little tree in foliage, with large bicoloured leaves, it bears tight waxy clusters of flowers ranging in colour from pale pink to deep red, often showing colour as early as January, and opening in succession during mild spells well into spring. *R. arboreum* is a parent of many hybrids, and there are also several cultivars with varying degrees of hardiness and range of flower colour.

R. Nobleanum An old hybrid with *R. arboreum* as one of its parents, this large but slow-growing shrub or small tree is appreciative of woodland garden shelter. As with its Himalayan parent, the dark evergreen leaves are clothed on their undersides with a contrastingly light buff down, and the broadly funnel-shaped flowers form tight clusters – a brilliant scarlet in the bud stage, typically opening to a rich shade of rose-pink, paling inside to white, and blotched or spotted with crimson. But there are varieties with flowers of almost pure white or an unmarked dark pink. During mild spells, flowers may be produced successively at any time between November and March, and in mild districts they normally open in January and persist until earliest spring.

Luculia gratissima   A fairly large Himalayan shrub, with downy twigs and long leaves which are usually deciduous but may sometimes be retained over winter in the mildest areas, or when grown under glass. Rather tender and unsuitable for cold districts, it makes a good subject for conservatory cultivation in Britain, flowering during the winter with clusters of sweetly fragrant, 2.5cm (1in) slenderly trumpet-shaped flowers in a bright pink.

Daphne mezereum, mezereon   This deciduous small upright shrub, a native of Europe, is one of the easiest of its genus to grow well, and likes sticky, limy soils. Its fragrant madder-pink flowers open in February and last well into March, clustered thickly on shoots of the previous year's growth. The variety *D. m.* Grandiflora has larger flowers with a longer season, appearing in the autumn and persisting, in mildish weather, throughout the winter.

D. odora   This 1.5m (5ft) evergreen bush, a native of China and Japan, needs a site open to the sun but sheltered from the worst winter weather. The fragrant purple-pink flowers are produced during winter and early spring. Although these are moderately frost-proof, the leaves are liable to drop, and the top growth may die back, following severe weather. The attractively variegated form Aureomarginata is stronger growing and though it often loses its leaves in winter, it is said to be the hardier of the two.

D. × hybrida (syn. D. dauphinii)   This small evergreen hybrid daphne is a notably hardy plant, better able than most of its genus to thrive in heavy clay soils. The fragrant purple-pink flowers appear in the autumn, often persisting until early spring.

D. BHOLIA 'GURKHA' ' JACQUELINE POSTLE'

Tamarix pentandra, tamarisk   This graceful Asian shrub forms a spreading fan of slender branches and fine, glaucous foliage, though pruning is sometimes necessary in early spring to retain a picturesque silhouette. Very hardy and wind-resistant, and a favourite seaside shrub, it can grow well in poor soils, and is covered in late summer and autumn with feathery rose-pink flower spikes. The selected form Rubra has equally prolific flowers in a darker pink.

Hamamelis × intermedia Ruby Glow. A somewhat variable hybrid witch hazel with winter flowers of an unusual coppery shade

Magnolia campbellii, pink tulip tree   This earliest-flowering of the magnolias, a native of the Himalayas, ultimately makes a large tree with widely spreading branches. It is magnificent when it eventually comes into its prime, though typical specimens do not begin to flower until about twenty years old. Some selected varieties flower sooner, however, in particular the Tibetan subspecies *M. c. mollicomata* and a garden hybrid between this wild tree and the typical species, given the cultivar name Charles Raffill; these start to flower at about ten years old. The flowers, like huge waterlilies, are a deep purplish-pink on the outside of the petals and a pale pink inside; the bare twigs of mature trees are usually well covered with blossom during February and March. Both the wild tree and its named varieties need a lime-free soil and, to protect the flowers, a site well sheltered from cold winds and spring frosts. A town garden with a moist peaty soil often provides ideal conditions.

Crimson and Purple

Rhododendron **Fulgarb**   One of the many garden hybrids of *R. arboreum*, this large evergreen shrub, sometimes grown as a small standard tree, needs the shelter of a woodland type of garden. There, in mild seasons, its small but numerous tightly packed clusters of bright crimson flowers appear as early as February, and remain on display until spring.

R. dauricum   This semi-evergreen rhododendron from the Far East is one of the earliest of the genus to flower, the bright rose-purple flowers often opening in January and lasting until March. It, too, really needs the protection of a woodland garden. Its cultivated variety known as Midwinter is hardier, usually remains fully evergreen, and carries numerous small clusters of phlox-purple flowers from New Year until early spring.

R. mucronulatum   One of the best known of the winter-flowering rhododendrons, and one of the most reliable. It loses its leaves in all but the mildest winters, but nevertheless is perfectly hardy, masses of funnel-shaped flowers of a luminous rose-purple appearing during January and February on the bare, upright, often neatly

Viburnum × bodnantense Dawn. A large and vigorous hybrid viburnum which flowers from autumn right through the winter

pyramidal twigs. It is often possible to provide temporary protection for the flowers during frosty weather (see p22).

R. Praecox   This hardy semi-evergreen hybrid also tends to lose its aromatic leaves in the winter, though the small but very numerous bright pink flowers are relatively weather resistant, and appear in ones and twos at the ends of the shoots as early as February, the opening buds at first a dark crimson-purple. A hybrid of *R. dauricum*, making a small, compact shrub, it flowers as a rule a month later than *R. mucronulatum*. The first crop of buds may be killed by frost, but a good display is usually evident only a week or two later; as with *R. mucronulatum*, it is often worth providing individual bushes with the temporary overnight protection of loosely tied newspapers when severe frost is expected. *R.* Praecox is unusual among rhododendrons in being able to tolerate a modicum of lime, but the soil nevertheless should be moist and fairly rich in humus.

Polygonum vaccinifolium, trailing knot grass   One of the most useful plants for a rockery or a sunny wall on account of its late flowering season. A shrubby prostrate herb from the Himalayas, with bright pinkish-purple heather-like spikes opening at the end of summer and lasting well through the autumn.

Hebe Autumn Glory   This small shrubby veronica hybrid makes a loosely bushy, evergreen mound, covered in the autumn with spikes of violet flowers which open in the late summer and last often until the end of January.

H. × andersonii   A naturally occurring hybrid from New Zealand which makes a fairly large, vigorous shrub. The numerous long spikes of tiny flowers, pale mauve at first, soon fading to white, are produced during late summer and autumn. Although they often do best by the sea and in the mildest inland areas, both these shrubby veronicas are reasonably hardy given a well-drained soil and, provided the woody topgrowth survives the winter, the flowers are fairly weather-resistant and usually do well even though they may be subjected to sharp frost.

The winter-flowering *Iris unguicularis* needs a fairly dry, sheltered site

Elsholtzia stauntonii   A small shrubby Chinese herb, with pointed deciduous leaves that smell, if crushed, of the mint to which the plant is related. Frost cuts the stems down to the ground during winter, but the plant is quite hardy and easily grown on any open, sunny site, where it produces numerous clusters of eye-catching lilac-purple flowers during September and October.

Hydrangea strigosa   A fairly large and comparatively rare Chinese shrub which grows slowly to a height of about 3m (10ft). It has distinctive, softly hairy shoots and foliage, the deciduous leaves dark green above and contrastingly grey beneath. The flowerheads of lilac and white are produced in the autumn, after most other hydrangeas have faded or changed colour. This species is winter-hardy, but the new season's growth appears very early in the spring, and some frost damage is liable to occur then.

Blue

Perovskia atriplicifolia, Russian sage   A small evergreen Himalay-an shrub, with finely cut aromatic grey foliage and glaucous white shoots, bearing long spikes of white-powdered lavender-blue flowers late in summer, the display lasting well into autumn. The variety known as Blue Spire has larger flowers of a warm lavender-blue. Russian sage thrives in any dryish soil on a sunny site, and its distinctive overall tone of blue-grey qualifies it for inclusion in planting schemes which use colour imaginatively.

Iris unguicularis, winter-flowering iris   A native of Algeria and a few other arid regions near the Mediterranean, this species is un-usual among irises in liking poor, dry soils. For best flowering performance it needs conditions as near as possible to the Mediter-ranean environment, where summers are hot and dry, and the rain falls mainly in winter – for example a gritty and preferably limy soil beneath a warm south-facing wall, where the rhizomes can ripen thoroughly in the reflected heat during late summer. Dead, matted vegetation should be cleared away and the green leaves should be shortened by half their length in mid to late summer, to help the ripening. A feed at this time may also help. The lavender-blue flowers are invaluable for winter floral arrangements, and flower specialists say they should be gently pulled off rather than cut, and last longer in bloom if taken while still in the unopened bud stage.

Caryopteris × *clandonensis,* blue spiraea   A hybrid of two Asian species, this small shrub makes a knee-high mound of greyish-green aromatic foliage, covered from late summer until the end of September with feathery clusters of bright blue flowers. It can occupy a sunny spot in any well-drained soil or be massed along a wall as a bright backing for other low-growing plants. Cultivated varieties include the popular Arthur Simmonds, with sky-blue flowers, and Heavenly Blue, which has flowers of a darker shade of blue and more compact growth.

Ceanothus **Autumnal Blue,** Californian lilac   One of the hardiest of the ceanothus hybrids, this fairly large evergreen shrub grows well in the UK, but appreciates a sunny, sheltered situation; its rich blue flowers give a glorious display from late summer well into autumn.

C. Gloire de Versailles   This hybrid Californian lilac is popular both in Britain and in continental Europe, and thrives in cool regions if given a sunny, sheltered site. A fairly large deciduous shrub, it may be restricted in size by cutting the previous year's growth back to conveniently placed lateral shoots during early spring. In late summer it is covered with large clusters of pale lilac-blue flowers, the display lasting well into autumn.

Ceratostigma willmottianum, hardy plumbago or shrubby lead-wort   This Chinese shrub eventually makes a fairly symmetrical dome of attractive foliage up to about 60cm (2ft) high, with bright sky-blue flowers from late summer well into autumn. A useful shrub for the front of the border, able to grow well in light, sandy and fairly dry soils.

Aster spectabilis   Like a dwarf Michaelmas daisy, but more intensely blue, and untouched by the mildew to which Michaelmas daisies are often prone; an American plant, making an ankle-deep carpet of deep-green leathery foliage. The striking, tightly clustered flowers last for a long autumn season.

3
Bulbs and Corms

Because of their remarkable capacity for storing food and moisture, bulbous plants are well adapted to grow and flower under difficult conditions. The difficulties they have had to face in their native habitat will vary. Perhaps they have been obliged to tolerate a regular season of drought, as tulips do, or a shortage of light during the growing season, as experienced by plants such as the winter aconites. For whatever pressing reason, bulbs and corms tend to flower and seed either at the close or at the beginning of the main flowering period for herbaceous and shrubby plants: so many bulbs are at their best in autumn, winter or very early spring.

Gardeners who work with chalky or limy soils, where many woodland plants cannot grow, know that bulbous subjects can usually flourish in these areas, and make up with their drifts of flower for the autumn foliage colours that such gardens often lack. Small bulbs should be planted for a massed effect which will stand out at a distance; the most spectacular results are achieved if species and varieties of a distinct colour are kept grouped and segregated. Only when a small number of bulbs are to be seen at close quarters should this basic rule be relaxed. A tiny front garden next to a pavement, for example, will gain little by careful grouping, and an abandoned motley may well be more appropriate.

Where the garden is large and the vista deep, planting should be carried out in a controlled but apparently random manner, for flowers of this type seldom look right if regimented into severe lines and symmetrical beds, except perhaps when used as part of a seasonal bedding display in a formal flower-bed. Even there, formal symmetry is less appropriate for small bulbs like crocuses than for large and brilliantly coloured spring flowerers such as the hybrid garden tulips. These are too tall and stiffly erect to give a natural appearance in an informal setting.

Random planting, by means of the time-honoured method of rolling the bulbs from a garden trug and planting them where they fall, gives a more or less natural appearance, although of course the curves and drifts which result can be made to follow carefully planned outlines without loss of effect. Artificial outlines can be used, for example, to form the edges of an open floral path across the grass, to be seen only during the flowering and leafing season of the bulbs, leading the eye if not the feet through the garden and towards some favourite seasonal vista.

Several useful bulbs and corms come into flower in the autumn, among them some true crocus species, the so-called autumn crocuses or colchicums, the yellow crocus-like sternbergia, cyclamens and leucojums or snowflakes, followed before the really cold weather begins by the tall semi-hardy nerines. The first snowdrops also appear in November, to be followed soon after Christmas by bulbous irises and the winter aconite, and later in the New Year by the earliest narcissi and tulips.

Crocuses are among the most important of the autumn and winter flowerers, apart from the ever-popular spring-flowering Dutch hybrids. The many wild species and their cultivated varieties available for garden use each have a distinct flowering season, enabling a succession of crocus flowers to be planned to last from September until spring. The display will improve year by year as the colonies establish themselves, become naturalised and start to increase naturally by means of the new corms which develop to replace the old, and also in many cases by seed. Drifts may be encouraged to spread in the required direction by lifting the young corms and replanting them at a slight distance; in the longer term, crocus seed may be collected as the flowers wither, sown immediately in a sandy compost and allowed to grow undisturbed in pots or boxes until the third year, by which time the corms will be ready for flowering and large enough for planting out.

One of the earliest autumn-flowering crocuses is *Crocus kotschyanus* (syn. *C. zonatus*), a native of the eastern Mediterranean, which produces globular rosy-lilac flowers early in September. The synonym *zonatus* refers to a distinctive zone of bright-orange spots running around the base of the petals. It is a satisfyingly easy species to grow, the introduced colonies increasing fairly slowly but steadily – more rapidly if you give a little assistance by digging up some of the new corms and replanting them further afield. Slightly later to bloom is the naturally occurring semi-albino variety of the species, *C. k. leucopharynx*, which, as the name implies, has a conspicuously pale throat in its lilac cup.

Next to flower is the beautiful *C. speciosus*, which has several popular varieties ranging in colour from white and lilac to deep

The autumn-flowering *Crocus speciosus*, with varieties ranging in colour from white
to deep purple, is one of the most reliable crocuses for naturalising

purple, intensified by a contrasting white throat. The typical species has delicately veined lilac flowers, but a few pure white specimens are usually in evidence. *C. speciosus* is one of the most reliable naturalisers, tolerant of any soil, acid or alkaline, between the extremes of a dry sandy loam and a wet sticky clay. It is useful also as a carpet beneath tall shrubs, provided the overhead leaf-cover is not too heavy. Seed is produced profusely and germinates readily, allowing the colonies to spread rapidly by natural seeding rather than slowly below ground – though mice may dig up the corms when other food is scarce. Mice often do greatest damage when a thatched mat of grass and clover has built up over the plot, allowing them to criss-cross the area with their runs and excavate the tops of the corms unobserved. Grey squirrels can be troublesome when the corms are newly planted and the soil is still soft and easily dug; once they have located a source of food like this they tend to return regularly until a cover of vegetation has established itself.

Late in September, the furled buds of *C. nudiflorus* show colour, and the large deep-purple flowers are fully open before the leaves start to appear above ground. A native of the Pyrenees and other hilly areas of south-west Europe, *C. nudiflorus* is hardy and grows well in Britain, spreading rapidly by means of underground stolons, to such an extent that it has become naturalised and achieved the status of an introduced wild plant in some parts of England, though it is not usually stocked by nurseries. Following it at the close of September and early in October is *C. salzmannii*, its buds developing with the leaves and opening to a pale shade of lilac with a contrasting deep yellow throat. Later in October another southern European crocus comes into bloom – *C. medius* from southern France and the Italian hills. The comparatively large flowers appear at the same time as the leaves, tinted a pale lilac outside the cup, heavily veined with purple towards the base of the petals and dark purplish-mauve inside, with conspicuous bright orange stamens.

Other October-flowering crocuses include two species from Greece: *C. tournefortii*, which has small lilac flowers lined with dark veins and centred with an orange throat; and the rare *C. hadriaticus*, which has fairly large flowers of creamy-white with a yellow throat. The former has the unusual and useful habit of staying open during dull weather when most crocuses are tightly furled. The latter species is a favourite with mice, probably because the corm is easily found, being rather large, flattened in outline and usually set shallowly in the ground. Crocuses such as these which originate in comparatively hot dry areas flower more freely if they can be shielded in some way

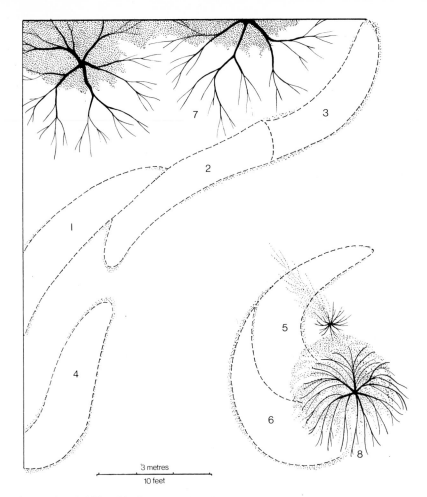

'3 metres
10 feet

Successional drifts of bulbs planned to delineate a broad visual path across a lawn:
1 *Crocus speciosus* Aitchisonii, and *C. chrysanthus* E. P. Bowles;
2 *Crocus salzmannii*, and *C. tomasinianus* Whitewell Purple;
3 *Crocus salzmannii*, and *C. chrysanthus* Blue Peter;
4 *Crocus speciosus*, and *C. tomasinianus*;
5 *Crocus kotschyanus*, and *C. chrysanthus* Blue Peter;
6 *Crocus speciosus* Aitchisonii, and *C. tomasinianus* Whitewell Purple;
7 *Galanthus* species – a selection of snowdrops beneath apple trees;
8 *Eranthis hyemalis* – winter aconites beneath the weeping cherry *Prunus* Kiku-shidare Sakura, and, surrounding the upright cherry, *P.* Amanogawa

from excessive rain during the latter part of the summer so that the corms are allowed to dry out and ripen thoroughly, as they do in their native environment.

The autumn-flowering crocuses have all completed their display by the end of November, and December brings a gap between the last of the autumn flowerers and the earliest of the spring-flowering crocuses. The earliest to resume the display is often the Greek *C.*

laevigatus, particularly its handsome variety *C. l. fontenayi*, which can open its buds by Christmas and is usually in full flower before the New Year, sporting a very bright shade of pinkish-lilac marked at the petal base with veins of dark purple. It is closely followed by *C. imperati* from southern Italy, its flowers usually pale buff with purple striping outside the petals, and a clear lilac inside. It commonly produces a range of seedling colour variants but, though it flowers well in Britain considering the seasonal weather, it seldom manages to set seed when grown unprotected outdoors. Next as a rule to bloom is *C. sieberi*, which comes from Greece and the neighbouring islands – a very free flowerer, with bright bluish-lilac cups made more conspicuous by a shading of rich golden-yellow in the throat and at the base of the petals. Then comes the very well known *C. aureus*, the original Dutch yellow crocus which features in the ancestry of numerous hybrid and variant forms, few of which come into flower much before March. The original *C. aureus* has many colour variations, in common with other species which lend themselves readily to hybridisation; but in its most typical form the flower is orange, lined outside the cup with streaks of grey.

Other crocuses to flower before the end of February when planted outdoors in Britain include *C. chrysanthus* from upland Greece and Turkey. Like *C. aureus* it has been widely cultivated for many years, and though it typically displays small orange flowers, striped and tinted with a bronzy metallic sheen, it has numerous named cultivars. Some of the best are: E. P. Bowles, with cups of bright butter-yellow, opening before the end of February and often persisting through March; Cream Beauty, with pale creamy-yellow flowers, comparatively large and freely produced; Lady Killer, with distinctively narrow flowers in a dramatically contrasting combination of dark purple and white; Snow Bunting, free-flowering, pure white centred with golden-yellow; Blue Bird, with large full flowers of greyish-blue centred with pure white; Blue Peter, a rich purple-blue, toned inside the cups with light blue and throated with golden-yellow; and Zwanenberg Bronze, with freely produced flowers of dark bronze, with rich golden-yellow inside the cup.

In common with the Dutch hybrids, these conspicuous crocuses sometimes have their flowers pecked off by sparrows; once the local birds acquire this annoying habit it becomes necessary to use a harmless bird-repellent such as Morkit. Mice and grey squirrels also damage the corms, but both the typical *C. chrysanthus* and its varieties are as prolific as they are hardy, and the annual increase in numbers usually outweighs such depredations.

One of the most determined colonisers among the late winter- or very early spring-flowering crocuses is *C. tomasinianus*, a native of the Adriatic region, with flowers of pale lavender-blue and silvery-white. Once established, it can seed itself almost everywhere, but it is well worth having in any but the most orderly garden, and is excellent for planting in a semi-woodland situation beneath trees and shrubs, where it can be left to itself permanently. A popular cultivated variety of *C. tomasinianus* with bright reddish-purple flowers is Whitewell Purple, which spreads as readily as the typical species and flowers freely, though at its best a little later, usually during early March. The disadvantage of free seeding and consequential rapid spread is the inevitable dilution of colour effect as different crocuses mingle in flower; for, like the sky-blue chionodoxas which follow in March, the species and their distinct colour variations are much more impressive in reasonably self-contained groups, so that the subtlety of their colours is not lost when seen from a distance.

Vegetative spread below ground, though usually fairly slow, varies greatly from species to species both in speed and extent, and the more prolific kinds, like the autumn-flowering *C. nudiflorus*, can be controlled by erecting some kind of barrier below ground level. On a small scale, it is traditional gardening practice to thrust pieces of slate edgeways into the ground, surrounding each group of corms. Where a fairly large area is being prepared for planting, or where a new lawn is being turfed or sown incorporating crocuses from the very start, a continuous strip of some rot-proof material can be laid under the surface in the exact shapes required to contain drifts of natural appearance. Roofing felt is convenient for this purpose and comparatively inexpensive, completely pliable, easy to cut into approximately 15cm (6in) strips up to the length of the roll, and quick to insert. In established turf, a shrub border or uncultivated ground, cut a continuous slit with a spade, following the required pattern of curves, and insert the material just below soil level so that it remains invisible; take care to close the soil edges together firmly by leverage with further spade cuts as necessary. Self-seeding over the edge of a drift boundary is inevitable with some species; should you wish to remove odd plants which are spoiling the effect, mark them with a label at flowering time, to be dug up and replanted elsewhere as soon as the leaves have withered. Some colour-blending at the edges of drifts may of course enhance the general appearance.

Similar in flower but belonging to a different family of plants are the colchicums, or autumn crocuses. Their genus includes the British wild meadow saffron, *Colchicum autumnale*, and the Middle Eastern *C. speciosum* – usually considered the most handsome of the wild colchicums, but a very variable plant with numerous colour forms, produced all the more freely as it grows readily from seed. Between them, *C. autumnale* and *C. speciosum* have given rise to numerous cultivars, with colours ranging from pure white to deep purple. Hybrids and cultivars include the very beautiful Water Lily, which has spectacular double flowers of pinkish-lilac; The Giant, with tulip-shaped flowers in a deep shade of lilac; Violet Queen, with pointed flowers of purplish-lilac marked with darker violet; and Atrorubens, with neatly shaped flowers of a warm, glowing crimson-lilac. Both species also have a separate and distinct pure white form known as Album, with beautifully globe-shaped flowers; unlike the darker varieties these need an open, sunny site.

Autumn-flowering colchicums are often called naked ladies or naked boys in allusion to the pale, leafless flowers which rise slenderly budded and seemingly blue with cold from the bare soil. They are as vulnerable as they look at this stage, and tend to collapse if subjected to rough weather, but they can be given some protection from storms by planting them in long grass to support their weight. The leaves, which grow in the spring, are vigorous and bulky, and can crowd out smaller plants, so site them well away. *C. autumnale* is less troublesome in this respect and, in its typical form, is better able to withstand the shade of branch-cover overhead; as the popular name, meadow saffron, implies, it flourishes in grass cover provided this is not too thick. Nevertheless, its weak flower stems and the bulky foliage in spring do limit the choice of possible sites; an ideal spot can be beneath apple trees growing in rough grass where rotary mowing, with the blades set high, can go on until the flower buds start to appear above ground.

Like a yellow autumn-flowering crocus, but in fact a European relative of the amaryllis, *Sternbergia lutea* produces its bright lemon-yellow flowers in October and November, and revels in a sunny and moderately dry site. It likes loamy soils which are slightly limy, but will do fairly well in mildly acid or even chalky soil. Colonies of sternbergia need to be left alone for a few years to become well established before flowering is reliable and prolific, but they can often be grown and flowered successfully as temporary pot-plants before planting out.

One of the first bulbous plants to flower in the New Year is *Cyclamen coum*, which often opens its buds around Christmas time and remains on display until the spring, with colour variations ranging from white through shades of pink to crimson. As with other hardy winter-flowering cyclamens, the roots tend to grow upwards from the corm and draw nourishment from the surface layers of soil, so these plants benefit greatly and rapidly from mulches and top dressings, and are particularly sensitive to irregularities in the water supply. On very dry sites they can tolerate being planted a little deeper than usual so that their feeding range is greater; conversely, on very wet sites they should be planted in a mound of soil, at or even slightly above the true surface level. In either case, a dressing of leaf mould brings greatest benefit when applied as the leaves are dying down, for it is whilst the leaves are fading that nutriments are most readily absorbed. A site beneath deciduous trees is often ideal, for the hardy cyclamens have the rare ability to grow over shallow tree-roots.

Cyclamen libanoticum follows *C. coum* into flower from February onwards, but it is not very hardy and in Britain does best in a cold greenhouse. Although it may survive outdoors, it seldom flowers as well as the hardier species and needs constant attention, with regular watering during autumn, winter and spring, and a covering of some sort during summer to allow the corms to dry out.

Cyclamen coum is one of the first bulbous plants to flower in the New Year, remaining on display until spring

The hybrid winter aconite, *Eranthis* × *tubergeniana*, has comparatively large, bright golden yellow flowers and attractive, bronze-tinged foliage

Cyclamen hederifolium (syn. *C. neapolitanum*) from southern Europe is one of the easiest of the genus to naturalise beneath the cover of trees, the pink or white flowers opening around August, followed a month or two later by the marbled leaves, and persisting on display until October or sometimes November. *C. hederifolium* is capable of flourishing beneath really heavy tree shade, such as that cast by conifers or beech, for the latter is still in leaf whilst the cyclamen flowers are out; and when the fallen tree leaves are swept up late in the autumn a pleasant green carpet of cyclamen foliage remains through the winter, fading only as the new beech leaves of spring appear.

Other autumn- and winter-flowering cyclamens include the pale pink *C. cilicium* from the Taurus Mountains and its albino form *C. c. alpinum*, which has tiny white flowers marked with silvery veins, especially attractive on close inspection – hardy plants suitable for naturalising, flowering for a comparatively brief period from the end of September to the end of October. In common with the Lebanese *C. libanoticum*, and to be found growing wild in the same Middle Eastern regions, the spectacular *C. persicum* is not quite hardy in Britain and really needs the protection of a cold greenhouse, unless you have a particularly warm and well-sheltered corner for it. The parent species of most modern greenhouse varieties, *C. persicum* flowers from the middle of February until spring – the showiest of all the wild cyclamens, with its large pink flowers and ornamental marbled leaves.

The winter aconite, *Eranthis hyemalis*, being a native of western Europe, is well adapted to the Atlantic type of climate and in Britain is one of the brightest and best of the true winter-flowering bulbs – or more accurately, tubers. The buds open during the first or second week in January, producing large flowers of a clear buttercup-yellow, clustered on 10cm (4in) stems, the size of the flowers being larger on moist sites. Excellent colonisers beneath trees or deciduous shrubs, winter aconites develop their leaves early in spring before the overhead shade becomes too dense, enabling them to flourish beneath even the heaviest deciduous cover. The southern European aconite, *E. cilicica*, is a shorter stockier plant, with equally eye-catching dark yellow flowers and bronzy, finely cut foliage. Hybrids exist between the two species, and both the naturally occurring *E. × tubergeniana* and the cultivar Guinea Gold have larger flowers of a brighter golden-yellow, and attractive bronzy foliage intermediate between the two.

Aconites like to be left undisturbed for as long as possible in a woodland-garden type of habitat, and the size of their colonies will increase slowly but steadily. Spread them by collecting the seed as it ripens and scattering it around the old plants, preferably on a patch of soil which has been lightly cultivated.

Snowdrops, the commonest single- and double-flowered types at least, are probably among the best known of the typical winter-flowering bulbs. But a more comprehensive collection, to include several of the distinct species and their varieties, can create a display to be admired throughout the season from early autumn to mid-spring. The earliest autumn-flowering snowdrops are often similar to, but not usually as vigorous as, the more familiar typical species, *Galanthus nivalis*. First to appear however is a geographical variant of this species, *G. n. reginae-olgae* – the sub-specific epithet having been given in honour of Queen Olga of Greece, grandmother of Prince Philip. The flowers of Queen Olga's snowdrop appear early in

Cornus alba Sibirica. The blood-red shoots of the Westonbirt dogwood make a cheerful display during the winter
The winter aconite *Eranthis hyemalis*, and the double snowdrop *Galanthus nivalis* Flore Pleno, both thrive beneath deciduous trees and shrubs

October, before the leaves emerge, and last until late in November, the leaves appearing only as the flowers start to fade. It is a handsome plant which likes a fairly dry situation, not necessarily in full sunlight, but it actively dislikes a damp soil, in which its bulbs will soon rot and disappear.

Queen Olga's snowdrop is followed into bloom by *G. elwesii*, which opens in November and remains in flower until March or so. This fairly well-known alternative to the common snowdrop has comparatively large flowers, more conspicuous than the daintier *G. nivalis* when a drift is to be seen from a distance. But though it is sturdy and thick-stemmed, with hefty leaves, clumps tend to thin and die out after a few years, and the bulbs need constant replacement. *G. elwesii* is longer-lived and more vigorous when sited in semi-shade where the sun strikes in the afternoon only at the peak of summer, and which in autumn is cool and shaded. The variety *G. e.* Cassaba, unlike the type, apparently prefers a site in full sunlight. It produces twin flowers rising from each pair of leaves, but they are much later than those of the typical form, usually not appearing until the New Year.

Another autumn-flowering snowdrop is the Aegean *G. corcyrensis*, which flowers in November. It is a fairly hardy plant, but needs as sunny a spot as possible, well sheltered from strong winds. Colonies tend to stagnate unless the clumps are lifted and divided fairly frequently, but their spread may be hastened after the flowers have faded by bending the stalks over and covering the green pods with soil, so that the protected seeds can ripen and finally germinate securely *in situ*.

By the New Year the true *G. nivalis* is in flower and so are several cultivars and hybrids, notably *G.* Atkinsii which blooms in January and February with long-petalled flowers rising on tall stems above its clumps of glaucous leaves, easy to grow, and tolerant of imperfect conditions; *G.* Brenda Troyle, equally easy to cultivate, and quick to establish solid clumps of glaucous green leaves with wide-spreading starry flowers, the petals opening all the wider in bright sunlight; and *G.* Dora Parker, which makes similar clumps of glaucous green leaves, but whose flowers droop distinctively, with particularly large rounded petals. Among cultivated varieties of the common *G. nivalis* the green-tipped *G. n.* Viridapicis is one of the largest flowered, not opening as a rule until March, each pair of leaves arching to form a hood over the sturdy-stemmed flowers, the vigorous glaucous green

Fothergilla major, an American relative of the witch hazels, in its autumn colours

foliage making a rather untidy clump when out of bloom. It is a greedy plant, thriving in richer, moister sites which it colonises eagerly and tenaciously.

Some species of snowdrop have forms differing chiefly in their flowering dates. One such is *G. caucasicus* – sometimes classified as a mere geographical form of *G. nivalis* – which has distinct early, mid-season and late flowering variants, all easy to grow, with handsome clumps of tall, upright blue-green leaves and large, regularly formed flowers which, in the latest-flowering form at least, are often double-petalled. After Christmas, the sequence of species coming into flower includes *G. graecus*, *G. byzantinus* and *G. rizehensis*, the last-named a particularly good eastern European plant with distinctively small, delicately scented flowers, easy to establish in the shade and able to flourish on a north-facing site, where it succeeds on many types of soil including chalk. Among the last to come into bloom before *G. elwesii* fades are the Crimean *G. plicatus* and its cultivar Warham Variety, which has particularly large flowers; the Turkish *G. fosteri*, very similar to *G. elwesii*; the hybrid *G.* Straffan; and last, as a rule, of all the snowdrops to flower, *G. ikariae*, an island native from the Aegean, which is still in full bloom at the end of April.

For snowdrops in general, a site amongst the stems and roots of deciduous shrubs can be made to accommodate them all, by selecting the sunniest or the shadiest spots and allocating them as appropriate. In this way they remain safely dormant during the summer months, out of harm's way beneath the low leafy canopy, which will have no effect except to keep the ground moderately dry and thus assist in ripening the bulbs. An annual sprinkling of bonemeal is beneficial as a slow-acting feed, to be imbibed mainly as the leaves wither. Snowdrops which need moving are best lifted after flowering is over, but whilst still in leaf. Once the foliage has become limp, bulbs newly planted 'in the green' will remain dormant for the remainder of the season and be ready to grow away and flower well the following year; dried bulbs, in which form snowdrops are usually bought, take a whole season longer to establish themselves properly because they are obliged to forfeit several month's visible growth whilst they form new roots.

Long, severe winters have the effect of drastically shortening the snowdrop's flowering season, but little can be done to counter this.

Snowdrop species, varieties and hybrids can be selected to give a continuous display from autumn to spring

Few of the species or varieties are very successful as pot-grown greenhouse subjects, and the snowdrop's best defence against a severe winter is a site chosen to suit individual requirements, as far as these are known.

Closely related to the snowdrops, the snowflakes, mainly from central and southern Europe, are almost as hardy, and two species in particular are autumn and winter flowerers. A native of Portugal, also found in parts of north Africa and the Greek islands, *Leucojum autumnale* – the autumn snowflake – produces its small and dainty drooping bells in September, clustered three or four on a 15cm (6in) stem, the petals white with only the lightest tinge of pink at their base. It is a rather inconspicuous plant, easily overlooked unless sited where the flowers stand out clearly against a contrasting background and the stems and somewhat delicate-looking leaves are in scale with their surroundings – the base of a dark path-side rockery often provides the ideal spot. Although easy to grow in a climate like that of the British Isles if given a reasonably sheltered site and a well-drained sandy soil, *L. autumnale* is slightly less hardy than the later spring- and summer-flowering species, and will not survive a bitter winter outdoors. Another autumn-flowering snowflake is *L. roseum* from Corsica, with tiny rose-pink flowers, but this species needs the protection of a cold greenhouse.

Hardier than the autumn snowflakes, the spring snowflake, *L. vernum*, a native of central Europe, flowers early, in mild seasons opening in February. Unlike the other species it prefers a moist or even a damp site amongst lightly foliaged deciduous shrubs, where it will readily naturalise itself and form a permanent colony. It has larger and more conspicuous flowers than the autumn snowflakes, with solitary fragrant white bells, the petals green-tipped like some of the snowdrops. Typically the foliage is rather thin and sparse, but its Austrian form, *L. v. wagneri*, is a taller and much sturdier plant with thicker foliage and larger flowers, usually borne in pairs.

Daffodils readily come to mind as typical of spring, but a few are definitely winter flowerers. The miniature *Narcissus minor*, which normally blooms early in spring, has a rarely seen cultivar known as Cedric Morris – a tiny trumpet daffodil some 22cm (9in) high, which opens its buds as early as January. Perhaps the best-known winter-flowering daffodil, parent of numerous varieties and hybrids, is *Narcissus tazetta*, which by nature comes into bloom during January and February, with large, strongly fragrant flowers of a bright lemon-yellow. Unfortunately, it thrives only in climates milder than that of mainland Britain. Most daffodils need a cold spell to allow the bulb to rest before coming into flower – the basis of the techniques of cold storage or chilling to induce early flowering – but *N. tazetta* does not. If the bulbs are given the requisite moisture and warmth, they will start into growth during autumn and make first-class pot-grown house blooms; but they can be brought into flower outdoors during winter if the soil is kept warmly cloched. In the Scilly Isles several cultivars of *N. tazetta*, in particular the very popular florists' daffodils Paper White and Grand Soleil d'Or, are traditionally brought into growth by burning straw over them to warm the soil. Most daffodil bulbs start to put out new roots early in the autumn, and for the best annual bedding results need to be planted before the end of September, considerably earlier than the traditional time for planting. When established in a permanent site, bulbs which need feeding should have top-dressings of bonemeal and garden compost early in the autumn during this period of root activity.

Amongst the less commonly seen small autumn-flowering bulbs is a dwarf sorrel from Chile, *Oxalis lobata*, little more than 8cm (3in) high with rosetted, black-spotted shamrock leaves and stalkless pale golden-yellow flowers. It is easy to grow on a sunny site in any reasonable soil, and is excellent in a rock garden.

Two relatives of the spring-flowering British bluebell or wild hyacinth which flower during the winter months are *Scilla tubergeniana* and *S. bifolia praecox*. The former is a hardy plant from the Iranian hills with starry little two-tone flowers striped in light and dark blue, clustered a few to a stem above a dainty covering of narrow leaves; the latter is the early-flowering form of a species native to the eastern Mediterranean, with rich blue flowers clustered on contrasting red stems. Hardy and easily established, either species makes an excellent, robust drift for the slopes of a rock garden, and both as a rule open their flowers in February.

Anemone blanda is a fairly well-known species of windflower from the mountains of Greece, which opens its many-petalled flowers in late February most years, individual plants displaying colours ranging from deep blue through white to pink. Perhaps the most striking of these colour variations is the very deep shade of blue seen in the geographical form *A. b. atrocoerulea*. *A. blanda* is followed into flower by the similar but uniformly pale blue *A. apennina* from southern Europe, and later by the buttercup-yellow *A. ranunculoides* from southern Europe and the Caucasus. Dwarf anemones of this type grow well in chalky soils and semi-shade, and are often at their most eye-catching on the edge of a border where they can enjoy some sunshine and still be viewed against a dark background. They naturalise well and, once firmly established, should be left alone to form a permanent colony.

Like the rhizomatous winter-flowering iris (see pp52–4), some of the dwarf bulbous irises are reliable winter flowerers. *Iris histrio aintabensis*, a native of Syria, thrives almost anywhere and reliably produces its delicate-looking but quite hardy light blue flowers in January and February. A native of Palestine, *I. histrioides* is a stockier, more robust plant with darker blue flowers which open in January. It establishes itself well, increases readily, and seems to be hardy if allocated a sunny site with a light, well-drained soil; but it is susceptible to the iris ink-disease, and will succumb unless treated regularly with an appropriate fungicide such as Baywood's Elvaron. *I. reticulata* is a 15cm (6in) tall Caucasian iris, able to thrive in any fairly light garden soil. The typical species has scented, dark purple-blue flowers which appear in February and are particularly eye-catching when the clumps are surrounded by a thin covering of snow, the patch of rich royal-blue standing out in vivid contrast. Several cultivated varieties of *I. reticulata* flower with the parent species during the winter including Cantab, which has pale Cambridge-blue flowers marked with an orange blotch; Harmony, which has sky-blue flowers marked with yellow; and J. S. Dijt, a Dutch variety with particularly fragrant crimson-purple flowers.

Many hybrid irises have *I. reticulata* as one of their parents; all are beautiful and provide a long succession of colour, but most are spring flowerers, from March onwards. *I. danfordiae* has a bright yellow flower which opens in January and February, but though the plant spreads actively below ground, buds are sometimes reluctant to form. In common with many other bulbous plants, it may be encouraged to flower more freely by feeding with bonemeal early in the autumn – a busy season in the garden when preparing for colour throughout the winter months.

4
Autumn Leaf Colour

The autumn foliage display, whether garish and spectacular or mellow and refined, results from a variable combination of factors, not least of which are the chemical reactions taking place within the plant cell-tissues. Deciduous plants store all the nutrient materials available before their leaves are shed for the winter. In the normal course of the growing season, the sugar which has been manufactured during daylight hours through the process of photosynthesis is moved around the body of the plant during the hours of darkness whilst the chlorophyll is inactive, and becomes stored within the living cells of stem, roots and twigs. A similar storing process takes place at the end of the growing season when days shorten and temperatures drop so that the creation of chlorophyll ceases, and this green product of the action of sunlight breaks down into minute yellow granules.

Whilst chlorophyll is the most important colouring agent in the vast majority of plants, stems and leaves contain a number of other pigments, their type and colour varying from species to species, sometimes differing even between individual plants of the same species. Pigments such as these are liable to accumulate during the autumn as a product of surplus sugar still remaining in the leaf, the most easily visible being those within the crimson and purple range of the spectrum – dark colours which, if present in a significantly large proportion, are able to mask the lighter yellow, orange and scarlet hues. Darker pigments are apt to appear most strongly during autumns characterised by mild, sunny days and still, cool nights, when a low temperature after dark has encouraged the rapid disintegration of chlorophyll and thus prevented the normal translocation of sugar from leaf to stem. Warm, overcast autumn nights, on the other hand, favour the dominance of paler yellow and orange tints – natural leaf colours which have often been present throughout the summer, but effectively obscured by the green mask of chlorophyll.

In addition to the variable pigments found in most plants, woodland trees and shrubs in certain parts of the world, in particular the eastern United States and Canada, possess a special type of tannin within their cell walls which can give rise to hues vivid enough in their turn to modify or mask the common leaf-pigments. These tannic elements largely account for the brilliance of the North American fall, with its spectacular maples, sumachs, red gum, tupelo, dogwood and poison ivy. Few plants native to Britain and western Europe possess these additional elements and, unless carefully managed on a garden scale, British leaf colour rarely approaches the North American spectacle. As a rule, good British displays occur only every few years, but what they lack in brilliance is gained in subtlety and diversity of hue, and the season of leaf-fall often lasts longer in the British Isles than elsewhere in the world.

Although some foliage plants hailed as spectacular in North America might prove disappointing when planted in England, several species or their selected varieties can be relied upon to provide a consistently bright show. The sweet gum, or red gum, *Liquidambar styraciflua*, which grows naturally on swampy ground in the eastern United States, performs best under cultivation in a moist loamy soil of good quality. It does not always colour fully in the British autumn, but a specimen planted near open water is always attractive, and frequently forms a spectacular cone of crimson and orange. As with many other trees, outstanding examples have been cloned to preserve their consistent autumn coloration – *L. styraciflua* Lane Roberts is one example. Other American trees and shrubs which colour reliably in British autumns include the tupelo, *Nyssa sylvatica*; the Canadian red maple, *Acer rubrum*; the scarlet oak, *Quercus coccinea*; the sorrel tree, *Oxydendrum arboreum*; *Fothergilla major* or the closely similar *F. monticola*, both of which produce a motley of scarlet, orange, crimson and yellow; and the spice bush, *Lindera benzoin*, which turns a bright golden amber.

Outside North America, leaf colour is particularly spectacular in parts of eastern Europe, in China and Japan. Eastern plants which colour reliably during the British autumn include a cultivated variety of the Japanese maple, *Acer palmatum heptalobum* Osakazuki, an intense red; and the Chinese maple *A. henryi*, a glowing orange. *A. palmatum* Senkaki and *A. palmatum heptalobum* Lutescens are also consistently colourful at this season, but in pure yellow. The Oriental azaleas or deciduous rhododendrons often produce bright red tints; the ericaceous shrub *Enkianthus campanulatus* always reddens brilliantly, as does *Photinia villosa*, *Stewartia pseudocamellia*, and *Cornus kousa*. The Korean hill cherry *Prunus serrulata pubescens* colours reliably, and often remains a vivid scarlet for several weeks. Most of the hybrid Japanese cherries take tawny-orange shades, beautiful but not spectacular, brightest perhaps in the British-raised *Prunus* Kursar, *P.* Okame, and *P.* Pandora. Few trees are brighter yellow than the maidenhair, *Ginkgo biloba*, or the Japanese hardy bitter orange, *Poncirus trifoliata*.

With so many factors varying from season to season and from site to site – the possible permutations of chemical process, the influence of soil and micro-climate, and the vagaries of the weather – it is not easy to forecast accurately the intensity of autumn coloration. In Britain, anticyclonic conditions of the type which sometimes produce an 'Indian summer' during October and the early part of November, usually culminate in the richest displays. In those parts of North America where foliage colour is most intense, the climate is fairly extreme, but the annual rainfall pattern usually ensures a moist growing season followed by a reasonably dry, sunny autumn during which the nights are characteristically cool. In Britain, it is often said that a sharp frost early in the season induces a good display, but this is not entirely true. Too sharp a frost will kill the leaves before nutrient materials have been completely transferred, and precipitate an early and rather colourless fall. A slight frost, on the other hand, usually damages only the lower leaves. This type of ground frost usually occurs overnight following clear, sunny days, and is predicted by a nip in the air at sundown, chilly enough to ensure a drop in air temperature to 7°C (45°F) or less – the crucial point at which the leaf-sugar in most deciduous plants ceases to be moved via the branches, but is converted instead to pigment. A temperature drop of this pattern early in the autumn, low enough to stimulate the necessary chemical reaction without damaging leaf tissue, followed by a few weeks of mild, sunny weather, usually results in a colourful long-lasting display. Much, of course, depends on the inherent persistence of the leaf, and high winds blow off many leaves before their time.

Healthy leaves tend to colour best, and bad weather early in the growing season can influence the quality of autumn tints by damaging young foliage. In Britain, at least, a sheltered site usually gives the finest results, and a lakeside garden is often ideal. It provides the necessary moisture, particularly important for many North American trees, is usually sheltered from cold winds early in the season, but tends to trap low-lying frosty air and so has comparatively cold nights during the autumn – all factors conducive to a colourful display, while the reflecting surface of the water presents a perfect setting.

As autumn colours result from a surplus of nutrient elements remaining in the leaf at the close of a growing season, they will be less intense where nutrition has been poor so that there is no surplus. Actual nutrient deficiencies often result in premature tinting, but such symptoms of ill-health seldom add to the decorative value of a plant, and the leaf-fall in such cases is often early and unspectacular. Infertile, dry and gravelly soils tend to provoke an early fall, and colour in any case seems to develop more strongly on moisture-retentive soils. Woodland soils in general, and moist ones in particular, are often acid by nature, and it has often been suggested that the presence of free lime reduces colour intensity. Many examples can be found to repudiate this, but it is a fact that a number of trees and shrubs which colour well in the autumn naturally choose to grow on humus-rich soils with an acid or neutral reaction, though such soils may have developed through the gradual accumulation of fallen leaves over a limestone base.

Irrespective of climatic and chemical factors, individual plants vary greatly in their capacity to produce bright colours, and a particular specimen may give consistently fine results. Mendel's law of heredity points out that a batch of seedlings raised from a notably colourful species is likely to include a proportion which will give better or worse results than their parents. Plants produced by vegetative propagation, on the other hand, will copy their parent faithfully in habit of growth and vigour, shape, and leaf and flower colour. Occasionally, a variety may be cultivated for the opposite reason – to provide green leaf-colour late in the season – and plainly if you are looking for a focus of bright colour in the autumn, this would be useless.

Plant vigour has some bearing on the capacity to colour well in the autumn, for whilst vigorous young plants tend to use up all their available leaf-sugar, older, slower-growing specimens often allow an excess to accumulate within their leaves. Light intensity clearly powerfully influences pigmentation, and the leaves of many species adopt shades of red in full sunlight and yellow in the shade. This happens with the Far Eastern Nikko maple, *Acer nikoense*, and that American relative of the witch hazels, *Fothergilla monticola*. It also occurs in the case of the European yellow-flowered deciduous azalea, *Rhododendron luteum* – a favourite woodland garden under-storey plant which patterns the shrubbery at leaf-fall with colours varying according to the density of the canopy over-

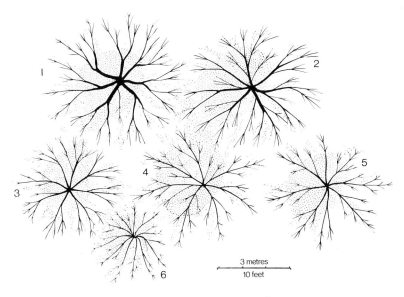

A grove of maples arranged for maximum autumn effect:

1 *Acer rubrum* Schlesingeri;   4 *Acer palmatum heptalobum* Osakazuki;
2 *Acer pensylvanicum*;   5 *Acer palmatum* Atropurpureum;
3 *Acer palmatum* Coreanum;   6 *Acer palmatum* Dissectum Atropurpureum

head. Only those few species which have a very high level of crimson pigment in their sap are able consistently to produce bright red colours in the shade, a characteristic which gives the Japanese maple cultivar *Acer palmatum heptalobum* Osakazuki a place of special value amongst small woodland trees. Open, sunny situations of the type which produce the best red tints of autumn also tend to have the lowest night temperatures, and the two factors undoubtedly combine and interact, cold sites usually affording the earliest colour, provided neither wind nor frost has been severe enough to damage plant tissue.

With the Japanese maples in particular, adequate rainfall evenly distributed through the growing season, followed by a dry, sunny autumn with calm days and cool nights, produce the most spectacular results. Too much rain is a disadvantage, and high-rainfall areas in general tend to produce poor colour unless the situation is remedied by a dry and sunny autumn. Conversely, drought results in early leaf-fall, before the colours have been able to develop fully, and an inevitable setback to the following season's growth. In Britain, much of the best combined maple display – a famous example is the maple grove at Westonbirt Arboretum in Gloucestershire – involves varieties of only two species: *Acer japonicum*, particularly the variety Vitifolium, which has wide-spreading, multi-lobed leaves, and *A. palmatum*, chiefly cultivars within the *heptalobum* and *dissectum* groups of the species.

At the opposite extreme, some of the palest autumn tints can play an important part in the creation of unforgettable garden scenes, and they should never be overlooked in the planning stage. It is useful to be able to select subjects according to their anticipated foliage tints, and the list that follows includes the most consistently reliable autumn-colouring plants, categorised by their colour, and ranging from some of the palest shades progressively through yellow, orange, scarlet and crimson to the darkest purple.

Yellow and Pink

Sambucus nigra, common European elder   Though often despised as a woody weed, the elder can make a wonderfully picturesque small garden tree with its rugged bark and spreading, arching branches. The form Aurea has yellow leaves through summer and autumn, but the common green type changes colour very early. The leaves become almost white, tinged with lemon and bordered with crimson, the crimson tinge varying in intensity – a beautiful setting for the large clusters of purple-black berries.

Euonymus alatus, winged spindle tree   This slow-growing shrub from the Far East, with characteristic corkily winged twigs, is one of those species whose pigmentation varies considerably according to the degree of shade. One of the brightest of autumn shrubs when grown in full sunlight, in shade its foliage turns a pale yellowish-white, stained with crimson-pink.

E. yedoensis   A larger, more vigorous shrub from Japan, also vividly coloured in full light, in the shade turning lemon-white stained with pink – a delicately beautiful effect when laden with bright pink seed capsules. The leaf colour also seems to be brighter on light, sandy soils, paler on heavy clays.

Cercidiphyllum japonicum   A large tree in the Far East, much smaller in frosty regions, for which the Japanese form is best suited. Autumn colour is one of the chief virtues of this elegant plant, most effective when viewed against a dark woodland background. The leaves are palest amber or lemon-white, sometimes straw-yellow, and flushed with a smoky-pink that ranges through shades of apricot and salmon, giving an overall effect of pale pastel mauve. In the spring the opening leaves again take on a pink tinge.

Prunus pensylvanica, wild red cherry A small North American tree with white spring blossom, and willow-like foliage which usually turns a pale lemon-yellow tinged with pink, contrasting in the fall with the bright chestnut-red bark, and the glossy, aromatic twigs.

Acer saccharinum, silver maple A fairly large North American tree which grows well in Britain, named for the silvery-white under-surface of its finely cut leaves, delicately beautiful in the spring when flushed with bronzy-orange, and turning a silvery lemon-beige in the autumn, lightly stained with crimson.

Yellow

Orixa japonica A rare, medium-sized Far Eastern shrub with pungently aromatic leaves. Bright green during the summer, they turn consistently to the palest lemon-yellow in sun or partial shade.

Carpinus japonica, Japanese hornbeam A graceful little tree, striking when outlined against a dark background. The deeply veined, fine-toothed leaves, vivid green during summer, turn straw-yellow deepening to a golden honey-buff, the colour lasting for a month or more before leaf-fall, especially in light shade.

Betula papyrifera, paper birch or canoe birch; *B. lutea,* yellow birch; *B. lenta,* cherry birch – three North American trees; *B. costata*; *B. platyphylla* – both from the Far East All are outstanding for their yellow autumn leaves, lighter and brighter than those of the British silver and white birches. Most of them are also of great value in winter for their ornamental bark (see p139).

Cornus nuttallii One of the largest tree dogwoods from western North America; good in an acid, woodland soil and always much admired when in flower during the spring. In very exposed situations the foliage sometimes turns red in the autumn, but usually it exhibits a pleasantly muted shade of yellow.

Prunus spinosa, blackthorn or sloe A small wild tree or hedgerow shrub familiar in Britain, and amongst the earliest to flower in the spring. It is also one of the earliest to turn colour in the autumn, adopting clear, pale daffodil-yellow tones in September and October.

Ginkgo biloba, maidenhair tree   A curious Chinese deciduous tree botanically midway between conifers and ferns, though it has the outward appearance of a normal broadleaved species. It grows vigorously into a tall, handsome cone, with fan-shaped leaves which turn a spectacular pale daffodil-yellow before falling.

Poncirus trifoliata, Japanese bitter orange   A hardy member of the citrus family, useful in the garden for its sweet-scented white blossom in spring, and the small yellow oranges that follow. The leaves turn a clear yellow before falling to reveal spiny green stems.

***Acer palmatum* Senkaki,** coral-bark maple   One of the most shapely clones of the Japanese maple, consistently forming a neat dome and strikingly beautiful during winter with its coloured twigs (see p147). The small leaves – bronzy-green during summer – turn clear, pale daffodil-yellow in the autumn.

Gymnocladus dioicus, Kentucky coffee tree   A small, slow-growing tree from the eastern and central USA. The large, compound leaves are a delicate shade of pink as they open in the spring, and eventually turn a clear daffodil-yellow before falling to reveal the light grey twigs which form a conspicuous feature over winter.

Prunus serotina, rum cherry   Sometimes a fairly large tree in its native North and Central America, usually much smaller when planted in the UK. It has white flowers clustered like those of the bird cherry, and thick, glossy dark-green leaves which turn a clear yellow before falling in the autumn.

Acer campestre, field maple or hedge maple   A small wild tree in Britain, often a constituent of old farm hedges. In late summer the yellowish winged fruits develop a reddish cheek like miniature apples, a tint which also touches the leaves before they turn clear yellow in the autumn.

A.* × *hillieri This small tree is a field-maple hybrid with small, neatly lobed leaves which also turn a clear yellow before falling.

***A. palmatum heptalobum* Lutescens** A variety of the Japanese maple, with handsomely divided leaves tinted a dark, coppery-green all summer, becoming a clear daffodil-yellow in the autumn.

Photinia villosa flava   This oriental relative of the hawthorns makes a large, broad-headed shrub which bears haw-like berries in the late summer. The typical species normally displays rich shades of red, but the foliage of this naturally occurring variety becomes pure daffodil-yellow in the late autumn.

Ostrya carpinifolius, hop hornbeam   A small hornbeam-like tree from southern Europe, named from the hop-like fruits which are on display in autumn as the large ovate leaves turn a clear shade of yellow.

O. virginiana, ironwood   An elegant small North American tree with similar hop-like fruits, and autumn leaves of a warm butter-yellow. Both trees are easy to grow in any garden soil.

Acer rufinerve   One of the Japanese maples, the specific name describing the leaf veins which have tufts of rufous hair in their axils. The large three-lobed leaves occasionally display a reddish, but more frequently a rich butter-yellow shade, very early in the autumn. When yellow, the leaves persist on the tree for about two months; but should the red tinge appear, they soon shrivel and fall, leaving the attractively striped bark as a winter decoration (see p156).

Corylus avellana, hazel   A common British woodland shrub, valued for its ornamental catkins in late winter (see p32), and which takes on pleasantly rich buttery-yellow foliage tints in the autumn. The variety Aurea is a less vigorous shrub with leaves of a soft yellow throughout the summer.

Rhamnus frangula, alder buckthorn   A small tree native to Britain and Europe, which likes to grow in fairly dark, damp corners. The rounded leaves turn bright butter-yellow before falling.

Sorbus aria **Chrysóphylla,** golden whitebeam   A cultivated variety of the European whitebeam, easy to grow and very useful on chalky soil, in exposed conditions, or near the sea. The oval leaves open a creamy-yellow in the spring, remain yellowish-green through the summer, and gradually turn a rich butter-yellow to give a long autumn display.

Liriodendron tulipifera, tulip tree or American yellow poplar   This large and well-known eastern North American tree is easy to grow in any garden soil. It bears peculiar yellowish-green tulip-like flowers in the summer, and odd-shaped leaves which turn a rich butter-yellow in the autumn.

Cladrastis sinensis, Chinese tallow wood   A sizeable tree closely related to the American yellow-wood. In summer it bears drooping clusters of fragrant pink and white flowers, and small leaves of a soft greyish-green which turn a rich butter-yellow very early in the autumn. This is usually the first tree of the year to lose its leaves – during September in the UK – and the last to break bud in the spring, often remaining dormant until June.

Acer saccharum, sugar maple   Not to be confused with *A. sacchar-inum,* the sugar maple is one of the finest trees in the USA for early colour in the fall, displaying a range of bright hues; but it seldom grows well in the UK and usually colours a bright butter-yellow. The clone Temple's Upright (see p92) is outstanding.

Acer platanoides, Norway maple   A native of Europe, it grows vigorously in Britain, where it produces bright butter-yellow autumn tints, magnificent when seen against a dark background, and particularly rich in the varieties Cucullatum and Schwedleri, both of which make large, upright trees.

A. cappadocicum, Cappadocian maple   A very handsome medium-sized Asian tree with a smooth, pale grey, sinuous trunk which produces suckers around its base. The large, glossy, prominently lobed leaves turn bright butter-yellow and remain on display for several weeks.

Gleditsia triacanthos, honey locust   A well-known little tree from the USA of rounded, umbrella-like silhouette with glossy brown pods and vivid light green feathery foliage which turns a buttery cadmium-yellow in the autumn. The variety Sunburst is an improvement, and deserves the luxury of a dark background to display the foliage to perfection.

Fraxinus excelsior **Jaspidea,** golden ash   The common British ash is not noted for its autumn colour, which is usually a nondescript brown. But the large, vigorous variety Jaspidea has a yellow tinge to its foliage throughout the growing season, turning a clear cadmium-yellow in autumn, and finally falling to reveal colourful shoots which remain a conspicuous golden-yellow over winter (see pp145–6).

Cladrastis lutea, yellow-wood   A beautiful little tree from the south-eastern USA, usually planted for the fragrant white flowers it produces in the summer. The small leaves, a vivid green during the growing season, turn cadmium-yellow before falling. A dark background in the garden adds to the charm of this tree.

Laburnum alpinum, Scotch laburnum; ***L. anagyroides,*** common laburnum; ***L.*** × ***watereri*** **Vossii,** hybrid laburnum   These small southern European trees and their hybrid are well known for their golden-rain flowers in spring and early summer. Their foliage starts to turn bright yellow near the branch-tips early in autumn, and develops slowly until the whole tree is a rich cadmium-yellow.

Parabenzoin praecox   A small deciduous shrub from Japan, related to the bay laurel and the American spice bush, and flowering on the bare wood in earliest spring. The bright green leaves turn a brilliant shade of yellow in the autumn.

Amelanchier florida, service berry   A small spreading tree from western North America, covered with clustered white flowers in early spring. The large, rounded leaves turn a rich dark yellow in the fall.

Acer nikoense, Nikko maple   This Far Eastern maple is one of the trees which produce red autumn tints in full sun, the more heavily shaded foliage turning a rich dark yellow without a trace of red.

A. pensylvanicum, moosewood   A small eastern North American tree with prettily striped bark (see pl55) and large, three-lobed leaves which usually turn a bright dark yellow in the fall.

Tilia mongolica, Mongolian lime   Few lime trees are at their best in the autumn, for their leaves tend to shrivel, turn brown and fall early. This small tree has a compactly rounded, densely twiggy crown of distinctively lobed leaves almost like those of an ivy – glossy and green during summer, turning bright dark yellow in the autumn.

Hamamelis mollis, Chinese witch hazel; ***H. japonica,*** Japanese witch hazel   These small Asian trees produce beautiful warm, dark yellow foliage tints in the autumn. The winter flowering habits of both species and their varieties are described fully in Chapter 2.

Betula pendula, silver birch; ***B. pubescens,*** white birch   The native birches of Britain and Europe. A charming shade of pale jade-green in the spring, they take on tones of deep golden-yellow in the autumn.

B. maximowicziana   This Japanese tree has larger leaves than any other birch, with similar autumn tints of dark old gold.

B. medwediewii, Caucasian birch   A shrubby, multi-stemmed tree with fairly large, rounded leaves which develop deep golden tints.

Crataegus monogyna, common hawthorn, quickthorn or may   This doyen of British hedgerows often becomes an unremarkable rusty-brown in the autumn, but in good years the foliage turns an attractive shade of old gold – a striking sight when laden at the same time with clusters of dark red berries (see p186).

Sorbus cashmiriana   A charming little rowan tree from Kashmir, notable for its pink spring flowers and the large white berries which last well into winter (see p191). The finely pinnate leaves turn a warm shade of old gold, but soon drop, leaving the berries clustered on bare branches.

Acer carpinifolium, hornbeam maple   This native of Japan is one of the last trees to colour in the autumn, the hornbeam-like leaves turning a fine warm old gold in mid-November.

***A. palmatum* Ribesifolium,** currant-leaved maple   Sometimes known by its Japanese cultivar name of Shishigashira, this large, distinctively upright shrub with high arching branches has boldly palmate leaves which are dark green during summer, and a deep shade of old gold in autumn.

Amber to Bronze

Koelreuteria paniculata, golden-rain tree   A small, wide-spreading Chinese tree which will grow well in most gardens but which needs a long, hot summer in order to produce its yellow flowers and peculiar fruit. The large, compound, ferny leaves, which open a vivid lobster red in the spring, moderate to a soft bronzy-green during the summer months, and turn a rich golden-amber in the autumn.

Lindera benzoin, spice bush   A deciduous relative of the bay laurel from the eastern USA, with spicily aromatic leaves which turn a brilliant golden-amber in the autumn. A very useful bush for partial shade and a lime-free soil.

Prunus maackii, Manchurian cherry   A vigorous small tree with ornamental bark (see p154), and drooping, pointed leaves which open a vivid yellow-green in the spring and turn amber and gold in the autumn.

Viburnum lantana, wayfaring tree   A large British wild shrub, and a common hedgerow plant in the south of the country. A striking dark bronzy-green in spring, its autumn leaves take on hues of warm greyish-amber and buff, darkened overall by a dull crimson backing.

Sorbus aria, whitebeam   A small, shapely British and European wild tree with bright bronzy-green foliage in spring. This passes through shades of greyish-white to bright green, contrasting vividly with a white undersurface, and finally turning amber-beige in autumn, in harmony with the deep crimson berries.

S. cuspidata, Himalayan whitebeam   A less hardy tree than most of its genus, unsuited to very cold regions. The very large leaves are felted in ash-grey, and startlingly white as they open in the spring on candelabra-like branches which are themselves white-felted at the tips, later to become purplish-brown as they lose their fur. The leaves change colour through beige and chocolate to a tawny amber, tinted with orange and crimson, before falling very late in the year.

S. japonica calocarpa   A type of Japanese whitebeam, and a fairly large tree with broadly rounded leaves, densely white-felted on their lower surface as on the twigs, displaying autumn hues of silvery amber-buff.

Malus glaucescens   A small, round-headed North American crab-apple which bears tiny, fragrant, yellow apples in late summer. The lobed two-tone leaves turn amber-buff in the fall, darkened here and there with a tinge of purple.

Sorbus torminalis, service tree   A native of Europe including Britain, this is a well-proportioned small or medium sized tree with ascending branches and picturesquely scaling bark. The lobed leaves, dark glossy green all summer, turn a dark bronzy-yellow before falling, to leave a few russet fruits hanging from woolly brown twigs.

S. aucuparia **Beissneri**   A handsome clone of the British rowan, selected not for its berries as are most of the mountain-ash cultivars, but for its handsome coloured bark (see p149) and the fine, ferny foliage which turns a warm bronzy-yellow in the autumn and persists on the tree for several weeks before falling.

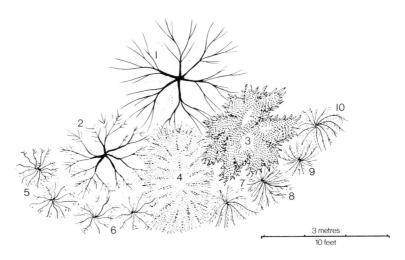

A group which retains its beauty through autumn and winter:

1 *Sorbus aucuparia* Beissneri;
2 *Euonymus alatus*;
3 *Stranvaesia davidiana*;
4 *Xanthorrhiza simplicissima*;
5 *Rosa nitida*;
6 *Rosa foliolosa*;
7 *Berberis* Bountiful;
8 *Berberis morrisonensis*;
9 *Berberis* Buccaneer;
10 *Berberis* Barbarossa

Viburnum sieboldii A large and vigorous Japanese shrub with attractive, strongly veined leaves which are a soft yellowish-green throughout summer, changing to a tawny, bronzy-yellow in the autumn. It is best not sited near a path, as the fallen leaves emit an unpleasant smell if they are stepped on.

Cornus sanguinea, common dogwood A native of Britain and Europe, and common in old farm hedges which it brightens in the winter with its dark red shoots (see p148). The greenish-yellow leaves turn tawny orange-bronze before falling.

Fagus sylvatica, European beech One of the finest native trees in the British autumn, displaying a wide range of hues, usually a tawny orange-copper. The foliage – a pale jade-green tinged with yellow – is also attractive when newly opened in the spring, but large beech trees cast too much shade for small garden use.

Quercus robur, English oak; *Q. petraea,* durmast oak The two native British oaks adopt autumn tones of tawny-buff and rusty-bronze. They are also attractive in the spring as the foliage expands in shades of olive-green and pale bronzy-yellow.

Brown

Taxodium distichum, swamp cypress or bald cypress This well-known deciduous conifer from the Everglades region of Florida grows well in all types of soil, including those which are too wet for anything else. It makes an impressive column of feathery foliage which turns a warm rusty-brown, in harmony with the fibrous tawny bark, before falling in the autumn.

Aesculus flava, sweet buckeye; *A. glabra,* Ohio buckeye; *A. neglecta,* red buckeye All three are small trees from the south-eastern and central United States, closely related to the horse chestnuts. Though the latter are more familiar in Britain, the buckeyes are as easy to grow and their size is better suited to the small garden. All are handsome in flower and leaf, and the cultivar *A. neglecta* Erythroblastos has the added bonus of spring colour from the young leaves, which are shrimp-pink at first, turning yellowish-green for the summer. In the autumn all adopt rich tawny hues, particularly bright and orange-toned in the case of the sweet buckeye.

Carpinus turczaninovii　A small shrubby hornbeam from China, excellent on chalky ground, with an attractively weeping habit. The small leaves are bright red as they unfurl in the spring, becoming tawny orange-brown in the autumn.

Quercus rubra, red oak　A well-known name which covers a range of closely related and very similar forms from eastern North America. When planted in Britain, red oak usually makes a large, fast-growing, broad-headed tree with long, drooping, coarsely lobed, dull-green leaves which turn tawny-orange early in the autumn, the colour fading progressively to a dusky tawny-brown before falling.

Acer grosseri; *A. hersii*　Two small closely related maples from China, the former with striped 'snakeskin' bark, the latter marbled and mottled (see p156). Both have variously lobed leaves which turn a bright tawny, orange-buff very early in the autumn.

Orange and Orange-Red

Sorbus americana, American mountain ash　A handsome little rowan tree with an ascending branch system, conspicuous in the winter when the twigs are crowned with bright red, sticky buds. The finely pinnate foliage turns a rich tawny-orange before falling.

S. anglica, shrubby whitebeam　A small bushy tree native to western Britain, with large rounded leaves, glossy green above and downy grey beneath, which adopt a similar tawny-orange hue, but mellowed by the paler undersides to a warm golden-russet.

Diospyros lotus, date plum　A small Asian tree which produces little purplish or yellow tomato-like fruits and bright tawny-orange leaf colours in the autumn.

D. virginiana, persimmon　An elegant, wide-spreading tree from North America, with picturesquely rugged bark, and bearing small, red-cheeked yellow fruits. This species also exhibits bright tawny-orange leaf colours in the autumn.

Prunus avium, wild cherry　A common woodland tree in Britain, adding each year to the spring scene with its white blossom and coppery-bronze young leaves. The foliage exhibits a variety of colours in the autumn – usually a tawny-orange tinged with golden and crimson hues. The double white-flowered variety Plena is quite as attractive as many Japanese hybrid cherries, most of which adopt tawny-orange autumn tints.

P. serrulata hupehensis, Chinese hill cherry   A fair-sized tree of ancient Chinese cultivation, with ascending branches and pale pink spring flowers. In autumn the foliage usually turns tawny-orange, with shades of yellow and scarlet.

P. **Kursar**   A garden hybrid between two anciently cultivated Asian species, this flowering cherry has prolific pink blossom very early in the spring, and is one of the brightest and most consistent cherry hybrids for its glowing autumnal tawny-orange foliage.

P. × *hillieri*   This small hybrid cherry and its fastigiate clone Spire are two of the most prolific flowerers, covered with pink blossom in the spring, and both exhibiting warm shades of tawny-orange in the autumn.

Stewartia monodelpha; *S. serrata*   Two small Japanese trees, valuable in woodland style gardens where the site can be partially shaded and the soil is rich in humus and free from lime. They produce exquisite white flowers in summer, and their rounded, leathery leaves turn a bright tawny-orange which is accentuated by the warm brown shade of the bark.

Acer davidii, Father David's maple   This beautiful small Chinese tree varies in the colour of its autumn foliage, which is usually a warm orange-buff. The large glossy, rounded leaves with their red stalks are always attractive.

A. capillipes   This small Japanese maple is equally beautiful, with striped bark and a rich flush of pink as the young three-lobed leaves are opening in the spring. Autumn coloration is usually a tawny biscuit-orange.

Quercus phellos, willow oak   A large tree from the eastern USA, and an inhabitant of moist, lime-free soil. It has slender branches and drooping, willowy leaves – glossy green on their upper sides – which turn bright yellow and orange-buff in the fall.

Sorbus commixta   A Japanese mountain ash with very small leaflets, and a narrowly ascending crown of branches which becomes a pillar of orange-buff tinted with yellow and crimson, the display commencing early in the autumn and lasting for two or three weeks.

S. chamaemespilus   An Alpine whitebeam from central Europe, which makes a densely branched, slow-growing shrub in British gardens. It stages a glowing display of orange, rich yellow and russet during the autumn.

Rhus typhina **Laciniata,** fern-leaved stag's-horn sumach   The fine foliage of this cultivar adopts a rich variety of orange and yellow shades, lighter and brighter than the scarlets and crimsons of the typical form. The display is early but brief, the leaves having fallen before many trees have started to change colour.

Hamamelis × *intermedia* **Jelena**   This cultivar of the hybrid witch hazel (see p27) usually exhibits bright autumn leaf colours of orange and yellow.

Acer nikoense, Nikko maple   Previously noted as adopting yellow tones in the shade, this smallish oriental tree with rounded, compound leaves usually exhibits vivid tints of flame orange in average garden conditions but, unless the site is well sheltered, the leaves drop quickly.

A. henryi   A small, wide-spreading Chinese tree with compound leaves which consistently adopt glowing orange hues in the autumn.

A. saccharum **Temple's Upright**   A strongly fastigiate cultivar of the North American sugar maple, it forms an impressive but slow-growing column, fiery-orange in the autumn.

A. macrophyllum, Oregon maple   A large western North American tree with enormous, deeply lobed leaves, dark glossy green during the summer, turning bright orange in the fall.

A. davidii **George Forrest**   A vigorous variety of Father David's maple from China, ornamental in the autumn when the red-tinged winged seed-cases are suspended along the branches, and the red-stalked leaves turn a vivid orange.

Nyssa sylvatica, tupelo   A slow-growing but fairly large tree from the eastern USA, often found in swampy land. Outside its home territory, a damp, loamy soil suits it best, and ensures that the glossy dark green leaves exhibit a glorious array of autumn tints. The variety Sheffield Park has been selected for its consistent performance in the UK, where it adopts vivid shades of orange two or even three weeks earlier than the typical species.

Berberis morrisonensis, Mount Morrison barberry   A low, densely growing Taiwanese shrub, attractive in late summer and autumn when laden with large red berries. The tiny leaves turn a brilliant orange, shaded with tints of scarlet and gold.

Photinia villosa   A small, broad-headed Asian shrub, related to the hawthorns, with small white spring flowers followed by red berries. All the photinias are good autumn-leaf shrubs, and this is one of the brightest. Very late to turn colour to a vivid orange composed of scarlet and gold tints, which last well into winter.

Euonymus yedoensis   A tall, vigorous deciduous spindle tree from the Far East. Its bright rose-pink fruits are conspicuously on display as the comparatively large leaves turn brilliant shades of yellow and red, to produce an overall vivid orange in full sunlight.

Acer griseum, paper bark maple   A very hardy, shapely little Chinese tree, with three-lobed leaves which turn red and yellow – from a slight distance looking like a blaze of orange – but which are only a shade brighter than the papery, peeling bark (see p153).

Enkianthus campanulatus   A fairly large Japanese ericaceous shrub of erect growth, easily grown in a lime-free soil in sun or partial shade, and attractive in spring when decorated with bronzy-yellow bell-flowers.

E. cernuus rubens   A similarly sized Japanese shrub, with a profusion of bright red fringed flowers in the spring. Both species are noted for their brilliant autumn coloration, overall a deep orange composed of countless shades of red and yellow.

Stewartia pseudocamellia   A small Japanese tree which thrives in a woodland garden situation where the soil is free from lime. Noted for its exquisite white summer flowers. The warm colours of the flaking bark (see p143) act as a perfect foil for the rich orange, red and yellow autumn tints of the foliage.

Sorbus sargentiana A Chinese rowan which makes a sizeable tree. Its stout, rigidly erect branches form a broad crown, conspicuous during winter when bearing large, sticky red buds like a conker tree. It features huge clusters of scarlet berries which are quickly stripped by birds, and a delayed leaf-fall. The large, red-stalked leaflets turn a brilliant orange-scarlet and crimson early in November, but after two weeks or so change colour again to a dark maroon before falling.

Liquidambar formosana A relative of the American sweet gum, this small Taiwanese tree has maple-like leaves of a delicate reddish tinge when they open in the spring. The autumn tints are quieter than those of the American sweet gum, displaying shades of dusky pink shading to red, tinged with orange and speckled with crimson.

Cotinus americanus, Chittam wood A small tree or large, rounded shrub from the southern United States. Similar to the smoke tree, but brighter in foliage than this or the related sumachs, it exhibits pinky-bronze tints in spring, and is said to be one of the finest deciduous shrubs in the fall, with vivid shades of scarlet, yellow, violet and orange.

Malus tschonoskii A smallish Japanese tree whose steeply ascending branches make a compactly conical silhouette. The spring blossom and tiny crabapple fruits are not conspicuous, but the autumn coloration is quite spectacular, the leaves turning a motley of brilliant tawny-orange, shaded with scarlet, yellow and purple.

Rhus typhina, stag's-horn sumach A well-known shrub or small tree from eastern North America, with wide-spreading, candelabra-like branches which, though of gaunt appearance whilst the bush is still small, eventually develop a well-furnished, flat-topped crown. The thick twigs are covered with red fur when young, and bear decorative conical crimson fruit-clusters in autumn. These are on display as the fine, pointed leaflets start to turn a fiery orange-scarlet, tinged with crimson and yellow. It is one of the most consistently reliable autumn-colouring shrubs in British gardens, where the leaves start to change sometimes as early as September. But the display is often short-lived, as the leaves fall readily.

Parthenocissus quinquefolia, Virginia creeper   A very well known climber which will clothe walls or trees. The leaves, composed of five separately stalked leaflets, turn a vivid orange-scarlet in the autumn before falling.

Fothergilla major   A compact, slow-growing, but ultimately fairly large shrub from the southern USA. Related to the witch hazels, it is easily grown in any lime-free soil. It bears conspicuous creamy-white flowers before the leaves open in spring, and takes on brilliant orange, scarlet and crimson autumn colours.

Cotinus coggygria, smoke tree or Venetian sumach   This southern European shrubby tree has rounded, grey-green leaves and smoke-like clouds of greyish-fawn flowerheads in summer. Both flower colour and autumn coloration are brightest in the variety Flame, whose leaves turn a glorious orange and scarlet before falling.

Stewartia koreana   A beautiful small woodland tree from Korea, with attractive flaking bark (see p144) and glorious white flowers in the summer. As a rule, the leaves turn a brighter shade of orange and scarlet than those of the other stewartias.

Sorbus **Jermyns**   A small hybrid rowan tree, with an upright crown decorated with sticky red buds during the winter, and bearing large clusters of deep amber-orange berries, as conspicuous as the tawny orange and scarlet autumn foliage.

S. alnifolia   A densely columnar Asian tree with purplish branches. Its rounded leaves, very much like those of a hornbeam, are pleasantly bronzed in spring, and turn a rich tawny orange-scarlet in autumn, blending well with the bright red fruits.

Vaccinium corymbosum, swamp blueberry   Also known as the high-bush blueberry on account of its impressive height, this eastern North American shrub forms dense thickets of erect stems, and is often grown commercially in lime-free soil for its large, black berries. It can be effective in British gardens if planted in drifts to form a waist-high ground cover, exhibiting conspicuous autumn tints of vivid tawny-scarlet, orange and bronze. Many of the blueberries, bilberries, whinberries, cranberries or whortle-berries turn bright tawny-orange or crimson in autumn leaf, and thus serve a useful dual purpose on sunny, acid soils.

Sorbus folgneri A small Chinese tree, rarely seen in gardens but very attractive with its spreading, arching branches and long, tapering leaves, dark green above and felted white on the underside. White felt also covers the young shoots throughout the winter, in stark contrast to the dark purplish-brown old bark. In late October or November the leaves turn a bright tawny orange-scarlet on their upper sides, retaining the silvery-white reverse; while large, drooping clusters of berries often add to the display (see p187).

Eucryphia glutinosa A beautiful little Chilean tree, with glorious white flowers in the summer. In humus-rich woodland garden soils it forms a shapely spire, the dark glossy green foliage turning bright shades of orange and dark red before falling in the autumn.

Acer grandidentatum, big-tooth maple A small, slow-growing tree from the southern United States. The leaves, similar to those of the British field maple, turn bright orange and dark red in the fall.

A. ginnala A very hardy small tree or large shrub from China and Japan, with bright green, three-lobed leaves which turn vivid orange and dark red in the autumn – a spectacular but fleeting display, as the leaves drop early.

A. ukurunduense A rarely seen, low, spreading bush from east Asia, whose long-pointed, deeply lobed leaves exhibit brilliant shades of dark red and orange in the autumn.

Prunus sargentii A fairly large, round-headed cherry tree from Japan, with single pink flowers in early spring, and dark chestnut-brown bark. It is one of the earliest trees to change colour in the autumn, the foliage taking on glorious tints of orange and maroon, often before the end of September.

P. incisa, Fuji cherry A shrubby little Japanese tree with white flowers very early in the spring, some varieties flowering during winter (see p44). The leaves are small for a cherry, and adopt rich tints of orange and maroon before falling.

Acer japonicum **Vitifolium** A cultivar of the Japanese maple, with large, fan-shaped leaves which colour beautifully in the autumn as a blaze of orange and crimson, with shades of purple and scarlet.

A. circinatum, vine maple   A large, densely foliaged shrub from western North America. The large, almost circular leaves are bright green during the summer, and begin to change colour very early in the autumn, when they turn a glorious orange-crimson.

Cotoneaster bullatus   A substantial Chinese shrub with large and noticeably crinkly, dark glossy-green leaves, and large clusters of bright red berries. The leaves take on rich tints of orange and crimson before falling.

C. ambiguus   Also from China, and a fairly large and vigorous shrub with rounded leaves, woolly on their undersides. The berries ripen to a purple-crimson shade which blends with the rich orange and crimson tints of the autumn foliage.

Berberis sieboldii   A small, suckering, deciduous Japanese shrub, with hairy-margined leaves that turn a rich orange-crimson in the autumn, blending beautifully with the clusters of glistening orange berries.

Oxydendrum arboreum, sorrel tree   A large shrub or small tree from the eastern USA, at its best in a woodland type of garden with an acid soil. During summer it bears drooping clusters of white lily-of-the-valley flowers which last until early autumn. The leaves, which have an acid flavour when chewed, exhibit brilliant shades of orange and crimson in the fall; the sorrel tree is one of the most consistent autumn-leaf shrubs for British gardens.

Vitis coignetiae   This immensely useful deciduous Japanese creeper has huge, leathery leaves which start to change colour slowly, the display developing over several weeks into an intense orange-carmine, tinged with scarlet and crimson (see p157).

Euonymus alatus, winged spindle tree   A fairly small oriental shrub with pairs of corky wings on its twigs. It has been mentioned previously for its unusually pale foliage tints in the shade; but when grown in full sunlight it is one of the brightest garden shrubs in the British autumn, exhibiting shades of blood-orange red with a tinge of pink.

Parrotia persica, iron tree   This useful little woodland tree from the Middle East, a member of the witch hazel family, has wide-spreading branches and stems, marbled and flaked in shades of green, grey and brown. In autumn the large leaves turn a glorious carmine crimson-orange, shaded with bronze and pink – yellow in the shadiest places. The weeping form, Pendula, makes a compact mound of foliage, equally brilliant in the autumn.

Rosa foliolosa   A low-growing, freely suckering shrub from the south-eastern United States, notable for the lateness of its bright pink, fragrant flowers (they last until September), which are followed by round red hips. The glossy, bright green leaflets turn orange-crimson and purple as the hips ripen, making a colourful display for the sunny front of a shrub border.

R. virginiana   A wild rose from eastern North America, which makes small, suckering thickets of slender, erect stems, the pink flowers of summer followed by little red hips. The glossy green leaflets turn purple, then orange, crimson and yellow in the fall.

R. nitida   Also from eastern North America, this shrub is conspicuous amongst roses for its vivid autumn colour. It makes a low, densely prickled thicket of arching, suckering stems, with large, bright pink flowers in the summer, followed by scarlet hips. The leaves exhibit a motley of amber, scarlet, purple and crimson-orange.

Berberis diaphana; **B. aggregata**; **B. georgei**; **B. jamesiana**; **B. wilsoniae,** Chinese barberries   All form very ornamental small, dense bushes, bright with red berries in the autumn, when the small leaves exhibit rich shades of orange, tawny-crimson and purple.

Sorbus hupehensis   A small rowan tree from China, and a compact pyramid of ascending, purplish-brown branches, noticeable in winter when crowned with maroon buds. One of the most ornamental of rowans – though the spring flowers have an unpleasant, fishy smell – with drooping clusters of pink-tinged white berries (see pp190–1). The comparatively large, bluish-green leaflets start to change colour at the end of October, displaying tints ranging from orange and dusky apricot to crimson and purple.

Viburnum opulus, guelder rose   A well-known wild plant in Britain and Europe, usually seen as a shapely bush of spreading habit, with white flowers in the summer and clusters of translucent, glossy red berries which often persist on the bare branches well into winter. The lobed maple-like leaves turn a bright rosy-carmine before falling. There are several garden varieties, such as Sterile with huge snowball-like flowers and a darker shade of autumn foliage with tints of velvety crimson-orange.

Red and Crimson

Hamamelis vernalis **Sandra**   A selected leaf-form of the Ozark witch hazel from south-central USA (see pp27–8), which displays an amazing variety of foliage colours in autumn, the overall effect being one of scarlet-flame.

Enkianthus perulatus   A fairly large and densely leafy, slow-growing ericaceous shrub from Japan, with clusters of prolific little white flowers in the spring. The small green leaves grouped at the ends of the shoots consistently turn a brilliant carmine-scarlet before falling, making this one of the most reliable autumn-colouring shrubs for planting in Britain.

Acer rubrum **Schlesingeri**   This clone of the Canadian red maple was specially selected for the brilliance of its autumn coloration, the two-tone leaves turning a rich carmine-scarlet before falling.

A. micranthum   A large, rarely seen shrub or small tree from Japan, with small three- or five-lobed leaves which display a bronzy shade of green through the summer, and turn bright carmine-scarlet very early in the autumn, the outer foliage contrasting with the more shaded leaves which remain a deep yellow.

A. palmatum heptalobum **Osakazuki**   A magnificent clone of the variable Japanese maple, with finely divided leaves which are colourful throughout the growing season, and turn a brilliant scarlet before falling.

A. japonicum, full-moon maple   There are several selected culti-vars of this Japanese tree, with varying leaf colour. The typical species usually adopts a glowing scarlet tone in the autumn.

Cotoneaster adpressus   A dwarf Chinese cotoneaster with wide-spreading shoots, bright red berries, and small leaves which turn a vivid scarlet before dropping in the autumn.

C. adpressus praecox   A larger variety of the same species, with arching branches, covered in the autumn with orange-scarlet berries, and equally vivid scarlet foliage.

Quercus coccinea, scarlet oak   A large eastern North American tree, and one of the finest for autumn foliage, though its performance is somewhat variable in British woods and gardens. As a rule, the broad, deeply lobed, glossy dark green leaves turn a glowing scarlet by degrees, a few branches at a time, the last to colour often lingering on the tree until after Christmas. The clone Splendens has been selected for its reliably rich scarlet coloration. Scarlet oaks need a lime-free soil, and are often planted here and there along the margins of British woodlands to add a little seasonal brilliance.

Stranvaesia davidiana   A vigorous, erectly branched evergreen shrub or small tree, a native of China, with dark green leathery leaves and bright red berries in drooping clusters – an excellent hedge or screening plant. The younger leaves remain green over winter, but the older foliage turns a bright scarlet in autumn.

× *Stranvinia* **Redstart**   A bigeneric hybrid between *Photinia* and *Stranvaesia*, raised by the British nursery firm of Hilliers. It makes a large shrub or small tree with ornamental, colourful foliage, a motley of glossy green and coppery-red during the growing season, turning brilliant scarlet in the autumn.

Sorbus **Embley**   A small hybrid rowan which develops an erect crown of branches, and bears large clusters of orange-red berries. The leaves consistently become a glowing scarlet-red fairly early in the autumn, and remain on display for several weeks.

S. esserteauana lutea   A small, open-crowned Chinese rowan tree noted for its clusters of bright lemon-yellow berries. The unusually dark leaves have a woolly-grey felt on their undersides, and exhibit autumn tints of a rich scarlet-red.

Berberis polyantha   A large, upright Chinese shrub with tiny deciduous leaves which turn a very reliable vivid red in the autumn, forming a striking setting for the drooping clusters of berries.

B. **Parkjuweel**   A densely twigged and very prickly hybrid barberry, with semi-evergreen leaves which turn a vivid red and persist on the erect branches almost until spring, to give a reliable and colourful winter display.

Cotoneaster horizontalis The common Asian cotoneaster, well known and useful for planting against low walls or banks. Before the leaves are shed they adopt rich red hues, the colour heightened by the numerous red berries.

C. lucidus A tall, upright Siberian bush, unusual amongst cotoneasters for its glistening black berries. The dark, glossy leaves turn a brilliant red in the autumn.

Prunus pumila, dwarf sand cherry   A low, spreading bush from the north-eastern USA, with white spring blossom and edible black fruits which are produced during long, hot summers. The narrowly ovate, greyish-green leaves turn bright red before falling.

***Acer platanoides* Reitenbachii**   A sizeable and rapidly grown tree, this cultivar of the Norway maple has large, five-lobed leaves which open with a strong reddish tinge in the spring, are bright green through the summer, and finally turn a rich dark red before falling.

Ceratostigma willmottianum, shrubby plumbago   A neatly compact, small Chinese shrub with a long flowering season, the rich blue flowers lasting until the autumn, when they contrast with the dark red foliage tints.

Sorbus serotina A small Korean rowan tree with erect branches, and clusters of small, bright orange berries. The glossy green leaflets turn a rich dark red before falling.

***S.* Joseph Rock**   A small hybrid rowan of outstanding beauty, at its best in the autumn. It forms a compact pyramid of erect branches, decorated with large clusters of yellow berries. These contrast vividly with the autumn foliage tints of dark red, often shaded with purple and coppery-crimson, in a long-lasting display during late October and November (see p171).

S. prattii A small Chinese rowan which often takes the form of a flat-topped shrub, notable for its long-lasting, white berries. The ferny foliage takes on dusky-red autumn tints.

Amelanchier laevis, June berry   A large shrub or small tree from eastern North America, very beautiful in the spring when the fragrant white flowers coincide with the young, opening leaves which are tinted a soft purplish-pink. The rounded leaves turn a dusky crimson-red before falling.

Viburnum furcatum   A large, upright shrub from Japan and Korea, with hydrangea-like flowers in the spring, followed by black berries. It thrives in a lime-free soil of the woodland garden type, when its large, rounded leaves will turn bright crimson-pink in the autumn.

V. cassinioides, Appalachian tea   An eastern North American viburnum which needs a lime-free soil, and makes a tall, rounded bush with leathery, dark green leaves tinted a warm bronze as they open in the spring, and crimson with tints of scarlet and pink in the fall.

V. prunifolium, black haw   A small, upright, eastern North American tree, named from its large, edible black berries. Before they fall, the bright glossy green leaves turn crimson, with shades of scarlet and purple.

Parthenocissus tricuspidata, Boston ivy   A very commonly seen, vigorous climber that will clothe both walls and trees. When grown on town houses it is usually mistaken for the Virginia creeper, but the leaves of the Boston ivy are quite distinct, rounded and three-lobed, and turn a brilliant scarlet-crimson before falling in the autumn.

Cyrilla racemiflora, leatherwood   A small evergreen shrub from the southern United States and Central America, hardy in Britain where it appreciates a sheltered position in lime-free soil. Its white flowers appear late in summer and last into autumn, and the pointed leaves extend the autumn display by turning crimson for the winter.

Malus toringoides   A small, shrubby, Chinese crabapple with gracefully spreading branches, beautiful in the spring when decked with creamy-white blossom, and later in the year when bearing conspicuous red and yellow fruits. The deeply lobed leaves take on rich crimson autumn tints.

Rhus radicans, poison ivy A rambling shrub which clings by means of aerial roots. It adds to the North American fall as its trifoliate leaves turn an intense crimson, but is best excluded from the garden as its touch can cause a painful rash.

Aronia melanocarpa, black chokeberry A small eastern North American shrub with white flowers in the spring, followed by glistening black berries. The dark glossy green leaves colour richly in the fall, but the clone Brilliant has been selected especially for its rich crimson autumn tints.

Stewartia sinensis This small woodland garden tree, a Chinese member of a largely Japanese genus, enjoys a lime-free soil and partial shade. It bears beautiful, fragrant white flowers in summer, and the bright green leaves turn a rich, dark crimson in the autumn before falling to reveal the flaking bark (see p144).

Acer japonicum **Aconitifolium** This cultivar of the Japanese maple has finely divided, deeply cut leaves which turn a rich, dark crimson in the autumn. During summer, the foliage is soft green, clothing a large, neatly rounded shrub which grows best if given a well-sheltered site in the garden.

A. palmatum coreanum, Korean maple A large shrub with a rounded crown and lobed leaves which are bright green during summer, turn a rich, dark crimson early in autumn, and remain on display for two months or more before falling to reveal attractively striped bark.

A. maximowiczii A small Chinese maple with striped bark and lobed leaves which are tinted red throughout the growing season. As autumn sets in they turn dark crimson.

Crimson to Purple

Viburnum lantana, wayfaring tree A wild shrub in Britain and Europe, often growing on chalk soils, and frequently seen in old farm hedges. It bears white flowers in the spring followed by black fruits, and the broadly rounded leaves turn a dark shade of crimson in the autumn.

V. acerifolium, dockmackie A fairly small, bushy shrub from eastern North America, with flowers and berries similar to those of the wayfaring tree. The maple-like leaves turn dark crimson with shades of purple before they fall.

V. alnifolium, American wayfaring tree or hobble bush   A fairly large eastern North American shrub with hydrangea-like spring flowers followed by black berries, and large rounded leaves which turn a deep crimson and purple in the fall. Unlike the British way-faring tree, it needs a lime-free soil for the best results.

Sorbus megalocarpa   A small, spreading Chinese tree with purplish-brown twigs and conspicuously large, red, sticky winter buds like those of a conker tree. The flowers appear very early in spring, and are followed by enormous brown berries which are still on display when the large, oval, dark green leaves turn dark crimson and purple in the autumn.

S. meliosmifolia   A small shrubby Chinese tree that makes an up-right crown of purplish-brown branches, eventually spreading bushily as it ages. The large leaves are a warm salmon-pink in spring, bright green during summer, and usually a rich, dark crimson with purple and scarlet highlights in autumn.

S. scalaris   A small, wide-spreading Chinese rowan tree whose fern-like leaflets – dark glossy green on the upper sides, downy-grey beneath – turn a rich motley of crimson and purple very late in the autumn.

S. gracilis   A shrubby Japanese rowan with rich crimson and plum-purple foliage, blending with orange-maroon berries.

Liquidambar styraciflua, sweet gum or red gum   A large tree from the eastern USA, recognisable in the winter by the corky bark of its twigs. The five- or seven-lobed leaves, a glossy bright green all summer, exhibit glorious shades of crimson and purple in the autumn, especially if the tree is growing in moist soil, or close by a lake. The clone Lane Roberts has been selected for the reliable brilliance of its autumn tints.

Disanthus cercidifolius   A fairly large shrub from the Far East, related to the witch hazels and sharing their tall, multi-stemmed, arching habit of growth, though the tiny purplish flowers are pro-duced in October. On lime-free soils it grows well in partial shade,

The American sweet gum, *Liquidambar styraciflua*, usually exhibits glorious tints of crimson and purple in the autumn but the most intense autumn colours are produced in full sunshine, and four or five specimens planted close together for a massed display can make a striking feature in the larger woodland garden. The display starts as early as August, when the bluish-green leaves turn golden-yellow, with a splash of crimson and scarlet here and there. As autumn approaches the crimson increases until the whole bush is a blaze of deep crimson-purple, a few coloured leaves persisting on the twigs well into winter.

Nandina domestica, sacred bamboo   An evergreen bamboo-like plant from China, India and Japan, with bright green leaves which are tinged purplish-red in the spring and colour again in shades of crimson, purple and red during autumn and winter. The much smaller, more compact variety, Nana Purpurea, has reddish-purple leaves all the year round. In both cases, a sheltered site in full sun produces the brightest colours.

Cornus florida, flowering dogwood   A small bushy tree from the eastern USA, much admired in spring for its beautiful bract-flowers, and conspicuous in the fall when the leaves turn a rich tawny-crimson. The variegated form, Tricolor, has creamy-white markings on the leaves during summer and adopts a subtle bronzy-purple tone, edged with pink and crimson, in the autumn. Flowering dogwood varieties with red bracts usually display bright purplish-crimson autumn tints.

C. kousa, Japanese kousa; *C. kousa chinensis,* Chinese kousa   Large oriental shrubs which produce their white bract-flowers later than the American species, but colour equally brightly in the autumn with a motley of dark crimson shades – the first-named highlighted in rich bronze, the latter with touches of purple and fiery red.

C. controversa   A Far Eastern dogwood of tree-like stature, valuable in planned garden design for its strikingly tabular, rigidly spreading branches laden with clusters of creamy-white flowers in the spring. It can boast a longer autumn display than perhaps any other plant, for when sited in full sun the more exposed leaves begin to turn purplish-crimson by mid-August, their silvery-grey undersides contrasting oddly. By the end of October even the more sheltered leaves have turned colour, ranging from yellow in deep shade to purple-crimson in the sun.

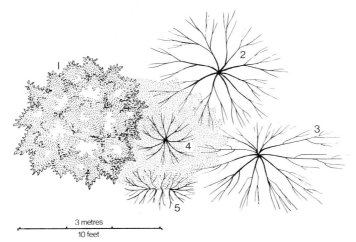

A sculptural group with autumn and winter colour in leaf, flower and berry:

1 *Viburnum tinus*;
2 *Viburnum opulus* Xanthocarpum;
3 *Viburnum plicatum* Mariesii;
4 *Morus alba* Pyramidalis;
5 *Viburnum opulus* Nana

Berberis yunnanensis   A fairly large Chinese barberry which forms a neatly rounded, dense crown of reddish twigs, bearing bright red berries and vivid autumn foliage tints of crimson and maroon.

Viburnum plicatum, Japanese snowball   A fairly large shrub from the Far East. Its cultivars Mariesii and Lanarth in particular can provide striking architectural features with their tabular, horizontal branch system, laden in the spring with snow-like flowers. The bright green leaves turn a dusky maroon-crimson in the autumn, persisting on the bush and retaining this colour for two months or so in the shade. The colour is not vivid, but provides an excellent background to accentuate brighter shades and contrasting shapes.

Acer rubrum Scanlon   An upright-growing clone of the Canadian red maple which forms a broadly compact cone. The two-toned lobed leaves consistently turn a rich tawny-crimson in the British autumn.

Pyrus calleryana   A wild Chinese pear tree with white spring blossom. The clone Bradford is a popular and hardy variety in the United States, where it makes a vigorous, medium-sized tree with glossy green leaves which turn tawny-crimson with orange highlights in the fall. The clone Chanticleer is the best variety for planting in Britain, where it makes a neatly upright, densely crowned column, pretty when in flower and conspicuous in the autumn when the foliage turns bright tawny-crimson and purple.

Viburnum* × *hillieri A semi-evergreen hybrid viburnum with wide-spreading, upward-sweeping branches, covered during summer with loose clusters of creamy-white flowers. The dark green leaves, which have a coppery tint in the spring, turn crimson-bronze in the autumn and remain on the bush all winter.

Fagus sylvatica purpurea There are many purple-leaved forms and clones of the common British beech, their foliage ranging from copper to almost black-purple during the summer, fading in the autumn to lighter shades of bronzy-crimson and copper.

***Prunus* Okame** A small hybrid cherry with carmine-pink blossom very early in the spring, and bronzy-crimson autumn tints.

***P.* Pandora** An upright hybrid cherry which displays large blush-pink flowers in spring when the young leaves are a rich shade of bronze-pink. Autumn foliage is usually a rich coppery crimson.

P. besseyi, sand cherry A small shrub from the warmer, drier parts of the central USA, with white blossom in the spring, followed by edible purple-black fruit. The greyish-green leaves turn a bronzy-purple shade in the fall.

Xanthorrhiza simplicissima, yellow-root A deciduous, suckering shrub from the eastern USA, which forms dense weed-excluding thickets of erect waist-high stems, with ornamental pinnate leaves which turn a glossy bronze-purple in autumn. It is attractive too in early spring when it bears clusters of small purple flowers, and does well in moist, heavy ground.

Sorbus reducta A dwarf suckering rowan from China and Burma, useful in the garden wherever a low thicket of slender, erect stems is needed – an excellent companion to winter-flowering heathers, or as a permanent feature for the front of a mixed border. The red-stalked, dark glossy green leaves turn a rich bronze and reddish-purple in the autumn – a fine setting for the small, pale pink berries which often last on the stems over winter.

Hydrangea quercifolia, grey beard A fairly small shrub from the southern USA. It bears white flowers in summer, but is of value chiefly for its magnificent autumn colours, when the large oak-like leaves are brilliant in crimson-tinted purple.

Cornus mas, Cornelian cherry This large European shrub, which flowers during the winter (see p30), is also attractive in the autumn when the small rounded leaves colour a crimson-tinged purple before falling.

Callicarpa bodinieri This substantial Chinese shrub adopts tints of ruddy pinkish-purple in the autumn, in harmony with the pale purple berries.

C. japonica, murasaki A small Japanese shrub with bright pinkish-purple autumn tints and attractive violet berries.

Sorbus vilmorinii A small Chinese rowan tree with gracefully spreading branches and clusters of pale blush-pink berries which last well into the winter (see p190). The numerous, tiny leaflets turn a bright ruddy-purple in the autumn.

S. × ***kewensis*** A small hybrid rowan, with huge bunches of bright scarlet berries which are at their best as the ornamental, ferny leaflets turn a rich claret-purple for the autumn.

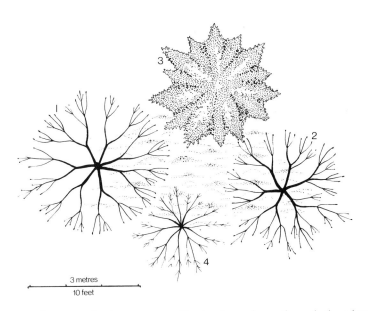

3 metres
10 feet

A spectacular group in the autumn, with pleasing colours through the winter:

1 *Fraxinus excelsior* Jaspidea;
2 *Fraxinus oxycarpa* Raywood;
3 *Cedrus atlantica glauca*;
4 *Acer japonicum* Vitifolium

Rosa farreri This wild Chinese rose makes a large, spreading shrub, with pale pink flowers in summer, followed by vivid coral-red hips which are on display while the ferny foliage turns claret-purple for the autumn.

Fraxinus chinensis, Chinese ash A fairly large tree with sweetly scented white flowers in the spring. The leaves usually turn plum-purple before falling.

F. oxycarpa **Raywood,** claret ash A selected clone of a small and graceful Middle Eastern ash tree, with a compactly rounded crown, excellent in a sunny garden. The small leaves turn a reliably consistent dark plum-purple before falling in the autumn.

Viburnum pubescens A large shrub from the north-eastern USA, with white flowers in the summer followed by blue berries, on display as the broadly rounded or heart-shaped leaves are turning a rich dark purple for the fall.

V. opulus **Nanum,** dwarf guelder rose A densely tufted little shrub, seldom seen to flower, but valuable in the garden for its lobed, maple-like leaves which turn dark purple in the autumn.

Acer diabolicum, horned maple A fairly large Japanese maple tree, quite spectacular in the spring when covered with pendulous clusters of yellow flowers, which develop later into reddish, winged 'nuts' armed with horn-like bristles. The large five-lobed leaves usually turn a dark purple in the autumn.

Cornus sanguinea, common dogwood A thicket-forming shrub often planted in roadside landscaping schemes on account of its coloured stems (see p148), and a frequent constituent of British hedgerows. Common dogwood is rarely planted in gardens, but as part of a semi-wild background it can be valuable in the autumn for the intense maroon-purple, almost black, tints of its leaves.

5
Evergreens

Even those who most love deciduous autumn colour and winter stems will not dispute that evergreen foliage lends shelter, textural warmth and visual depth to the winter garden. If the garden is sufficiently large, evergreen plants can be used to form virtually a continuous framework, threading through the beds and borders, without the need to bother overmuch about the colour or texture of their foliage. In small gardens, however, or in self-contained compartments within larger gardens, the most striking visual effects are often the result of careful siting according to the colour, shape, size and texture of individual subjects. Particular regard may therefore be paid to the tonal variation of the evergreens, to the darkness of purples or plain greens, and the brightness of silver and yellow variegation. Colourful displays, whether of flowers during the growing season, or of the bark and stems of deciduous trees and shrubs in winter, need a dark background to be appreciated fully, and a selection of evergreen shrubs can provide this.

One of the darkest of all shades of green is furnished by the foliage of the European yew, *Taxus baccata*, an attractive tree when freely grown, but not usually so useful in this form within the context of a garden. One of the yew's most useful qualities is its response to clipping, for it can be restricted to almost any size or shape, and is one of the few conifers that can send out fresh green shoots after being cut ruthlessly back to the old wood. As a hedge it is unsurpassed for a finely textured, utterly peep-proof screen. Moderately slow-growing, it takes twenty years to achieve a solid hedge height of 3m (10ft), but it will make a closely clipped screen in five to ten years – the sort of time period it is worth planning for in gardens of substance.

Amongst the broadleaf evergreens, one of the darkest of greens belongs to the Portugal laurel, *Prunus lusitanica*, a screening plant that has an advantage over common laurel in its ability to thrive on chalky soils. It is also generally hardier, escaping damage during winters that have cut back or even killed the commoner, brighter green species. Portugal laurel can readily be clipped to shape and makes a splendid hedge but, if allowed to form a single stem, grows into a picturesquely branched, round-crowned little tree that looks very ornamental rising from shrubbery of contrastingly coloured evergreens, backing some colourful scheme.

The flowers of Portugal laurel are quite attractive but not spectacular. Some dark-foliaged evergreen shrubs, suitable for backing winter stems and providing a continuous evergreen thread through the garden, have magnificent flowers, the camellias being an outstanding example. Some of them even qualify as winter flowerers through their habit of displaying a few odd flowers long before their main spring season. Rhododendrons are far better known and more widely grown, in British gardens at least, but camellias are often quite as hardy, and even more beautiful when in bloom.

Camellias usually do best in the sort of site favoured by woodland rhododendrons. They are tolerant of a wide range of conditions, and will usually survive in sun or shade, in occasional excesses of moisture or drought and such extremes of heat and cold as occur in the cool temperate regions of the world; they only suffer leaf damage when subjected to a sudden temperature drop to below $-18°C$ ($0°F$). A mild, moist climate grows the best camellias, and in southern Britain the performance of a species or cultivar improves – in size, flowering capacity and vigour – in progression from the colder, drier east to the milder, moister west. The ideal site for camellias is light shade. In too densely shaded a site growth is weak and straggly, flowering is poor. Camellias planted amongst small standard trees, partially shaded beneath the light branch-cover, usually give excellent results. The north-facing wall of a house is suitable provided it does not flank a wind funnel, for draughts ruin the flowers. A south-facing wall, unless it is shaded by nearby trees or shrubs, usually dries out too quickly and drastically for camellia roots, and east- or west-facing walls sometimes offer a useful compromise. An east-facing aspect is often ideal during the growing season, but east walls can be subject to over-rapid thawing out following frost – dangerous whilst the surrounding ground temperature remains below freezing, and a frequent reason for the failure of flower-buds.

Early camellia flowers may be browned by frost, and though new ones are often produced in rapid succession, the display as a whole is marred unless the unsightly brown petals drop quickly. Bushes sited beneath the branches of trees usually escape frost damage to the buds; but whether in flower or not, when severe overnight weather is expected it is prudent to provide small bushes at least with a temporary covering of newspapers or polythene sheets. Damage to the foliage may not become evident for several weeks, even when fatal, as the leathery leaves may take a long time to wither. Severe frost damage may be exacerbated by the effects of dryness at the roots, and wall plants in particular should always be watered thoroughly if doubt exists concerning soil moisture; mulching is an important safeguard against drought on all sites in full sunlight.

Before planting camellias, a generous quantity of coarse peat should be dug in during the summer if the soil is short of humus. At planting time a general-base fertiliser should be forked in, and after planting the root area should be mulched with a further layer of peat. Bonemeal, incidentally, is not good for camellias, as they dislike both calcium and phosphate in excess. Established camellia plants should be fed regularly to keep them healthy and free-flowering, by applying a well-balanced fertiliser or liquid feed three or four times a year. Alkaline soils are not suitable, though special planting holes can be prepared. Even if the soil is acid and full of humus, some camellias tend to produce strong vegetative growth without flowering. This tendency can be corrected by lifting and replanting in a solid container, large enough to contain the root-ball comfortably but small enough to restrain the roots, using a compost made of good loam, leaf mould and peat. It is often convenient to move permanently container-grown small plants around the garden, placing them to best effect, standing them on the patio, or even bringing them indoors temporarily when in flower. Like rhododendrons, camellias can be moved comparatively safely, and come into flower even when quite small.

White-flowered camellias are usually the tenderest, both in bud and in bloom, and single varieties of all colours are generally hardier than double. Species and cultivars with red flowers seem, as a rule, to be more resistant to frost than the whites or pinks; but one rather exceptional camellia which flowers regularly from October through December is the Japanese *Camellia sasanqua* Narumi-gata, which has very freely produced single white flowers faintly flushed with pink. The individual blooms do not last long on the bush, but this saves spoiling the display, as they fall before frost can turn them brown. *C. sasanqua* usually does best in countries warmer than Britain, and needs prolonged summer sunshine to harden the growth against winter frosts; but amongst its cultivars Narumi-gata is one of the most consistent performers.

Amongst the numerous cultivars of *Camellia japonica*, Donckelarii is probably the hardiest. One of the regular winter flowerers, it sometimes opens its buds in November and continues in flower for two months or more, occasionally displaying its rosy crimson-pink blooms in the snow. *C. japonica* varieties are all glossy-leaved evergreens of ornamental value throughout the year, and some of the best camellias for foliage effect are hybrids with *C. japonica* featuring in their ancestry, including the white-flowered Charlotte Rothschild, which has a neatly compact shape, and the very free-flowering Henry Turnbull, with a more picturesque, rangy form.

Hardiest, most prolific in flower, and probably the easiest to grow in Britain, are the *C. × williamsii* group of hybrids, which sometimes start flowering in February or earlier. These hybrids include the now famous Donation, which weathers the winter well, thriving in a shady spot where it will reach a compact 3m (10ft) in height and the same across, covered with large, semi-double pink flowers which remain on display for at least a month. Perhaps the hardiest camellia hybrids of all are the frost-resistant J. C. Williams, which provides a mass of single pink blooms and loses the flowers quickly as they fade, so that the bush is always tidy and fresh; and the equally weather-resistant Cornish Snow, one of the prettiest of camellias, with small but prolific pure-white flowers set amongst attractively bronzed foliage. Both are suitable for districts such as the north-east of England where winters are hard and summers tend to be cool. Another hardy variety is November Pink, which always produces flowers in time for Christmas, despite frosty weather. But to do well it needs sheltering from the wind.

The mahonias must rank among the most beautiful and hardiest of dark evergreen shrubs, ranging from tall and solidly upright to low, spreading ground cover, many of them also highly regarded as winter flowerers (see pp28–9), and valued for their ability to grow in alkaline soils. Good mixers, the various kinds lend themselves admirably to slotting in here and there, wherever there is a vacant space. The Japanese *Mahonia japonica* is probably the hardiest of the Asian mahonias, and an impressive screening plant, adopting a tabular silhouette with its horizontal or slightly drooping compound leaves composed of holly-like leaflets in an interesting shade of dark, mat green, with the slightest cast of bronze on the youngest foliage. The symmetrical shape of this dark evergreen is ideal for masking the hard edges of brick walls, blending masonry into border in a most unobtrusive way. Seen from close quarters, the leaves towards the base of the stem are quite colourful, with tints of scarlet and pink. The primrose-yellow flowers are freely produced in 30cm (1ft) drooping or horizontal clusters, on display between November and April, and usually at their best in February and March, their fragrance reminiscent of lilies-of-the-valley. This is an excellent shrub for siting in the shade of large trees, provided the soil does not become too dry; a splendid planting companion in summer for low, spreading plants with large, rounded leaves such as bergenias and hostas; and beautifully colour-matched in spring when fronted with daffodils.

Hybrid mahonias include *M*. Charity, a superb all-round plant, and perhaps the finest flowerer of the genus in Britain, often blooming from the end of October until the spring, checked only by the very worst winters. Even then the unopened buds usually escape damage, the flowers clustered in erect spikes, opening a rich lemon-yellow with a delicious fragrance. The spiny, dark green leaflets are on brittle stalks, and some shelter from strong winds is desirable. Magnificent under large trees as it prefers a modicum of shade, excellent when sited against a north-facing wall, and with the elegant proportions that complement architectural features, *M*. Charity grows fastest and best on light soils, whether acid or alkaline, which have been made fibrous with an admixture of peat or leaf mould.

The best-known low-growing mahonia is the western North American *M. aquifolium*, the Oregon grape, an excellent evergreen for covering odd corners in very shady sites, beneath trees or large shrubs. The compound leaves, a rich and glossy dark green in summer, have a metallic bronzy tinge when young, and a purplish cast over winter. More colourful leaves are often to be seen, for as they mature they turn crimson or scarlet at any time of the year and fall in ones and twos. The dense clusters of scented yellow flowers usually open in February or March and last through the spring. The Oregon grape associates well with ground-cover plants such as periwinkle, pachysandra and sarcococca, and prefers a well-sheltered, woodland type of site, for the leaves tend to become discoloured and scorched if subjected to cold winds, especially in late winter and early spring.

Other, taller species of mahonia include *M. lomariifolia*, which has a vast number of spiny holly-like leaflets, stiff and leathery like a huge evergreen fern, as the specific name implies. It needs a site facing towards the mildest, sunniest quarter, where in November it sometimes becomes covered with deep yellow flower clusters. A large tree in its native Burma, it makes a 3m (10ft) shrub in Britain, leggy and drawn-up when in woodland conditions, and at its best in full sunlight, where it retains a bushily compact shape. The leaf stalks, however, are easily broken if exposed to strong winds. *M. pinnata*, native to the south-western USA and moderately hardy in Britain, can grow 4m (13ft) high in sheltered gardens, with vigorous sea-green foliage, tinted bronze when young, the whole bush sometimes covered during the winter with rich yellow flowers. *M. acanthifolia*, from the Himalayas, is rather tender, and does best as a wall plant in a sheltered garden. Well-developed specimens are magnificent, with stiff foliage of a dark glossy green, and long, drooping clusters of bright lemon-yellow flowers in autumn and winter, a dozen or so spikes arranged like enormous stars at the branch-tips.

Another magnificent wall shrub, with similarly bright, dark green foliage, but completely contrasting leaf shape, is the climbing magnolia or bull bay from the southern USA, *Magnolia grandiflora*. The large, leathery, glossy leaves are coated on their undersides with a soft tawny down, particularly noticeable in the beautiful variety Exmouth. The species qualifies as an autumn flowerer, the enormous creamy-white flowers with their delicious lemon-like fragrance appearing late in the summer and remaining on display until October. In a sheltered, sunny spot it will make a round-crowned, free-standing tree, but the branches are liable to be broken by heavy falls of snow.

The larger, more vigorous rhododendrons are always of great value when planning background screens with a seasonal bonus of spectacular flower. As a foreground evergreen thriving in the humus-rich acid soil favoured by such rhododendrons, and with similar but, on average, smaller, finer, glossy dark green leaves, the Chinese *Pieris formosa forrestii* is attractive throughout the year. Its red buds are carried through the winter contrasting with the dense, dark green foliage, and the bright red young leaves of spring are followed by white lily-of-the-valley flowers. The hybrid *Pieris* Forest Flame is equally attractive during the winter, but is particularly noted for its display of fiery-red young foliage in the spring.

A screening evergreen in a somewhat similar category, with fairly large dark green leaves, is the loquat, *Eriobotrya japonica*, a native of the Far East. Sometimes cultivated for its fruit, it is ornamental when grown against a wall, where it is valued not only for its fragrant white flowers (which do not always appear in the British summer), but for the interesting silhouette formed by its branches, and for the colour and strangely crinkled, leathery texture of its leaves. Grown for the same purpose in the garden, though of contrastingly different appearance, the Japanese *Fatsia japonica* has

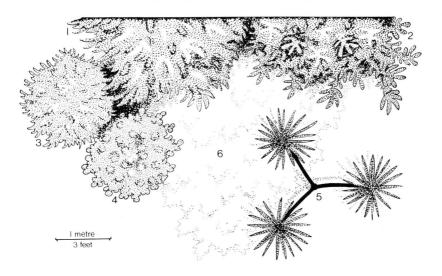

For a mild, sheltered area against a sunny wall, an evergreen group of luxuriant, tropical appearance:

1 *Eriobotrya japonica*;
2 *Fatsia japonica*;
3 *Viburnum tinus* Aureo-marginatum;
4 *Eucalyptus gunnii*, clipped to a bush;
5 *Cordyline australs* Atropurpurea;
6 × *Fatshedera lizei*

wide-spreading branches and large glossy leaves arranged like the fingers of a hand. This sub-tropical bush associates admirably with such uncompromisingly exotic plants as the hardy palms, or with sword-shaped foliage such as that of the yuccas, and brings a Mediterranean fig-like appearance to the shadiest site when grown against a whitewashed wall. It qualifies, too, as an autumn flowerer, for the globular clusters of off-white flowers are at their best during October. There is also a partially variegated form, Variegata.

The Japanese spotted laurel was popular with the Victorians, but the plain-green *Aucuba japonica* is less well known, though a useful evergreen capable of growing in fairly dense shade, where it will make a solidly round bush up to 3m (10ft) high, with handsome, dark glossy-green foliage. In a similar category but for open, sunny spots, the Japanese privet, *Ligustrum japonicum*, is a good screening evergreen with shiny dark green leaves, the compact and very dense foliage piling up to 3m (10ft) or so. The variety *L. j.* Macrophyllum has broader, glossy leaves of very dark green, almost like one of the camellias.

Several conifers have foliage of a bright, dark green which stands out clearly in the middle distance. One of the largest and most spectacularly columnar of these is the incense cedar, *Calocedrus decurrens*, from the south-western USA. It is a favourite constituent of arboreta, where contrasting height is needed to balance low,

spreading trees and rounded-crown shapes. Its foliage grows in distinctively tiered sprays, and it makes a very handsome and symmetrical tree, although far too large for most gardens. More often to be seen in homely surroundings are the numerous cultivars of the western North American Lawson's cypress or Port Orford cedar, *Chamaecyparis lawsoniana*. Amongst those with the brightest green foliage are *C. l.* Kilmacurragh, one of the narrowest of coniferous trees, and *C. l.* Erecta, a very old cultivar with closely set, bright green foliage arranged in a pointed shape like a candle-flame. The latter needs wiring to prevent it flopping apart under a weight of snow, and eventually it becomes bare of greenery at the base, but nevertheless it has a wonderful dark shape for inclusion in a backing group.

A conifer of quite different shape and growth-style, but with similarly bright, dark green colour, is a cultivar of the Japanese Hinoki cypress, *Chamaecyparis obtusa* Nana Gracilis – a small tree which takes many years to grow to 2m (6ft) tall, and which is ideal for the rock garden because of its picturesque shape, with curving sprays of foliage. Again of similar colour, but contrasting utterly in vigour and habit, is the famous Leyland cypress hybrid, × *Cupressocyparis leylandii*, which grows more rapidly than any other conifer commonly planted in gardens. It is useful when a large, rapidly grown screen is required, but rather too vigorous for a small garden. More interesting perhaps than the Leyland cypress, and better suited to small gardens, the Mediterranean cypress, *Cupressus sempervirens*, especially its cultivar Green Spire, makes a closely compact column of dark green foliage, narrow enough for use in confined courtyards, and irresistible for associating with Mediterranean-type architectural features. It is hardy in southern Britain, though rather tender while still small.

Some of the spruces have dark, bright green foliage and a narrow, neatly compact cone shape, though they may take a few years to thicken out and take on a substantial appearance. Most often seen in Britain is the Norway spruce, also known as the Christmas tree, *Picea abies*. A similar tree is the Serbian spruce, *P. omorika*, differing mainly in its soil preference, for Norway spruce needs an acid soil, while Serbian spruce naturally prefers an alkaline one. The typical Serbian spruce is a very graceful tree, more narrowly upright than the Norway spruce which, however, has a closely spire-like variety,

Fatsia japonica Variegata, a partially variegated form of this useful, autumn-flowering evergreen shrub

P. abies Pyramidata, which takes up very little room. Most beautiful and graceful of all spruces and, many would claim, of all conifers, is Brewer's weeping spruce, *P. brewerana*, which comes from a very limited area of mountain forest in the Pacific region of western North America. It needs a fair amount of room to develop its drapery of hanging foliage, and in a large garden, set dramatically amongst bare winter stems, it is one of the most spectacular trees.

The bay laurel or sweet bay, *Laurus nobilis*, a native of the Mediterranean shores said to have been the crowning laurel of ancient heroes, has dark green aromatic foliage and makes a densely textured pyramidal shrub reaching about 2m (6ft). Well known as a tub-plant, and excellent as a hedge, it thrives especially in mild coastal regions and is somewhat subject to frost damage in cold districts. A hardier form of the species is the willow-leaf bay, *L. n. angustifolia*, which has long, narrow, leathery leaves of a paler green. But both need a sunny, sheltered site. Another medium-sized shrub with aromatic leaves – noticeable when crushed – is the Mexican orange blossom, *Choisya ternata*, which is able to thrive in sun or shade. With its glossy three-piece leaves it makes a handsome and neatly rounded dark green dome, bearing sweetly fragrant flowers in spring and summer. Of similar height but contrasting shape, another densely foliaged evergreen is *Cleyera japonica*, a Far Eastern shrub which needs a lime-free soil, where it grows slowly to 2.5m (8ft) or so, its stiffly wide-spreading branches and leathery, dark green, glossy leaves adopting interesting shades of red and pink during winter – a good associate for heathers, as it appreciates a covering of low shrubs over its shallow roots.

The South American *Desfontainea spinosa*, a 2m (6ft) evergreen shrub suitable for sun or shade, is a winter-hardy plant that could almost qualify as an autumn flowerer, for the tubular orange, scarlet and yellow flowers often last until October, set vividly against the dark green, prickly, holly-like foliage. In a similar category, the escallonias have numerous hybrid cultivars suitable for garden use, on average making 2m (6ft) of glossy evergreen foliage, flowering in the summer and early autumn, and excellent for hedging or screening against sea breezes to which they are immune. Not all these natives of South America are, however, hardy inland.

The hollies of course make magnificent screens with their dense and prickly dark green foliage; and a good holly hedge is as impenetrable as any. They are easy to please in the garden, and make either low shrubs or fairly large trees. The dead leaves which often cover the ground can be uncomfortable when one is gardening nearby – being even spinier than the live green ones. Another large screening evergreen with small, dark, glossy green leaves is a Mediterranean buckthorn, *Rhamnus alaterna* – a rapidly grown bushy shrub which bears bright red holly-like berries. But it is not in the same class of hardiness as the hollies, and is better restricted to milder districts and seaside gardens.

A smaller evergreen screen is provided by the Japanese *Euonymus japonicus*, a densely foliaged bush, typically with dark green leaves, though several excellent variegated cultivars exist. The green and silver kinds are able to grow well in the shade, but the yellow forms such as *E. j*. Ovatus Aureus need sunshine to retain their colour. The species is not always completely hardy in cold districts, but it does well in southern England and is excellent by the coast. Similar in some ways, but a little less bulky overall, attaining perhaps 1.5m (5ft) in height and with smaller leaves, the densely foliaged Chinese evergreen honeysuckle *Lonicera nitida* makes an excellent low hedge. Its variety Ernest Wilson has tiny leaves on wide-spreading, drooping branches – an effective border shrub, but easily damaged by cold weather. More usually seen in gardens is the larger-leaved yellow form, *L. n*. Baggesen's Gold, yellowish-green during the winter months.

The firethorns, or pyracanthas, are small-leaved evergreens often grown on house walls where they make a useful patch of dark green in the winter, many displaying colourful berries until the spring. One of the most suitable for training as a small standard is the Chinese *Pyracantha atalantioides* Aurea, a tough little tree tolerant of all types of soil, and able to thrive under exposure, its yellow berries glowing against a dark background (see p172). Even comparatively hardy plants like this are liable to be cut back during exceptionally severe winters such as that of 1981–2, but the firethorns rank among the best subjects for north-facing walls and similar shady spots.

Phillyrea decora from Asia makes a large dome of glossy, leathery leaves up to 3m (10ft) high; and the smaller-leaved *P. latifolia* from southern Europe makes a closely textured screen of evergreen foliage and wide-spreading branches, readily forming a small and unusual standard tree. Similar in leaf is the common European box, *Buxus sempervirens*, also a large shrub which can be trained as a small tree. The vigorous, large-leaved variety, *B. s*. Arborescens, is particularly useful as a tall screen and, at the other extreme, the dwarf edging box, *B. s*. Suffruticosa, now seldom seen, has leaves of a cheerfully bright green and makes an effective clump at the front of a border.

Much smaller than the typical box, and one of the most useful evergreens for creating thick clumps of foliage in deep shade, is butcher's broom, *Ruscus aculeatus*, a native of Europe found growing wild in England. A very unusual plant with spiny leaf-like stems, it is reputed to have been used by butchers for cleaning their chopping blocks. The southern European *R. hypoglossum*, a much dwarfer shrub which forms a dense ground cover of broadly clumping foliage, is also useful for providing winter greenery in the shade.

One of the largest and most vigorous broadleaf, evergreen, screening shrubs is the common laurel or cherry laurel, *Prunus laurocerasus*, originally a native of Turkey and eastern Europe, and very tolerant of the shade beneath tall trees. Its several varieties offer a selection for different situations: *P. l.* Mischeana slowly forms a flat-topped mound of dark, glossy leaves; *P. l.* Rotundifolia makes a domed bush with rounded leaves, is one of the best laurels to tolerate regular clipping, and a good hedger; *P. l.* Magnoliifolia and Latifolia both have huge leaves 30cm (1ft) long, the latter with narrow, the former with rounded, glossy leaves, both eventually forming very large shrubs; *P. l.* Zabeliana is the smallest, narrowest-leaved variety, useful to the forefront of a dark evergreen scheme where it grows low and spreading in the shade.

An unusual screening shrub, and one of the most ornamental of evergreens, is the Chinese *Viburnum rhytidophyllum*, which has strangely corrugated, dark glossy leaves covered on their undersides with a fawn-coloured felt. The spring flowers are quite attractive, but the species excels as a foliage plant, particularly useful in limy and chalky soils. A contrasting companion for this shrub in mild localities is *Griselinia litoralis* from New Zealand, a densely leafy shrub with leathery, bright green foliage. The cultivar Dixon's Cream has attractively variegated leaves, and either type will make a fine hedge at the seaside, though they are less hardy inland. A glaucous sea-green shrub sometimes grown for the sake of its silvery evergreen foliage is *Atriplex halimus*, the tree purslane, a native of southern Europe hardy in southern and western Britain at least, and excellent by the coast. It makes a useful associate for *Maytenus boaria*, a graceful small tree or large shrub from Chile, the small narrow leaves a contrastingly bright glossy green.

Two hardy palms which introduce a suggestion of tropical summers to a temperate winter are the southern European *Chamaerops humilis*, the stemless dwarf fan palm which survives the coldest winters, and the taller *Trachycarpus fortunei*, the Chinese

The sword-like leaves of a yucca look no less exotic thrusting through the snow

Chusan palm, which has enormous fan-shaped leaves and will also withstand cold winters. Although hardy, these palms are best reared in pots and grown under glass for a few years, to give them a good start, before hardening off and planting out.

The cabbage tree, *Cordyline australis*, from New Zealand, is also an exotic-looking small tree suitable for mild temperate areas. A favourite seaside tree in southern and western Britain, it is somewhat palm-like in appearance, with a single stem and stiffly ascending branches, each crowned with a cluster of long, sword-like leaves. The New Zealand flax, *Phormium tenax*, also comes into this category, with thick, rigid swords held 2m (6ft) high, the typical species forming clumps of soft grey green. Yuccas also lend a sub-tropical evergreen effect to sunny gardens in Britain, with their sword-like leaves and tall lily-like spires of flowers in summer. Several species from Central America and the southern USA are hardy: *Yucca filamentosa* forms dense, stemless clumps of greyish-green leaves margined with curly white threads; *Y. flaccida* also forms stemless clumps of long glaucous green leaves which droop distinctively at their tips; *Y. recurvifolia* has a short stem bearing long, tapered leaves which curve outwards; and *Y. gloriosa*, well known as Adam's needle, has a stout stem up to 2m (6ft) high, with straight, stiff, viciously pointed leaves. Several of these exotics have variegated cultivars (see p128).

Conifers with a similar shade of glaucous sea-green foliage include several of the cypresses, notably *Chamaecyparis lawsoniana* Pottenii and Allumii, both of which make compactly upright spires, the former with soft, juvenile-type foliage and the latter with mature, upright sprays. Equally striking in colouring is the weeping Nootka cypress, *C. nootkatensis* Pendula, also from North America, and one of the most beautiful of medium-sized conifers, with gracefully pendulous foliage, at first sight similar to that of the weeping spruce, hanging down like the folds of a curtain. It is a tree to be grown fairly well isolated from other conifers so that it can develop its full potential without crowding, perhaps among birches, where it will contrast dramatically with the stems of winter.

Another weeping blue-green tree is *Juniperus recurva coxii*, a remarkable Asian juniper with long, drooping sprays of foliage, picturesque against shaggy brown bark. Several junipers have the glaucous green look, especially *Juniperus chinensis* Pyramidalis, a variety of the Chinese juniper, and a strictly conical, rather prickly little tree; *J. communis* Hibernica, the Irish juniper, which forms a narrow pillar of very slow-growing greenish-grey foliage, the stems tending to separate under the weight of snow and sometimes in need of wiring; and *J. virginiana* Skyrocket, a variety of the North American pencil cedar, probably the narrowest of all conifers, similar in foliage to the Irish juniper but so slender as to fit in well to the smallest garden. These spire-like junipers need an unshaded site that will allow them to develop firm foliage and a straight carriage.

One of the best-known small garden shrubs with evergreen greyish-green foliage is rosemary, *Rosmarinus officinalis*, a native of southern Europe well suited to a dryish site in a sunny border. Also from southern Europe and a shrub for full sunlight is *Cistus parviflorus*, one of the hardiest of the sun roses, forming a grey-green bush some 45cm (1½ft) high and 1m (3ft) across, bearing beautiful pink flowers in midsummer. Other grey-foliaged shrubs which recall the Mediterranean hills with their sunloving habits, and which still manage to look reasonably presentable in the depths of a more northerly winter, include some of the rock roses, hebes, lavender and phlomis. Particularly useful in the garden over winter is the southern European *Santolina chamaecyparissus*, lavender cotton or cotton lavender, a woolly evergreen that is almost obligatory in any sunny, dryish site, and its dwarf form Weston – whiter, woollier and more compact than the type, and ideal for the front of a south-facing border.

Senecio greyi and *S. laxifolius* have been much confused in nomenclature, but however these popular New Zealand natives are classified – now often grouped under the general head *Senecio* Sunshine, to cover a range of closely related garden hybrids – they are useful foliage plants for sunny sites. They will grow well in the shade, but they then lose their grey hairy covering and become green and uninspiring, and old leaves also turn green with age if the plants are allowed to become straggly. The weedy yellow flowers are not to everyone's liking, and as these plants seem to be less hardy after expending their energy on seed production, they are best clipped or pinched periodically to keep them healthy and frost-hardy, and the foliage grey and compact.

Some of the hardy eucalypts rank amongst the most dramatic blue-grey evergreens, but their colour often depends on the maturity of the foliage. *Eucalyptus gunnii*, one of the hardiest of the Australian gum trees, has two distinct foliage phases: the rounded young leaves are a bright silvery blue, but the old leaves change their shape and colour, becoming green and contrastingly sickle-shaped. The beautiful blue juvenile foliage can be retained permanently by keeping it trimmed back as a bush, and in this form it makes a wonderfully colourful hedge for a sunny site, clear blue and reliably hardy if trimmed regularly in the spring and kept to a height of 1–1.5m (3–4ft).

Blue-grey conifers include the well-known blue Atlantic cedar, *Cedrus atlantica glauca*, a wild form from the Atlas Mountains; and the smooth Arizona cypress, *Cupressus glabra* Pyramidalis, its beautiful foliage studded over winter with tiny yellow male flowers. *Pinus parviflora*, the Japanese white pine, has blue-green leaves lined with white; and the blue Colorado spruce, *Picea pungens* Koster – a very popular, perfectly cone-shaped little tree – has dense, prickly foliage of an intense bluish silver. Several cypresses come into the same colour category, including a variety of the Japanese Sawara cypress, *Chamaecyparis pisifera* Boulevard, which makes a soft, blue-grey dome; varieties of the North American Lawson's cypress such as *Chamaecyparis lawsoniana* Pembury Blue, a fairly large conical tree with fine blue foliage; *C. l.* Columnaris, fairly bluish in its foliage and compactly spire-shaped; *C. l.* Fletcheri, which makes a thickly foliaged, stiffly upright dome of bristly foliage; and the small *C. l.* Ellwoodii, a very slow-growing little tree, its bluish colour particularly bright during the winter.

Amongst variegated evergreen shrubs, hollies provide a good selection, and are popular in the garden (see pp184–5). A similar but denser screen, at least as attractive, is supplied by the variegated osmanthuses, particularly the Japanese *Osmanthus heterophyllus* Aureomarginatus which has small dark green leaves edged with bright gold, and *O. h.* Latifolius Variegatus, which has larger leaves marked with silver, white and shades of green. These large hardy shrubs produce their small fragrant white flowers in the autumn and early winter (see p40).

Another winter-flowering evergreen with good leaf variegation is the southern European laurustinus, especially the silver-variegated *Viburnum tinus* Variegatum and the gold-variegated *V. t.* Aureomarginatum, both slightly less hardy than the green type, but succeeding in most moderately sheltered gardens. Both variegated forms sometimes produce dark blue berries late in the autumn, and these look fine against the light leaf colours.

The large elaeagnus species make fast-growing shelter bushes with handsome evergreen foliage, and often bear unspectacular but very fragrant flowers in the autumn. *Elaeagnus × ebbingei* is a vigorous hybrid with large silver-backed leaves, the Japanese *E. macrophylla* has rounded silvery leaves, and both readily form a large, wide-spreading screen. The former has a very attractive variegated form

(*above left*) *Osmanthus heterophyllus* Lati-folius Variegatus. A large, holly-like shrub variegated in shades of green and silver, bearing tiny, fragrant white flowers in the autumn; (*right*) *Elaeagnus × ebbingei* Gilt Edge, a very attractive gold-variegated shrub which will make a vigorous evergreen screen

Elaeagnus pungens Maculata is one of the handsomest of screening evergreens for winter colour

E. × *e*. Gilt Edge, of fairly recent introduction, and this seems to be hardy and vigorous. The Japanese shrub *E. pungens* is best known for its beautifully gold-variegated form *E. p*. Maculata. The typical species has green leaves backed with brown-speckled white felt, and is more vigorous than the variegated form. *E. p*. Maculata tends to revert to the green type, and when green shoots appear they should be pulled off before they can gain vigour and swamp the golden leaves. The variegated form is one of the handsomest of evergreens for winter foliage colour and, provided green shoots can be kept at bay, is vigorous enough, once well established, to form an excellent screen which rarely needs cutting back.

One of the most unusual non-variegated evergreens with good foliage colour is the golden chestnut, *Chrysolepis chrysophylla*, from the western USA. A small tree or large shrub related to the European chestnut, it has pointed leathery leaves, dark green on their upper surfaces and yellow beneath, making a shady, spreading screen.

Variegated cultivars of the common European box include *Buxus sempervirens* Elegantissima, which makes a fairly low, thickly foliaged dome, with creamy-white leaf margins; *B. s*. Gold Tip, which looks rather like an ordinary green box yellowing slightly at the top of the bush; and *B. s*. Latifolia Maculata, perhaps the best variety for screens or hedges, with compactly dense foliage, and a colourful plant in full sunshine with its comparatively large leaves blotched with yellow, but greener in the shade. Box can grow well in heavy shade, but variegated forms lose much of their colour.

Species and varieties of pittosporum make attractive evergreen screening shrubs, especially suitable for the seaside or for sheltered sites in mild inland areas. One of the best variegations in the genus belongs to *Pittosporum tenuifolium* Garnettii, a cultivar of the New Zealand species, which makes a dense dome of foliage, the greyish-green leaves variegated with silver, margined with white, and tinged in the winter with a warm shade of ruby-red.

Some of the yuccas from the south-eastern USA have excellent colour variegations: the 2m (6ft) high *Yucca gloriosa* has Variegata, its dangerously sharp swords marked with stripes and margins of creamy-white; the stemless *Y. flaccida* has the cultivar Golden Sword, which displays a broad central yellow stripe on the curving-tipped leaves; and *Y. filamentosa* has particularly attractive forms in Bright Edge and Variegata, which have yellow margins to their spreading leaves, set in dense, stemless clumps. Somewhat similar, with their narrow sword-like leaves, are the phormiums. The New

Hybrid phormiums with brightly variegated evergreen leaves, grown in tubs as ornamental patio plants

Zealand flax, *Phormium tenax*, has the bronzy purple variety Purpureum, and Variegatum with yellow stripes on the rigid blades. Hybrid phormiums include *P.* Dazzler, with somewhat limp leaves tinted overall in deep reds and pinks – a wonderfully tropical-looking plant for a completely unshaded site – and Bronze Baby, which has long, drooping-tipped leaves of bronze, hardy in all but the coldest areas. The New Zealand cabbage tree *Cordyline australis* has the variety *C. a.* Atropurpurea, which is even more exotic than the green type, with its purple yucca-like leaves on stout stems. Away from the mild south and west, the purple cabbage tree needs well-sheltered conditions, and will not grow in the colder districts.

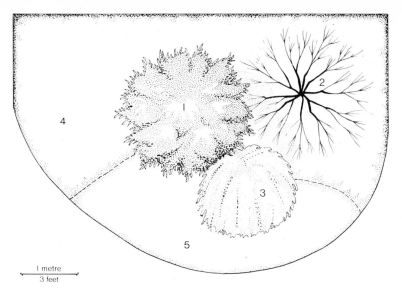

One of the most striking foliage groups, beautiful throughout the year:
1 *Cleyera fortunei*;
2 *Euonymus alatus*;
3 *Berberis × stenophylla* Pink Pearl;
4 *Calluna vulgaris* Arran Gold;
5 *Erica herbacea* Loughrigg

One of the most attractive small evergreen shrubs for the forefront of the border is the beautifully variegated *Berberis × stenophylla* Pink Pearl, a cultivar of the popular hybrid between two South American barberries. Its arching branches bear narrow little leaves mottled in shades of green, pink and cream, with new young shoots emerging throughout the year. The youngest leaves are pure cream on rose-red stems, and the variably coloured flowers, usually rose pink in the bud, opening white, make the bush a mass of bloom in the spring with an occasional bonus of a few flowers on display through autumn and winter. This hardy little shrub is suitable for both sunny and shady sites, in all types of garden soil.

Several yellow-foliaged or gold-variegated conifers provide excellent contrast amongst plain evergreens, but they should not be overdone in any design or the colourful effect is easily lost. They contrast best with dark green foliage and bluish or purple evergreens. The yellow cultivars of the North American Lawson's cypress include *Chamaecyparis lawsoniana* Stewartii, a very old variety and a full-sized tree, which forms a symmetrical cone of flattened golden sprays but, though striking during the summer, the colour is much less intense in the winter; *C. l.* Lutea, an even older cultivar, wider-spreading and more limply foliaged than Stewartii, colourful in the winter, with large, soft sprays of golden-yellow; *C. l.* Lanei, a narrow, shapely spire, with sparse but elegant sprays of golden-yellow, excellent in the winter; and *C. l.* Winston Churchill, fairly slow growing, but one of the best Lawson's cypresses for colour, making a neatly stocky column of dense foliage of a bright amber-yellow, particularly beautiful in winter. Amongst the dwarf varieties of Lawson's cypress, *C. l.* Minima Aurea is outstanding. A slow-growing globe of dense, finely soft, golden-yellow foliage, it is an excellent shrub for the rock garden, where it glows against the grey rocks and makes a good companion for the low-spreading junipers.

Amongst varieties of the Japanese Hinoki cypress, *Chamaecyparis obtusa* Crippsii makes a small tree with wide-spreading branches, forming a broad, loose cone of golden-yellow foliage; and smaller but equally beautiful, *C. o.* Tetragona Aurea is a slow-growing, almost dwarf bush with wide-spreading sprays of feathery foliage in golden amber-yellow. The Japanese Sawara cypress contributes *Chamaecyparis pisifera* Filifera Aurea, which makes a bush of drooping, whip-like golden-yellow sprays; and *C. p.* Plumosa Aurea, a small densely foliaged tree or large, domed shrub, with soft, feathery yellow foliage, darkening in the winter to a bronzy shade of gold.

Golden varieties of the Californian Monterey cypress make fairly large and very beautiful trees. Especially worthy of note are *Cupressus macrocarpa* Goldcrest, a narrow column of feathery foliage in rich bright yellow; and *C. m.* Donard Gold, a broad cone of rich golden-yellow foliage. Other similar varieties of Monterey cypress include Golden Cone and Golden Pillar, all thriving in southern Britain, but not reliably hardy in colder districts.

Among the spruces, *Picea orientalis* Aurea, a golden form of the Caucasian or Oriental spruce, retains shrub-like proportions, its spiky yellow foliage more colourful during spring and summer than in winter. Pines include the golden Scots Pine, *Pinus sylvestris* Aurea, a small, slow-growing tree which, by way of contrast, is most brightly coloured during the winter months, at which season the needles display a conspicuous, orangy-golden yellow.

The North American western red cedar or arbor-vitae, *Thuja plicata*, has a few gold-variegated forms which make fairly large trees, notably *T. p.* Zebrina – a vigorous, evenly textured cone of beautiful green and yellow foliage. Two dwarf bushes of the same species, *T. p.* Stoneham Gold and Rogersii, are splendid bronzy-gold shrubs for the rock garden; but among the best-known rock-garden shrubs of this genus is the American arbor-vitae, *Thuja occidentalis* Rheingold. One of the most popular dwarf conifers, it is especially beautiful in winter with its feathery foliage of golden-yellow, and is one of the best associates for low-growing dark evergreens, such as the prostrate junipers and the winter-flowering heaths and heathers.

The European common yew has several good golden-yellow forms. Amongst these are *Taxus baccata* Elegantissima, which displays a better colour in spring and summer than it does in winter; *T. b.* Semperaurea, a similarly shaped, upright-branched bush with orangy-yellow foliage in winter; *T. b.* Fastigiata Aureomarginata, the well-known golden Irish yew, which eventually makes a stout pillar of dense yellow-tipped foliage; and *T. b.* Standishii, another upright columnar variety, better coloured than the golden Irish yew, and a more convenient plant for the small rock garden as it is slower-growing.

At the opposite extreme, fastest-growing of all the golden-foliaged conifers, is the Castlewellan Leyland cypress, × *Cupresso-cyparis leylandii* Castlewellan, which can with equal facility make a tall tree substantial enough for park or arboretum, a closely clipped hedge, or part of a dense, peep-proof backing screen, where it will associate well with a wide range of green and blue foliaged conifers.

The creamy bark of the Himalayan birch, *Betula utilis*, stands out boldly above a carpet of winter-flowering heaths

6
Winter Stems

The luminous stems of white and silver birches seem to typify the rigours of a northern winter. So characteristic are they, that they have even penetrated the mythology of a cheerless season in the folklore of three continents, for their cold colours are as vivid when seen through the murk of short sub-arctic days in Canada, Scandinavia or Siberia as they are when gleaming in the chilly sunshine of a Himalayan mountain forest.

By inference, other white or grey barked trees and shrubs also have a cold and wintry look – the beeches with their smooth dark grey, the ashes with their lighter, mistier shade of grey; the violet willow with its purple-tinted white bloom; the whitewash brambles and the white-stemmed raspberries. Leafless, all suggest the depth of winter, and in this are at variance with those evergreen plants which have leaves of white or grey, for these irresistibly suggest long, dry summers – and many of them are Mediterranean sun-baskers – for their often woolly leaves have a warm, sunny look and seem out of place on damp, sunless days.

Warm colours in winter are seen in the browns and mahoganies of stems and twigs – of the cherries especially. Few plants magnify the weak sunshine of a winter's day as readily as the wild British cherry and the numerous Asian species and their cultivars, or even the North American cherry birch which, with several other American birches, bridges the gap very neatly between the two different trees. Trees with dark, shaggy bark can only look warm, even on the coldest day, and those with chestnut and cinnamon hues, like the strangely tattered paperbark maple, seem to take some of the chill out of the air. Many maples carry a suggestion of coolness, with their smooth olive or green and white snakeskin stripes; but the coral-bark maple, *Acer palmatum* Senkaki, surely ranks amongst the sunniest of all trees, the curious animal-pink of

The remarkable, flaking bark of the paperbark maple, *Acer griseum*

its twigs seeming to distil some essence of the colours surrounding it, glowing as it catches the haziest rays of the sun.

The basic rules of harmonious colour association are not as inflexible with winter stems and foliage as their exponents insist they are with the flowers of summer. Scarlet is always a difficult colour to blend successfully, in the flower border as elsewhere, but the brilliant stems of the scarlet willow *Salix alba* Chermesina will draw nothing but admiration when sited next to a yellow-stemmed willow, a cinnamon maple, a purple cherry-plum, a crimson dogwood or even a sheer white birch. Birches of the silvery-white type, incidentally, are prone to lose something of their purity through ill-matched company in winter or summer, and if given too staring a contrast can take on a cheap and nasty look.

The integration of awkward elements is often best arranged in stages. Black goes well with all colours, and the rough black base which frequently develops on silver-birch stems not only enhances their beauty but can help to blend the colours of adjacent and low-carpeting plants. Similarly, the darkest tones of purple, yew-green, and sepia-brown can mediate between the gaudier colours, and dark purple in particular can successfully link conflicting blues and reds – a discord which sometimes sets crimson and scarlet at odds – and the frequently contentious yellow and crimson. Yellow and orange shades associate as well with white as they do with black, and always look right against birch stems, which seem to take on a sunny reflected glow under their influence. A grove of silver birch associating with a coppice stool or two of the golden willow *Salix alba* Vitellina will well illustrate this point, especially if the background is as contrastingly black as it can be made, with shadow or dark evergreen foliage.

A difficult piece of wasteland or a boggy patch, adjacent to the garden, can be a godsend when planning a winter vista, for many trees and shrubs with outstandingly beautiful bark can thrive in such areas. Birches, willows, dogwoods, golden-speckled alder, hazels and whitewash brambles are perfect for the job. The wildest, boggiest patch can support a flourishing grove, full of birds and green leaf in summer, and a focus of spectacular beauty during the winter months.

Few gardeners find themselves in the fortunate position of having to deal with such a 'problem' area! The mixed border, on the other hand, comes into everyone's province, and here some of the smaller shrubs with coloured bark can be used to form a basic framework, with an eye to shape and texture as well as colour. Background is bound to influence choice, and where the border is sited against a wall, the colour of the wall may prove significant enough to be taken into account. Bark shades of light red and orange tend to lose their effect in front of red brick; similarly, yellow stems as well as yellow foliage may seem insipid when viewed against Cotswold stone, and grey or white stems will be well camouflaged against a background of grey granite, or Portland or Wenlock limestone. Sometimes, however, one distinctive focal point of similarly coloured stems will have the opposite effect, and cogently bring out the colour if placed some little distance from the backing wall. When planting is under way, container-grown plants in particular can be placed temporarily in position, and the results studied before making a permanent commitment. In this way, the most carefully prepared paper plan may well be overruled in favour of immediate practical effect.

Plant colours can undergo subtle changes depending on light, temperature and humidity. The age and condition of the plants will have their effect, too, and colours also frequently vary quite widely from individual to individual, the wild species and long-cultivated garden varieties being particularly prone to inequality. Clones or named cultivars are more stable, but even so there would be considerable jostling for position if all were lined up for colour gradation. In the list which follows, a selection of trees and shrubs with outstanding winter stems are arranged by colour, commencing with sheer white and progressing through shades of yellow, red, brown and orange, including motleys and stripes, to the spring-like green shoots of flowering nutmeg and kerria.

White

Betula jacquemontii   A fairly large, wide-spreading birch tree native to the western Himalayan forests. One of the most conspicuous trees during winter, with paper-thin bark peeling in strips to leave a smooth surface of dazzling white, barely darkening to a warm shade of cream in the branches and twigs.

B. caerulea-grandis   A native of North America, this small and rather stiffly upright birch tree has almost pure white bark which stands out conspicuously against any kind of dark background – a particularly attractive tree in the spring when laden with countless large yellow catkins.

B. pendula, silver birch   A native of Europe, and one of Britain's best-known wild trees, thriving in poor, dry soils, this beautiful woodlander is such a winter feature as to almost compel inclusion in a large garden, and is often most strikingly effective when several are arranged to make a small group. The silvery-white stems with their contrasting, rough-barked black base and gracefully pendulous dark reddish-black twigs, seem right in any informal setting. A smaller and more fully weeping cultivar of the silver birch is Young's weeping birch, *B. p.* Youngii, which grows very slowly, gradually mounding itself into a dome of curtain-like shoots. Young's weeping birch is often more appropriate than the wild species for planting in a small garden, though less suitable for underplanting because, like a weeping willow, the leaves and shoots if left untrimmed will cover the ground closely, keeping it dry and shaded over a mat of shallow, fibrous roots.

Other cultivars of the silver birch include *B. p.* Fastigiata, which, by virtue of its narrowly upright habit, takes up less room than the others, is easier to plant under, and equally attractive in colour of bark, though some may say it lacks the pendulous grace of the wild tree; *B. p.* Tristis, a fairly tall, slender birch which grows into a neatly symmetrical weeping tree with branches as well as shoots and twigs drooping gracefully; and the Swedish birch, *B. p.* Dalecarlica, its bark very like the typical silver birch, and similarly making a fairly large, broadly crowned and partially weeping tree, differing chiefly in the leaves, which are comparatively long and attractively

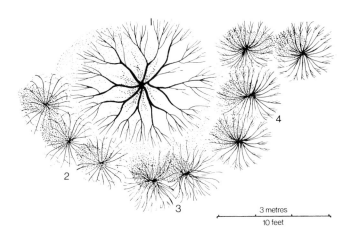

For a wild area, a striking collection of winter stems:
1 *Alnus incana* Aurea;   3 *Cornus stolonifera* Flaviramea;
2 *Rubus cockburnianus*;   4 *Cornus alba* Sibirica

deep-cut. For year-round beauty, *B. p.* Dalecarlica is one of the best birches to make a small clump in the medium-sized garden.

B. platyphylla   A large birch tree from the Far East, very similar in winter appearance to the European silver birch, with silvery-white bark and darkish twigs, but with a more widely spreading and somewhat less symmetrical crown. *B. platyphylla szechuanica*, Chinese white birch, and *B. p. japonica*, Japanese white birch, are two regional forms of the species. Both are tall, slender trees which tend to display a chalky or somewhat greyish-white bark rather than the typical silver, with contrastingly dark twigs.

B. pubescens, white birch   A well-known native of Britain and Europe, this medium-sized, fairly wide-spreading tree, is a common constituent of woodlands on poor, wet soils. The peeling bark is conspicuously dead white on mature stems, and dark reddish brown or copper on the large branches and younger stems, with downy reddish-black twigs.

B. populifolia, grey birch   This small birch tree is a woodland native of eastern North America, where it is widespread and common on poor land, and particularly familiar in winter with its conspicuous greyish-white bark.

Rubus cockburnianus (syn. *R. giraldianus*), whitewash bramble   A vigorous Chinese thicket-forming bramble which produces edible blackberries in late summer. The stems grow stiffly upright and arch at the top in a tangle of twigs, their true bark purple but overlaid with a thick white bloom, fascinating when viewed against a dark background, and sometimes eerily vivid on moonlit nights. Although incorrigibly informal, whitewash bramble is not difficult to keep under control; once their bark has lost its bloom, the old stems should be cut to the ground early in spring, to be replaced by startlingly white young shoots.

R. biflorus   The very vigorous, sprawling stems of this Himalayan bramble have green bark overlaid with a vivid, waxy-white bloom which wears off after a few months. The stems bear edible orange-yellow berries as they mature and start to turn dark green or brown, but the chief value of the plant lies in the colour of its young shoots, and these fruiting stems are best cut out as soon as new bloomy shoots appear at their base. Left uncut, the prickly stems form a

The Chinese white-wash bramble, *Rubus cockburnianus*, produces a thicket of startlingly white young stems

dense and almost impenetrable thicket, and sucker so freely that the plant can become invasive.

R. thibetanus A thicket-former from the Chinese and Tibetan mountains, which in late summer bears edible raspberries amongst its fine lacy foliage. The somewhat sprawling stems are similar in overall effect to those of the whitewash bramble, purple-barked and heavily coated with a bluish-white waxy bloom. These ornamental brambles or raspberries can be very effective during winter in a semi-wild garden, or isolated on a piece of rough ground, and they will do well on difficult, chalky soil; but they must be kept firmly under control, and there is really no place for them in a well-ordered small garden.

Salix daphnoides, violet willow   Native to a vast area of northern Europe and central Asia, including the Himalayas, this small, spreading and very graceful tree is hardy and quick-growing. Though barely large enough to do damage to house foundations, like all willows its roots explore the subsoil deeply and draw off

moisture during periods of drought; to avoid the danger of subterranean shrinkage in clay areas, it is best not planted too near
buildings. Vigorous young shoots of the violet willow have purple
bark overlaid with a sheer white bloom, appearing pale violet
where the deep purple shows through. To ensure a vivid, fan-shaped
display every winter, all the shoots should be cut back to the stump
in the spring. It is also effective when grown as a small standard
tree, the shoots pollarded to the base of the crown every other year.

S. irrorata   A vigorous, shrubby willow native to the southern
United States, similar to the European violet willow in its long,
whippy young shoots with purple bark heavily bloomed with
white, and, like the European species, producing a good display of
silvery-grey catkins very early in the spring before the leaves start
to sprout. Its size and vigour make it ideal for coppicing annually or
biennially in the spring, and a useful companion for a pollarded
violet willow if coppiced to ground-level close by the larger species.

Buff

Betula papyrifera, paper birch or canoe birch   This large birch tree
from North America, well known through Indian folklore, makes
an interesting addition to gardens big enough to accommodate it.
An exceedingly handsome tree in winter with its creamy-white,
paper-like bark, peeling in large flakes to reveal a tinge of orange
and buff beneath.

B. costata   A fairly large, vigorously spreading birch tree from
China and Siberia, with greyish-brown or creamy-white bark in
papery layers which flake away in large greyish-brown patches.

B. Jermyns   A fairly large, wide-spreading hybrid birch tree
recently raised at Hilliers' famous English nurseries, and proving
popular as an ornamental garden tree. It is a useful colour in
winter, the older bark of warm orange-buff peeling to an un-
blemished creamy-white, shaded with coppery tints among the
lower branches, and contrasting with the dark twigs of the crown.

B. utilis, Himalayan birch   A medium-sized tree of upright stance,
with bark peeling uniformly on both stem and branches in pale
creamy buff, shaded with copper and orange. There is also a dark-
barked form of the species.

Betula ermanii tends to be heavily limbed and wide-spreading, with a shredding bark of pinkish apricot-buff

B. × caerulea   This small birch tree is a hybrid between *B. caerulea-grandis* and *B. populifolia*, with characteristics somewhat intermediate between its two American parents but richer in bark colour, the overall creamy-white and buff tinted amongst the lower limbs with dark orange-brown.

B. ermanii   A fairly large wide-spreading birch tree from north-eastern Asia, noted for its extremely beautiful bark in a creamy shade of pinkish-apricot, peeling in thin strips and exposing patches of dull white shaded to dark buff and orange-brown. Its Japanese geographical variety, *B. e. subcordata*, has bark which peels in strips mainly of cream and white, shaded where it reaches the lower branches to a warm coppery-brown.

B. albo-sinensis septentrionalis   Another fairly large, conically crowned birch tree from China, often claimed to be the most ornamental of all the birches by virtue of the subtle coloration of its peeling bark which is a pale, glossy orange-brown tinged with copper and bloomed with shades of pink and grey.

Eucalyptus niphophila, snow gum   This small Australian gum tree, a native of cool mountainous regions, is one of the hardiest of the genus. It makes a slow-growing, shrubby but picturesque little evergreen tree, with bark beautifully patterned in a smoothly peeling patchwork of cream and white, green and pinkish-buff, the branches attractively framed at all seasons by the curved, leathery leaves, their dark greyish-green contrasting with the orange-brown shoots. Frost and low temperatures do not, as a rule, harm the snow gum, and it will survive winters severe enough to kill the other eucalypts. Nevertheless, for healthy growth it needs some shelter from cold continental winds, and looks better on a site open enough to allow free development of its natural shape without crowding by more vigorous trees.

Stewartia pseudocamellia   A small Japanese tree which flourishes in a woodland type of garden with a lime-free soil, always greatly admired in summer for its glorious yellow-centred white flowers, and for the bright autumn foliage colours that follow (see pp93–4). The bark is very attractive in winter, flaking into a pattern of fawn-grey, with smooth patches of cream and bright green.

The Australian snow gum, *Eucalyptus niphophila*, is one of the hardiest of the genus, and makes a picturesque little evergreen tree

S. koreana   A similar but smaller tree from Korea, with flaking two-tone bark in shades of pale and dark brown, and excellent autumn colours (see p95).

S. sinensis   A small, fragrant-flowered Chinese tree noted for its autumn colours (see p103), and attractive when leafless during the winter with its bark flaking into patches of green, buff and cream.

***Pinus bungeana*, lace-bark pine**   In some ways, this Chinese pine has more the appearance of a broad-leaved tree than a conifer, with its low, heavy limbs and smooth bark patterned like that of a London plane, flaking into a patchwork of buff, cream, green and grey. The lace-bark pine makes an admirable small evergreen tree, sometimes hardly more than a large shrub, but always highly ornamental in garden surroundings with its picturesque bark and cheerfully bright pale green foliage.

Rhododendron barbatum   A tree rhododendron from the mountain forests of Nepal and northern India, its large, dark evergreen leaves contrasting with the conspicuously bright yellow-buff twigs, the bark of lower branches and stem peeling picturesquely in shades of brown, cream and buff. It produces clusters of spectacular crimson flowers quite early in the spring, and needs shelter to protect these from the weather. A woodland garden with an acid, peaty soil and partial overhead shade, provides the ideal site.

***Parrotia persica*, iron tree**   A native of Iran and the Mount Ararat region, this small, spreading tree features strongly in many woodland gardens, largely for the sake of its vivid autumn foliage colours (see pp97–8). It is attractive, too, in the bare winter months, with its fawn-grey bark peeling in a patchwork of cream, green and brown.

Platanus × ***hispanica*, London plane**   This large hybrid tree is a well-known feature of city streets, easily recognised in winter by its mottled bark, peeling in patterns of cream, buff, green and brown, and by the dry, round seedheads hanging in little bunches from the wide-spreading (and frequently pollarded) branches.

***P. orientalis*, the Oriental plane**   A native of southern Europe, similar in appearance to the London plane but larger, with heavy limbs supporting a broadly spreading crown, clusters of bristly seedheads, and similarly dappled bark, peeling into a patchwork of cream, green and buff.

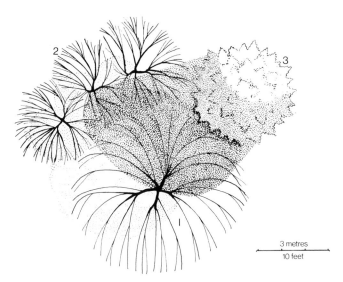

A substantial group which presents a fascinating blend of gold, white and blue through the winter:
1 *Salix × chrysocoma*; 2 *Betula pendula*; 3 *Chamaecyparis lawsoniana* Pembury Blue

Yellow

Betula lutea, yellow birch   A native of eastern North America, where it grows into an upright and fairly substantial tree valued for its timber. It can make an interesting addition to a large garden, particularly during the bare winter months when the bark is conspicuous, peeling into a smooth, glossy pattern of gold and amber.

***Cornus stolonifera* Flaviramea,** yellow dogwood   A densely thicketing, medium-sized shrub from North America, eager to make a suckering tangle of slender yellow and yellowish-green shoots. It is useful for patches of rough or boggy ground, and an excellent companion for the red-stemmed dogwoods and coppiced willows. Like the willows, if cut back periodically in the spring it will send up rampant growths of new shoots.

***Tilia platyphyllos* Aurea,** yellow-twigged lime   This variety of the large and vigorous European broad-leaved lime makes an ideal town tree for park or road verge, but is too large for most gardens. In winter the long, whippy yellow shoots of the current year's growth are conspicuous against the olive-green older branches.

***Fraxinus excelsior* Jaspidea,** golden ash   This variety of the common British ash has a vigorous and fairly wide-spreading crown, with yellowish bark on the young branches shading into bright golden-yellow shoots, making a striking combination with the sober grey bark of the limbs and main stem.

Salix alba **Vitellina,** golden willow   Ultimately, if left to grow naturally, this variety of the common European white willow makes a medium-sized tree with wide-spreading limbs. Usually, however, it is treated either as a coppice bush or a small pollarded tree, the branches being cut back to the stump or crown base every second year in the spring, ensuring a display of vigorous, richly coloured yellow shoots with a symmetrically fan-shaped silhouette.

S. × **chrysocoma,** golden weeping willow   This cultivar probably originated as a hybrid between the golden willow and *S. babylonica*, the old-fashioned weeping willow of Babylon. One of the best known and most popular of garden trees, the golden weeping willow grows to a large size, with wide-spreading, high-arching branches of a mellow buff-brown, supporting a continuous ground-sweeping curtain of long, slender, golden-yellow shoots.

Red, Pink and Purple

Salix Decipiens, cardinal willow   This hybrid cultivar probably includes in its ancestry the two common British riverside trees – *S. alba*, the white willow, and *S. fragilis*, the crack willow. It makes a large symmetrical bush or small, cone-shaped tree, with glossy yellowish-grey twigs tinged with scarlet on the side most exposed to the sun.

S. Basfordiana   A hybrid willow, larger than but closely related to the cardinal willow. All the young shoots darken through the growing season to a distinct orange-red in winter, but some individuals are much more brightly coloured than others, and when cuttings are taken they should be selected from the best specimens.

S. alba Chermesina (syn. S. a. Britzensis), scarlet willow   The best willow to plant for a spectacular display of red shoots in the winter. The wand-like stems grow about 2m (6ft) each year if the old shoots are cut hard back to the stool in the spring. To make a substantially larger bush, this coppicing operation can be carried out every second year, just before the buds break in March. The scarlet willow is also effective as a small pollarded standard tree, the branches cut back to the base of the crown some 2m (6ft) above ground-level, every other spring. Grown thus, it makes an excellent companion for the golden willow and several coppicing dogwoods.

Acer palmatum **Senkaki,** coral-bark maple   In this beautiful cultivar of the well-known Japanese maple the glossy, reddish coral-pink bark colour of the young shoots during winter is distinctive, most unusual among shrubs and small trees. Quite rapidly growing, it eventually makes a fairly symmetrical dome-shaped tree something over 6m (20ft) tall, covered with the colourful, densely interlacing branchlets.

A. pensylvanicum **Erythrocladum,** pink moosewood   A somewhat uncommon clone of the snake-bark maple from eastern North America, and one of the most ornamental of small trees for the colour of its bark in winter. It is not so easily grown into a good specimen as the coral-bark maple, and does best in a sheltered, moist, woodland garden. The young shoots are a bright coral-pink tempered with paler stripes, and the mature branches and stem are a pale salmon-pink, sometimes described as the colour of rosé wine, with overtones of beige and grey.

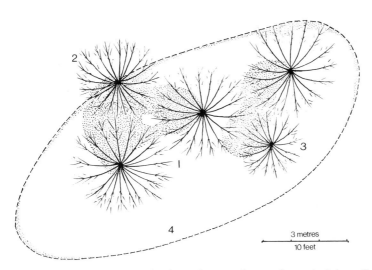

A memorable scheme for a patch of rough ground – scarlet and violet willows carpeted with purple Siberian squill:

1 *Salix alba* Chermesina;	3 *Salix irrorata*;
2 *Salix daphnoides*;	4 *Scilla sibirica*

Cornus alba, red-barked dogwood   A native of north-eastern Asia, and completely hardy, this shrub will thrive in most soils, wet or dry, and makes a cheerful display of bright-red shoots during the winter months. If left untended it can form a thicket some 3m (10ft) high, but it may be pruned hard back in the spring to produce a new flush of young shoots, bright green during spring and summer, darkening to a rich crimson by the time the leaves fall in the autumn.

C. a. **Sibirica,** Westonbirt dogwood   This cultivar of the red-barked dogwood makes a thicket of bright crimson-red shoots. Though highly ornamental, Westonbirt dogwood is not as tenacious as the type species, and tends to die out after several years. For this reason it is probably best not to coppice the shoots completely but merely to thin them out by removing about half the total number early in March.

C. a. **Spaethii**; *C. a.* **Argenteo-marginata**; *C. a.* **Aurea**   Three variegated forms of the red-barked dogwood, noted for the beauty of their foliage during spring and summer. Their dark plum-crimson stems are attractive in winter, but these cultivars are not so robust as the type species, and should not be pruned too severely. Like the Westonbirt dogwood, they should merely be thinned early in spring to encourage a proportion of new shoots to grow from the base, without detracting from the effect of the earliest foliage.

C. sanguinea, common dogwood   A wild shrub in Europe, and a frequent constituent of copses and old farm hedges in Britain, where it adds a touch of sombre beauty to the winter scene. Common dogwood makes a thicket of dark crimson shoots on stems of greenish-brown, and is eminently suitable for planting in areas of waste ground, or where a clump can make a pleasant but unobtrusive background to the garden.

C. controversa   A horizontally branched Asian tree up to 15m (50ft) tall, almost as tabular in form as the much smaller but better-known *Viburnum tomentosum* Mariesii. The stem bark of the mature tree is brownish-red streaked with grey, and the young stems and twigs a dusky purplish-red. It is spectacular as the leaves change colour in autumn (see p106), and attractive in spring when it produces numerous clusters of small white flowers.

Tilia platyphyllos **Rubra,** red-twigged lime   A tall, columnar variety of the European broad-leaved lime, not suitable for the small garden but a popular choice for planting as a commemorative specimen tree. The long, whippy young shoots are a bright brownish-red, symmetrically arranged on fastigiate branches.

Prunus cerasifera **Pissardii,** purple-leaved cherry-plum   This well-known little Middle Eastern tree makes a strikingly attractive garden feature all the year round, not least during winter after the purple-crimson leaves have fallen to reveal a compact framework of dark purplish-brown shoots.

P. c. **Nigra,** black cherry-plum   A well-known, wide-spreading but symmetrically crowned little tree which is ideal for hedging, regular clipping creating a dense thicket of dark blackish-purple shoots. In winter, a black cherry-plum, grown either as a standard tree or a coppiced bush, makes a charming companion for some of the yellow or red barked trees and shrubs.

P. c. **Rosea,** pink cherry-plum   A small, broadly round-headed tree, very ornamental in flower and leaf, with long, whippy shoots of a dark puce-purple.

Betula lenta, cherry birch   A tall tree in its native eastern North America, in British gardens usually small but gracefully picturesque, useful in autumn for its pleasant yellow leaf tints (see p81), and very noticeable in winter with its smooth aromatic bark, more like a cherry than a birch, in dark maroon-purple and glossy mahogany-red.

Sorbus aucuparia **Beissneri**   This cultivated variety of the British and European mountain ash is an erect little tree with closely compact branches. Attractive throughout the year, with finely divided light green foliage and large clusters of crimson berries in late summer, it is particularly noticeable in winter, with conspicuous coppery-orange and mahogany bark, the crown silhouetted by young shoots in a dark shade of coral-red.

Prunus avium, wild cherry or gean   The wild European and British tree is most noticeable in blossom along the margins of woodlands in spring. The bark peels in a motley of colours and textures, mainly a smooth, glossy grey and bright mahogany-red, becoming dark and roughly fissured with age at the base of the tree.

✳ *P. serrula* This native of western China and Tibet is one of the brightest-barked of small cherry trees, with heavily lenticelled trunk, and limbs of a glossy mahogany-red. During late summer and autumn the old bark peels off in strips, leaving the polished young bark to look its best over winter, gleaming a coppery red-brown in the weak sunshine. Many specimens are marred when they develop large, dark, warty patches on the bark, especially in the region of pruning scars; and care should be taken to treat *P. serrula* as a clean standard tree from the very beginning by removing all side branches as they develop. Unnecessarily large scars with their unsightly calluses can be avoided.

P. dielsiana A small Chinese cherry tree with slender, gracefully arching branches well laden in the spring with drooping clusters of pale pink flowers. In winter, the dark mahogany-red, lenticelled bark of stem and branches makes an eye-catching feature.

Brown and Orange

Prunus sargentii A large, vigorous Japanese cherry tree, particularly valued for its autumn leaf colours (see p96), and noticeable in the winter with its open framework of dark chestnut-brown branches.

Betula nigra, river birch or red birch A small but fairly broad-crowned tree from the eastern United States. Like the British white birch it can grow in poor soil and boggy places, and is excellent on the banks of a stream or in a moist woodland garden. Attractively foliaged in summer with grey-backed, glossy grass-green leaves, the river birch makes an interesting feature during the winter as its dark chocolate-brown bark peels in shaggy strips to reveal the smooth, creamy pinkish-buff young bark beneath.

Betula papyrifera humilis, Yukon birch An Alaskan variation of the widespread paper birch. Instead of the distinctive paper-white flakes of the typical species, this large tree sheds its peeling bark in rich shades of tawny chestnut-brown.

The Boston ivy, *Parthenocissus tricuspidata,* is one of the best-known vines for house walls, colouring brightly in the autumn
Hedera helix Gold Heart is the best of all variegated forms of the British ivy, particularly valuable in the winter

Myrtus apiculata   A South American species of myrtle that grows well in the milder parts of the British Isles and the more southerly states of the USA. It makes a very handsome little evergreen tree with dark coppery-green aromatic leaves, and bears numerous white flowers in summer followed by edible red and black berries. The bright cinnamon-red bark peels to reveal young bark in contrasting patches of pale cream.

Acer griseum, paperbark maple   A native of China, and one of the most beautiful of small maple trees. Often multi-limbed, the branches originate low on the stem and rise steeply to form an upright-fan silhouette, ultimately some 7m (23ft) high. It has a pleasantly cool aspect in the summer, with little three-lobed leaves that appear blue-grey when seen from below, turning in the autumn to gorgeous tints of flame (see p93). As a winter feature the bark is fascinating – orange and pale greenish-brown, flaking off in large papery tatters to reveal the glossy orange-brown of the smooth young bark beneath.

Alnus incana **Aurea,** golden-speckled alder   A yellow-leaved variety of the grey alder, found in many northern countries. It is beautiful in summer and outstanding in winter, with yellowish coral-pink catkins on twigs of the same colour, the branches and main stems a warm orange-buff. A tree that grows well in poor soils and in cold, exposed situations, it makes a perfect planting-companion in boggy places for the coloured-bark willows.

Sorbus aria **Lutescens,** yellow whitebeam   A cultivar of the British and European common whitebeam, the pale young leaves coated with a creamy down as they open in the spring, and the twigs forming a closely knit, compactly rounded crown. The bark on trunk and branches is a warm yellowish orange-buff.

Betula maximowicziana   This fairly substantial and rapidly grown birch tree from Japan has a wide-spreading crown and distinctively large leaves which develop pleasant old-gold autumn tints. The bark is particularly ornamental, orange-brown on the main stem, maturing to grey near the base of the tree.

Cotoneaster Cornubia, one of the heaviest croppers among tall, tree-like cotoneasters

✳   ***Prunus maackii,*** Manchurian cherry   A small but fairly vigorous, wide-spreading tree from eastern China and Korea, pretty in spring when bearing its tiny clustered white flowers, and almost equally attractive when leafless in winter, its light golden-brown bark tinged with shades of orange and yellow. On mature stems the bark flakes, peeling into glossy horizontal bands, making a striking contrast with the bright yellowish-green of the young leaves as they unfurl early in the spring.

Betula utilis, Himalayan birch   Certain forms of this species have creamy-buff bark (see p141), but the Far Eastern form has peeling stems of a dark, coppery orange-brown. Ultimately fairly large, young trees are susceptible to annual damage by late spring frosts until they have grown above the layers of freezing air which tend to build up near ground-level. For this reason, a sloping site is often best. Said to grow particularly well on chalky soils.

Stewartia monodelpha   This Japanese shrub makes a 5m (16ft) spreading cone of dark branches on main stems of orange, brown and cinnamon. It is attractive when leafless for the winter, and beautiful when in flower during the summer. It needs the protection of a sheltered woodland garden with a moist, lime-free soil.

Arbutus menziesii, Californian madrona   A native of Pacific North America, this relative of the European and Irish strawberry tree needs a sheltered site where the large evergreen leaves will not be damaged by cold winds. The madrona is a picturesque tree with shredding bark which peels to expose the smooth pale green beneath; the young bark darkens gradually to warm cinnamon.

✳   ***A. × andrachnoides***   A hybrid between the Greek and the Irish strawberry trees, this small hardy evergreen tree adopts a very picturesque appearance while still quite young, the cinnamon bark on its gnarled and spreading limbs contrasting beautifully with the dark glossy green leaves.

Prunus rufa, Himalayan cherry   A small tree with wide-spreading branches, bearing attractive pink blossom as the leaves open in the spring. But it is often at its best in winter, when the old bark peels and hangs in long strips ranging in colour from dark brown to amber and russet-red, revealing the glossy, prominently lenticelled young bark beneath.

P. salicina, Japanese plum   A small bushy tree with good autumn foliage colours. Interesting as a contrast-former during the winter, with its glossy, dark brown twigs.

Arbutus unedo, strawberry tree   A native of southern Europe and western Ireland, this beautiful and moderately hardy little tree makes a valuable contribution to the garden scene throughout the year, with its white bell-shaped flowers, edible strawberry-like fruit in autumn, leathery, dark evergreen leaves framing gnarled limbs, and rough-shredding dark brown bark.

Corylus colurna, Turkish hazel   A large tree of pyramidal outline. This hazel's neatly symmetrical crown of upright branches is made especially interesting in the winter months by the corky, scaling, brownish-grey bark.

C. chinensis, Chinese hazel   The largest of all the hazels, this Chinese tree grows to an enormous size, with vigorously wide-spreading branches and ornamentally furrowed bark of a light greyish-brown. Too large for most gardens, both these hazel trees are hardy and able to grow well in all normal types of soil.

C. avellana, European hazel   The well-known nut tree of British woodlands has interestingly toned bark of a warm khaki-brown, especially attractive early in February when catkins are hanging from the fan-shaped sprays (see p32).

Olive-brown and Green

Acer forrestii   This small, spreading Chinese maple, like most of its genus, is an attractive little tree in summer, its finely lobed leaves a dark green, mottled with lighter tones. In winter the long, arching shoots display quiet shades of pink, the colour darkening on branches and stem where the old bark is striped in a pattern of yellowish-olive and purplish-brown.

A. nikoense, Nikko maple   A small, spreading tree from Japan, whose unmaple-like compound leaves have glorious autumn tints (see p85). After the leaves fall the Nikko maple is still attractive, with a smooth greenish-grey bark that stands out well on dull days.

A. pensylvanicum, snake-bark maple or moosewood   A native of eastern North America, this beautiful little tree has large lobed leaves, conspicuously coloured in autumn (see p85). It is also one of the most attractive maples during the winter, famed for its fascinating bark, striped white and silver against a background of pale jade-green, in a pattern reminiscent of a snake's skin.

A. rufinerve   This small Japanese maple tree is of the snake-bark type, somewhat similar to the moosewood in leaves and bark. Predominantly the stem colour is a silvery grey-green, the young bark bright green, conspicuously striped with white, the outer branchlets a contrasting reddish-pink covered with a glaucous bloom. Overall, this is one of the prettiest of small trees, at its best in winter, particularly when set in front of a dark background.

A. hersii   A small Chinese maple with a distinctively upright stance, the main branches rising steeply before arching gracefully outwards. An attractive little tree in summer with its dark, almost blackish-green, barely lobed leaves on pink-tinged young shoots. It is beautiful, too, in winter, its olive-green bark marbled with white and pale green, the pattern well developed on both young and old wood.

Leycesteria formosa, flowering nutmeg   This well-known ornamental shrub, originally from the Himalayas, makes a fan-shaped bush of slender, arching shoots. If coppiced each spring like a willow, these 2m (6ft) wands retain their vivid green coloration during the winter months, and are useful in association with dark brown stems.

Kerria japonica   This well-known Far Eastern shrub, and its beautiful and more vigorous double-flowered form *K. j.* Pleniflora, are commonly grown chiefly for their long-lasting bright yellow flowers. But these shrubs can be very valuable in winter, too, their arching, light green stems reaching some 2m (6ft), looking especially tall and neatly fan-shaped when grown against a wall.

7

Climbers

Many of the tendrilled or self-clinging and aerial-rooted vines are grown mainly for their vivid autumn colours, and are described more fully in Chapter 4. They include several members of the genus *Vitis*, one of particular note being the spectacular *Vitis coignetiae* which has the largest leaves of any vine, some 30cm (1ft) across, more rounded than many of the genus and only shallowly lobed. It is a remarkably vigorous plant, said to climb to the tops of lofty trees in the forests of its native Japan and Korea; but it can readily be controlled and kept within a small area, such as a trellis or shed wall, by the simple expedient of pinching out the growing tips at regular intervals to make a bushy plant. Its enormous leaves make it one of the most useful subjects available to landscape gardeners when some kind of dramatic impact is needed rapidly.

A hardy fruiting vine is *Vitis* Brant, which will grow some 10m (33ft) tall and is equally happy scrambling through a tree or climbing with the aid of tendrils up a wired wall. The ornately lobed leaves provide vivid autumn tints, and it bears numerous little bunches of sweetly aromatic, bloomy black grapes. Another hardy grape vine is *V. vinifera* Purpurea, the Teinturier grape, usually grown for the beauty of its colourful foliage rather than its fruit. Others are *V. amurensis*, a vigorous Siberian vine with large, deeply lobed leaves; *V. davidii*, a vigorous Chinese climber with heart-shaped leaves and viciously hooked thorns; and *V. pulchra*, with broadly rounded leaves, bright green on reddish stems during the summer, tinted scarlet in both spring and autumn – a vigorous, hardy climber of unknown origin, probably closely related to *V. coignetiae*.

Perhaps the best-known vines normally grown on house walls in Britain are the Virginia creeper and the Boston ivy. The first-named, *Parthenocissus quinquefolia* from the eastern USA, is a self-clinger with leaflets characteristically arranged like five fingers; the latter, *P. tricuspidata* (often miscalled the Virginia creeper), has three-lobed leaves. Both are equally brightly coloured in the autumn. Other species in this genus include *P. henryana* from China, a very useful

self-clinging wall climber with dark green leaves, bronzy when young and scarlet in the autumn; *P. himalayana* from the Himalayas, a strongly growing climber which performs better on trees than on walls; and *P. inserta*, a vigorous, tendrilled vine from the eastern USA. The latter is a woodland plant most at home when allowed to scramble over small trees and large shrubs, with leaves similar to those of the true Virginia creeper, a bright glossy green in the summer, highly coloured in the autumn.

Most typical of evergreen climbers are the ivies, sometimes overlooked in summer and particularly valuable in winter; unobtrusively useful in the wild when clothing deciduous woods with a warming evergreen mantle, and equally but more noticeably useful in the garden when providing a close cover of green or variegated foliage. One of the smaller-leaved species is the British ivy, *Hedera helix*, and this has numerous cultivated varieties with beautifully variegated leaves, often grown indoors as pot plants. Amongst these are Chicago and Chicago Variegata, with cream-edged leaves; Golden Chicago, with light golden-yellow leaves; Glacier, with comparatively large leaves narrowly bordered with silver; Adam, with dainty little deeply lobed leaves edged with white; Lutzii, with distinctive yellow spots; Little Diamond with, as its name implies, a diamond-shaped central mark surrounded by contrasting white margins; Angularis Aurea, with comparatively large yellow-variegated leaves, an occasional one being pure yellow; Silver Queen and Marginata, which are almost identical cultivars, and have white-margined leaves daintily bordered in the winter months with pink; and best of all variegations of the British ivy, Gold Heart, which has an eye-catching central blotch of bright golden-yellow. Caenwoodiana is a non-variegated, dark green variety with very finely lobed leaves; and Hibernica is the so-called Irish ivy, a bright green, non-variegated selection which rarely climbs. It has larger leaves than the typical species, and makes a very vigorous evergreen ground cover.

The largest-leaved ivy is *Hedera colchica*, the Persian ivy from the Middle East, typically a vigorous climber with leathery, dark green, somewhat rounded leaves. The species is usually represented in gardens by the cultivars Dentata, with larger and more strongly lobed, light green leaves, and Dentata Variegata, perhaps the favourite large-leaved ivy, variegated in shades of green and yellow,

Vitis Brant will provide vivid autumn tints as well as small, edible grapes

A variegated form of the large leaved Persian ivy, *Hedera colchica* Dentata Variegata

grey, cream and white. The cultivar Paddy's Pride, also known as Gold Leaf, has similar, rather rounded leaves boldly variegated with golden-yellow and several shades of green. Both Paddy's Pride and Dentata Variegata, especially if grown in the shade, sometimes produce leaves that are entirely cream or yellow, and sprays of these leaves are useful as accompaniments to winter flowers for vase decoration, making a particularly fine foil for blue flowers such as *Iris unguicularis*. Grown freely on a wire-netting fence, varieties of the Persian ivy will make a beautiful, narrowly proportioned evergreen hedge.

Hedera canariensis, the Canary Islands ivy or Algerian ivy, is not quite as hardy as the similar Persian ivy. The typical species has bright green leaves which adopt a warm bronzy tone in winter, forming a welcome addition to indoor arrangements. The variegated form Gloire de Marengo, also known as Variegata, is attractive, its red-stemmed glossy green leaves margined with grey, white and pink; but it is even less hardy than the green type. Outside its native western Mediterranean and sub-tropicalAtlantic islands, it should be restricted to a warm patio wall and, during winter, may not survive unless taken indoors as a pot plant.

The British wild honeysuckle which opens its flowers in June has normally finished its display by September, but the variety known as the late Dutch honeysuckle, *Lonicera periclymenum* Serotina, produces its sweetly fragrant flowers – reddish-purple outside the trumpet and creamy-white inside – between July and the end of October. Most hybrid honeysuckles flower rather early, but *Lonicera* Dropmore Scarlet, a vigorous climber related to the hybrid scarlet-trumpet honeysuckle, produces clusters of scentless but beautiful bright scarlet flowers from July to October. An unusual evergreen honeysuckle is the Chinese *L. alseuosmoides*, which produces broad clusters of small trumpet flowers, yellow outside the trumpet and purple inside, also lasting from late summer well into October.

Other late-flowering climbers include *Senecio scandens*, the trailing groundsel, a vigorous semi-evergreen scrambler from the Far East. Its small yellow daisy flowers, taken individually, look like any of numerous common weeds in the genus; but they are produced in such impressively large clusters that they provide a conspicuously colourful display during October and November, persisting until the first frosts cut them back. Trailing groundsel needs a sheltered site where, though the scandent stems may be killed by heavy frost like a herbaceous perennial, it will recover in the spring. It can often be placed most effectively where the roots are protected beneath vegetation and the top growth can scramble in the open, perhaps over a small tree. *Solanum crispum* Glasnevin is a South American climber which makes a vigorous cover for a fence or the sunny, sheltered wall of a small building. Usually evergreen, it may lose its leaves in cold winters. It bears large clusters of really beautiful lilac-purple flowers of the potato type, with a yellow staminal beak, produced over a fairly long season from July to late October.

From the Far East comes the deciduous twining shrub, *Celastrus orbiculatus*, which climbs vigorously with thorny, twining shoots to reach a height of 12m (40ft) or so in a tree or on a wired or trellised wall. Related to the spindle trees, it has inconsequential flowers but conspicuous seedheads which, like those of a euonymus, consist of small brown pods that split open to reveal a yellow lining and scarlet seeds – an interesting combination of colours in the autumn when seen against a background of yellow leaves, the seeds often remaining in eye-catching clusters to decorate the bare, thorny branches over winter.

Several of the wild, or small-flowered, clematis species come into bloom fairly late in the season. Best known as a wild native plant in Britain is *Clematis vitalba*, the old man's beard or traveller's joy. This untidy, vigorous climber often literally smothers small trees and shrubs along the woodland edge, especially in chalk and limestone regions. With its heavy, blanketing vegetation and tiny, greenish-white flowers from July to September, followed by masses of woolly seedheads which persist rather drably into winter, it is not a plant for the garden, but many other wild, small-flowered clematis species, away from their native habitat at least, are both more attractive and better-behaved. One or two flower early enough in the season to be classified as late winter flowerers, like the truly winter-flowering *Clematis cirrhosa* (see pp37–8). One such is *C. calycina* from southern Europe, an evergreen climber which will reach 4.5m (15ft) or more, with fern-like foliage at its most handsome in cold weather, when it adopts a bronzy-purple tone. If the temperature falls too low, however, the plant is liable to be cut back to the ground. It likes a cool, shaded site and, like *C. cirrhosa*, often does best on a north-facing wall. The fairly small and faintly fragrant, nodding flowers are a greenish-yellow speckled with maroon, on display from January until the spring.

Late summer and autumn flowering clematis species are numerous. One is *C. flammula* from southern Europe, which grows vigorously to 4.5m (15ft) or so, and produces luxuriant dark green foliage and vast numbers of small, fragrant, cross-shaped white flowers from August to October. Another is *C. orientalis*, the orange-peel clematis, a vigorous Asian species climbing to 6m (20ft), with bright yellow flowers, usually bell-shaped but sometimes wide-opening. The best form is the now well-known clone collected in Tibet and listed under Ludlow and Sherriff collectors' number L&S 13342. This has thickly fleshy, broadly bell-shaped flowers of orangy-yellow with reddish-purple filaments and white anthers from midsummer until the end of October. Also to be included are *C. paniculata*, a vigorous Japanese species which climbs to 9m (30ft) or more, with dark glossy green leaves, and profuse clusters of small cross-shaped sweetly scented white flowers, produced mainly in October; *C. rehderana*, a vigorous Chinese clematis climbing to 6m (20ft), with distinctively downy leaves and shoots, and clusters of small, straw-yellow, cowslip-scented flowers from August to October; *C. tangutica*, from China, a vigorous climber reaching some 4.5m (15ft), with dark yellow bell-shaped flowers and feathery seedheads on display from June until November (see pp30–1); and *C. viticella*, a vigorous southern European climber with nodding purple flowers from July to September.

Amongst the small-flowered hybrids, autumn flowerers include *C. × jouiniana*, a hybrid between the wild British old man's beard and a herbaceous species. This non-clinging herbaceous shrub scrambles to a height of 3m (10ft) or so; its large leafy clusters of star-like flowers, from late August to October, are inconspicuously greyish-white with grey-blue sepal tips. Its cultivated variety, Côte d'Azur, of similar flowering season, bears clusters of small, pretty sky-blue flowers. Another is *C. × triternata* Rubromarginata. Selected from a series of natural hybrids between the two southern European species *C. viticella* and *C. flammula*, this cultivated variety makes a vigorous climber reaching some 4m (13ft), with inconspicuous but sweetly scented pale purple flowers from August to October.

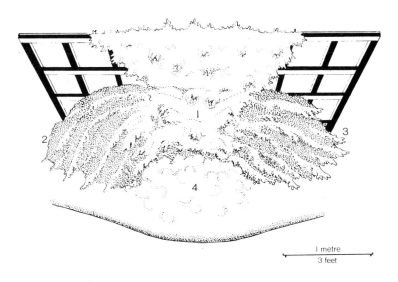

1 metre
3 feet

A climber mingling with thicketing shrubs can produce excellent autumn effects:
1 *Clematis tangutica*;   3 *Pyracantha* Soleil d'Or;
2 *Cotoneaster microphyllus*;   4 *Aster*, dwarf Michaelmas daisies

Most of the large-flowered hybrid clematises flower in the spring or early summer. Some of them produce a second and usually less spectacular display later in the year, and these varieties can often be encouraged by pruning to save their best flowers until the autumn. If you have several suitable plants, you could treat, say, half in this fashion, and thus extend the flowering season.

Some of the climbing hydrangeas are ideal for partially clothing deciduous trees during winter, with a bonus of creamy-white flowers in late summer and autumn. They relish a shady aspect, and flourish beneath summer foliage, or on the north-facing wall of a house. The evergreen *Hydrangea integerrima* (syn. *H. serratifolia*), less well known than the deciduous climbing hydrangea *H. petiolaris*, is a native liana in the Chilean rain-forests, where it festoons tall trees, climbing up through heavy shade to open its flowers in the sunlight above. In southern and western Britain it thrives in sun or shade, though if the site is in direct sunshine it needs a regular mulch of leaf mould to keep the roots cool and moist. It is one of the best evergreen climbers for a completely shaded wall, where it clings with aerial roots, making a warm cover of dark green leathery leaves, and cascades of creamy-white flowers in the late summer.

An evergreen climber related to the hydrangeas is the Asian *Pileostegia viburnoides*, with similar aerial roots that cling tenaciously to a wall or the bark of a tree. As efficient as *Hydrangea integerrima* in clothing a north-facing wall with dark green leathery leaves, it is covered during late summer and autumn with dense clusters of small, creamy-white flowers. Another evergreen climber is *Ercilla volubilis* from Chile, a fairly hardy plant that thrives at least in southern and western Britain, where it makes a close cover of rounded, leathery leaves, decorated in the spring with upright spikes of small, purplish-white flowers. It originated in a habitat similar to that of the evergreen climbing hydrangea, and appreciates having its roots and lower stem shaded all the year round, though the uppermost shoots and foliage may be exposed to full sunlight – conditions one might have on a shady house-wall or in an old tree. Yet another species from the Chilean rain-forest is *Asteranthera ovata*, which also thrives on a north-facing wall or a shady tree in the milder districts of Britain. It is not a high climber but, like some of the ivies, a trailing evergreen that creeps about in the shade, forming a mantle of tiny bright green leaves which clothe the lower stems of trees and make an interesting ground cover. The vivid scarlet flowers are rarely seen in British summers.

Not dissimilar in summer foliage, a self-clinging evergreen climber from Asia is *Trachelospermum majus*, which produces fragrant jasmine-like flowers in the summer. It is ornamental throughout the year, the small, rounded leaves turning scarlet for the winter and reverting to bright green in the spring. It will grow at least in most southern and western areas of Britain, reaching a height of some 7m (23ft) on a wall, which it covers in the winter like a densely leafy, colourful ivy.

8

Autumn Fruits

It is not always easy to find good comprehensive displays of autumn fruits. Contrary to expectations, botanic gardens seldom provide the opportunity to admire collections of fruiting plants at this season, because as a rule all the seeds are collected as soon as they ripen, either for propagation by the resident staff or for distribution to associated gardeners. In the countryside, human despoilers usually keep to traditionally edible wild berries such as brambles, occasionally turning to elderberries for wine-making or holly and mistletoe for Christmas decoration; but on a more destructive scale, massed displays of hips and haws are often eliminated by the farmer's practice of tractor-trimming his hedges in early autumn, before the land becomes too wet. In well-kept gardens many shrubs are dead-headed or pruned after flowering, and thus prevented from setting fruit. The best berry collections are often found in the least formal private gardens.

Waiting in the background are those birds which rely on berries to see them through the winter. They tend to eat the softest, darkest berries first, such as those of the elder and the guelder rose, and these, too, are the kinds most vulnerable to frosting, so they are unlikely to persist many weeks after ripening. Though frost appears to have little outward effect on hard berries such as hips, haws, cotoneaster and holly, it probably softens their pulp and makes them more palatable; certainly birds do not usually eat them until after a sharp frost.

Most wild berries of the soft but thick-skinned kind are fairly dark in tone – usually in shades of red or purplish-black – and those with the lightest colours, such as mistletoe and snowberry, tend to be less attractive to birds and so last longer on the plant. The same rule applies where distinctive cultivars of trees and shrubs have typically hard but unusually light-coloured berries, such as the yellow-fruited forms of holly, and among moderately soft-berried species such as the pink or white fruited kinds of rowan; but whether this discrimination reflects the palatability of

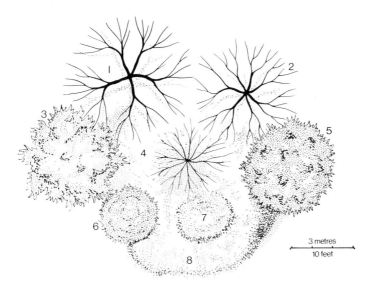

A group of small trees and shrubs selected particularly for their long-lasting fruits in a subtle blend of colours:

1 *Sorbus hupehensis*;
2 *Sorbus cashmiriana*;
3 *Stranvaesia davidiana* Fructuluteo;
4 *Decaisnea fargesii*;
5 *Viburnum henryi*;
6 *Skimmia reevesiana*;
7 *Symphoricarpos × doorenbosii* Mother of Pearl;
8 *Symphoricarpos × chenaultii* Hancock

the fruit, or merely its visual appeal, is a point for the ornithologist to decide.

Amongst the many garden trees belonging to the genus typified by rowans and whitebeams, the British mountain ash, *Sorbus aucuparia*, fruits more prolifically than most foreign species, and wild as well as cultivated specimens are often spectacularly laden with bright red berries during late summer and autumn. But birds strip the branches bare when cold weather sets in. Apparently the yellow form is not so palatable, for these berries often last well into winter. In a largely red-berried genus, *Sorbus hupehensis* stands out amongst the Chinese rowans for its pale pink or white fruits which last untouched through the winter; and *S. cashmiriana* is another Asian rowan with white berries which last well, largely ignored by birds. *S. vilmorinii*, also from China, has berries which are crimson at first as they set in August and September, slowly fading until they are pale pink or near-white by October and November, and they too sometimes last unscathed through the winter, festooned like beads along the bare branches. Incidentally, this species is hardier than most Asian rowans; it thrives in a cool, moist climate, and does particularly well in Scotland.

Most hawthorn berries are dark red, sometimes verging on

crimson, but those of the hybrid *Crataegus × lavallei* are of a much lighter orange-red, large and showy, and last well through winter, ignored by birds which are usually very partial to haws; though even these may be eaten as a last resort if the weather is exceptionally severe. Notable among the firethorns are the hybrid *Pyracantha* Watereri with orange-yellow berries, and two large Chinese species – *P. crenatoserrata*, which bears small but very numerous berries of a light coral red; and *P. angustifolia*, covered early in autumn with green berries which gradually turn yellow, and finally a conspicuous orange-red. All three mount a longer-lasting display than most other firethorns, though a bitter wind or a spell of icy weather can cut them back, and not only spoil the berries but kill the bushes themselves. They are best grown as wall shrubs for protection, but they should be trained to shape whilst the thorny branches are still young and pliable.

Amongst the cotoneasters, those with the lightest, brightest berries provide the most persistent displays, in particular *Cotoneaster conspicuus* Decorus, its semi-prostrate mounds covered with masses of brilliant scarlet fruits often until May. Bushes bearing the name *C. × watereri* usually have very numerous orange-scarlet berries which persist at least until mid-winter. The tree cotoneaster, *C. frigidus*, also produces long-lasting berries, bright red in large clusters, on a par with its yellow-fruited variety *C. frigidus* Fructuluteo. The scarlet berries of the well-known *C. horizontalis* usually persist well after the leaves have fallen, and the tall evergreen *C. glaucophyllus* has orange-red fruits which do not ripen until around Christmas, and last thereafter through the winter. The two closely related hybrid cotoneasters, Exburiensis and Rothschildianus, are large evergreens with pinkish-yellow berries, somewhat longer-lasting on the former; but both have usually lost them all by the first few weeks of the New Year.

Rose hips do not seem to attract birds, being rather hard and dry, and most of them remain on the bushes for months after they are ripe. The wild British dog rose, *Rosa canina*, provides bright hedgerow colour even in the depth of winter. The sweet briar or eglantine, *R. rubiginosa*, also native to Britain and Europe, bears bright red hips which similarly persist well through the winter. Amongst other rose species, the Chinese chestnut rose or burr rose, *R. roxburghii*, is unusual with its prickly, chestnut-like burrs; *R. moyesii*, another Chinese species, sometimes said to be one of the most beautiful wild roses in garden use, has large flask-shaped, waxy-crimson hips; and the ramanas rose, *R. rugosa*, a native of

Asia often naturalised in Europe and a parent of numerous garden hybrids and cultivars, has large, bright red, apple-like fruits which persist for several months. Amongst hybrid shrub roses, *R.* Highdownensis has flask-shaped hips of an eye-catching orange-scarlet, and these last well through the winter. The hybrid musk roses Cantab, Wilhelm and Will Scarlet all ripen their hips very late – around Christmas time – and offer a bright scarlet display through winter until spring. The hybrid damask rose St Nicholas is also notably long-lasting, as are the semi-climbing roses Allen Chandler and Cupid, which have very large, scarlet hips, Dusterlohe which is vivid orange, and Penelope, which has soft green hips, flushed as they ripen with coral-pink and bloomed with grey – the prettiest of pastel colour schemes when seen at close quarters, and useful for vase decoration through the winter.

The berries of some species are too variable to classify positively by their colour. In *Pernettya mucronata*, a South American evergreen heath, berry colours of the several cultivars range from pearly-white through shades of pink, mauve, crimson and scarlet, and in any combination they rank amongst the brightest of fruiting ground-coverers for lime-free soil. The berries are largely birdproof, but heavy frost is liable to spoil them, though the plants themselves are quite hardy. As they are typically one-sex plants, a non-fruiting male is usually needed to pollinate a group of females, but this characteristic is variable. Both the dark-red berried Bell's Seedling and the group of pernettyas known collectively as Davis's Hybrids regularly bear heavy crops without the assistance of a non-berrying pollinator.

The hollies are typical one-sex plants which, in the wild at least, need pollination to enable the females to produce good crops of berries, although here again some clones bear freely, apparently without the need for nearby males. Various shrubs and trees in different parts of the world have had to take the place of holly for nostalgic immigrant populations celebrating Christmas, and some quite unrelated species have been given popular names which reflect this. But the original and probably the best for traditional Christmas decoration is the European common holly (its natural range extends eastwards into mid-Asia and southwards as far as North Africa).

Associated with Christmas celebrations almost as closely is the mistletoe, the strange parasitic plant of ancient Druidic rites, originally the European *Viscum album*, though other species (in particular the North American *Phoradendron flavescens*) have from time to time usurped its place in popular folklore.

Autumn fruits other than berries which are attractive in the garden include the ornamental pods of several trees, shrubs and climbers. Notable are those of the Indian bean tree, *Catalpa bignonioides*, which measure up to 45cm ($1\frac{1}{2}$ft) long and hang like dark brown stalactites beneath the canopy of a well-developed tree. And in mild areas the long, tapering pods of *Wisteria sinensis*, in a velvety, silvery green, are particularly effective when the plant has been allowed to run wild and unpruned in a sparsely branched tree. Vine fruits are also beautiful, especially those of the more consistently fertile hardy grape vines such as *Vitis* Brant, which produces numerous bunches of sweetly edible grapes, a bloomy dark purple amongst the autumn leaves.

In the selection that follows, some of the most consistently reliable autumn fruiters have been arranged according to the colour of their fruits, ranging from creamy-yellow through shades of orange, red, purple and blue, finally returning to the palest shades of pink and pearly-white.

Yellow

Cotoneaster **Rothschildianus**   A large, vigorous evergreen hybrid shrub with spreading, arching branches and light green foliage, covered during autumn and winter with clusters of creamy-yellow berries.

C. salicifolius **Fructuluteo**   A tree-like, willowy-leaved Chinese evergreen shrub which bears heavy crops of pale yellow berries.

Poncirus trifoliata, Japanese bitter orange   A small deciduous Chinese citrus tree, hardy in cool temperate areas where commercial oranges and lemons will not grow, and greatly admired in the spring for its beautiful and sweetly scented white flowers. The small oranges that follow remain green for some time before turning a pale golden-yellow in the autumn. A bushy, stiffly branched plant with dark green, long-spined stems, it can be grown as an ornamental hedge or trained and pruned as a wall plant.

Malus **Wintergold**   A small hybrid crabapple with a compactly rounded crown. Covered with white blossom in the spring, it is a prolific bearer in the autumn, the small, clear golden-yellow apples lasting on the tree well into winter.

M. **Golden Hornet**   A compactly domed little hybrid crab, noted less for its white spring blossom than for its large crops of bright golden-yellow apples which persist tenaciously on the bare branches, and dazzle the eye when bathed in winter sunshine.

Sorbus **Sunshine**   A hybrid rowan tree with an upright stance when young, spreading quite widely later, and drooping each autumn beneath heavy clusters of golden-yellow berries.

S. **Joseph Rock**   A small hybrid rowan with a compactly erect crown, laden in autumn with large clusters of bright golden-yellow berries, conspicuous against the brilliant foliage tints (see p101) and lasting well into winter after the leaves have fallen.

S. folgneri **Lemon Drop**   One of the most graceful of the Chinese sorbus trees, with wide-spreading, arching branches which droop at their tips and two-toned leaves, dark green above and white on the undersides, making a choice display setting for the rather large bright yellow fruits. The leaves remain green during autumn before finally falling, leaving the berries clustered on bare branches over winter.

Cotoneaster Exburiensis. This large hybrid evergreen cotoneaster bears its apricot-yellow berries throughout the winter

***Stranvaesia davidiana* Fructuluteo**   A wide-spreading semi-ever-green shrub from China. The typical form has dark red or crimson berries; this smaller, almost prostrate, variety with dark green leathery leaves has drooping clusters of bright yellow berries which last through the winter untouched by birds.

Euonymus grandiflorus   A large semi-evergreen shrub from China and the Himalayas, noted for its purple autumn tints and for its conspicuous yellow seed-capsules, which together form a charming colour blend in the autumn. The capsules split to reveal bright scarlet seeds, and continue their display well into winter.

***Ilex aquifolium* Bacciflava (syn. *I. a.* Fructuluteo),** yellow-fruited holly   The common European holly thrives over so wide a range of soils and climates that it grows readily in most gardens within cold and temperate regions, and this variety is just as easy. It makes a large (though slow-growing) shrub, with glossy, dark evergreen prickly leaves.

***I. a.* Pyramidalis Fructuluteo**   One of the handsomest of hollies. An upright, conical, vigorous shrub which develops eventually into a substantial tree, with dark glossy-green spiny leaves, and huge clusters of bright, deep yellow berries which stand out conspicu-ously against the foliage.

***Pyracantha atalantioides* Aurea**   The yellow-fruiting form of a large Chinese firethorn and a splendid, vigorous free-standing tree or trained shrub suitable for a north-facing wall. The long-lasting berries are a rich, deep yellow, displayed amongst glossy dark evergreen foliage.

***P. crenatoserrata* Knap Hill lemon**   The selected form of a large Chinese evergreen shrub. Very similar to *P. atalantioides*, this densely branched cultivar produces large bright yellow berries that persist well over winter.

***Viburnum opulus* Fructuluteo**   A variety of the guelder rose of Europe and Britain. A large, vigorous, wide-spreading shrub which bears long-lasting pink-tinged yellow berries.

Sorbus aucuparia, the familiar native rowan or mountain ash, is a small, elegant tree which has large bunches of bright-red berries in autumn

V. opulus **Xanthocarpum**   A form of the guelder rose which bears clear golden-yellow fruits without a trace of pink, darkening to a translucent chrome-yellow when ripe. In both cases the large clusters of berries last well into winter, and are conspicuously ornamental on the supple grey branches long after the lobed leaves have fallen.

Cotoneaster **Exburiensis**   A large, hybrid evergreen shrub with spreading, arching branches and clusters of pink-tinged, apricot-yellow berries which persist among the light green foliage over winter.

Sorbus **Apricot Lady**   A small hybrid rowan with a wide-spreading crown of bright green foliage and large clusters of apricot-yellow berries which ripen in late summer and persist on the tree after leaf-fall.

S. **Ethel's Gold**   A small, fairly wide-spreading hybrid rowan tree with bright green leaves and clusters of golden-amber berries which persist on the bare branches throughout most of the winter.

S. aucuparia **Xanthocarpa**   A yellow-fruited form of the common British rowan. The amber berries, produced in large, showy clusters, last longer on the tree than the red types.

Malus **Professor Sprenger**   A small hybrid crabapple which develops a densely branched crown with a profuse display of spring blossom, pink at first, opening pure white; it is laden in autumn with prolific crops of glossy amber fruits which persist on the tree a month or so after the leaves have fallen.

Pyracantha angustifolia   A fairly large Chinese evergreen shrub with narrow, grey-backed leaves, and heavy crops of bright orange-yellow berries which last throughout the winter.

P. **Buttercup**   A fairly large, spreading, evergreen hybrid firethorn, with small berries of a rich orange-yellow.

Hippophae rhamnoides, sea buckthorn   A native of Europe and Britain, this slender-stemmed little tree or large shrub has long, narrow, willowy deciduous leaves of a soft, silvery sage-green, and becomes covered in autumn and winter with masses of orange-

Sorbus Apricot Lady. A small hybrid rowan which carries its apricot-yellow berries from late summer until long after the leaves have dropped

The sea buckthorn, *Hippophae rhamnoides*, bears masses of orange-yellow berries which persist after the silvery sage-green leaves have fallen

yellow berries, apparently ignored by the birds. After leaf-fall, their light colour glows brightly against the dark stems. Sea buckthorns are one-sex plants, and a male is needed to pollinate the berry-bearing group of females. When small plants have been raised from seed, the males may be distinguished in spring by the buds which are prominent in their leaf axils; the females at this stage are smooth. And female plants as they develop tend to be more twiggy and spreading than the male.

Orange

Elaeagnus umbellata   A large, vigorous deciduous Asian shrub, with wide-spreading buff-coloured branches bearing leaves of a soft green, backed with silver. In the autumn, the bushes are covered profusely with small orange berries which combine with the leaves to give a subtle, silvery effect.

Berberis sieboldii   A small, compact Japanese shrub of suckering habit, noted for the autumn tints of its deciduous leaves, and bright with glossy orange berries which persist into the winter.

***Sorbus* Signalman**   This closely columnar small tree, a cross be-tween the European service tree and an American mountain ash, is spectacular in autumn when bearing dense clusters of large, bright orange berries.

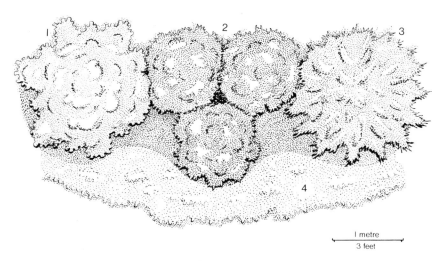

l metre
3 feet

With an evergreen carpet of rose of Sharon to give colour in the summer, these shrubs are spectacular in autumn berry:

1 *Elaeagnus umbellata*;   3 *Hippophae rhamnoides*;
2 *Callicarpa bodinieri*;   4 *Hypericum calycinum*

Malus **Almey**   A small hybrid crabapple with a broadly rounded crown and attractive red and white spring blossom. The fruits which follow are orange-red tinged with crimson, and stay on the tree during winter.

M. **John Downie**   This well-known hybrid crab forms a small, spreading tree with pink and white spring blossom followed by fairly large, edible apples in bright orange and red.

Crataegus × lavallei   This small hybrid hawthorn has a dense, spreading crown of glossy dark green leaves which often remain on the tree until Christmas – a pleasing background for the profuse crops of bright orange-red berries which persist far longer than on most thorns, often remaining intact through the winter.

Sorbus **Embley**   A small hybrid rowan with an erect, open-branched crown, displaying large, heavy clusters of glistening orange-red berries. It is spectacular in the autumn when the leaves turn a glowing red (see p100).

S. × kewensis   This small hybrid rowan with a densely branched, spreading crown is one of the most spectacular trees in fruit, the huge bunches of orange-red berries causing the branches to droop beneath their weight.

S. **Jermyns**   A small hybrid rowan with a compactly upright crown, laden in the autumn with large clusters of berries coloured at first a deep amber, slowly ripening to orange-red.

S. commixta   A Japanese rowan with a compact, strictly upright crown, and one of the best of the genus for autumn foliage (see p92). It bears large, erect bunches of small scarlet-orange berries.

S. aucuparia **Fastigiata**   This vigorous, stiffly upright form of the European mountain ash makes a narrow column of dark green foliage, decorated in late summer and autumn with large clusters of berries, orange at first, ripening to a bright scarlet-orange.

S. aucuparia **Sheerwater Seedling**   A vigorous, upright clone of the European mountain ash, popular as a street tree with its compactly conical and very shapely silhouette, and spectacular in the autumn when bearing large clusters of orange-red berries.

Pyracantha **Orange Glow**   A large hybrid evergreen firethorn which makes an excellent wall shrub, well covered in the autumn and through the winter with masses of bright orange-red berries.

P. coccinea **Lalandei**   A vigorously erect firethorn, usually heavily laden each year with large, bright orange-red berries which last through the winter.

Berberis **Pirate King**   This small hybrid deciduous barberry makes a vigorous, upright mound of fine foliage and dense twigs, covered in autumn and winter with bright orange-scarlet berries.

Cotoneaster **Firebird**   A large, spreading, hybrid shrub with glossy dark green foliage, and dense clusters of large orange-scarlet berries which persist on the branches long after the leaves have fallen.

C. adpressus praecox   A small but vigorously wide-spreading, ground-covering shrub, with arching branches, small deciduous leaves and unusually large orange-scarlet berries.

C. salicifolius **Autumn Fire**   One of several varieties of a tall evergreen Chinese cotoneaster, but much smaller than the type, with loosely spreading, almost pendulous branches, which carry numerous clusters of bright orange-scarlet berries in autumn and winter. The dark green leaves tend to fall during harsh winters.

C. × watereri   A group of variable hybrids, mainly large shrubs or small trees, with vigorously spreading branches and distinctively long, semi-evergreen leaves, mostly bearing heavy crops of bright orange-scarlet berries.

Scarlet and Shades of Red

Pyracantha atalantioides   The typical form of this vigorous Chinese firethorn sometimes makes a small tree. It is excellent also as a wall shrub for clothing the sunless side of a house with large, oval, dark, glossy evergreen leaves and masses of bright scarlet, long-lasting berries. *Laton.*

Malus **Crittenden**   A small hybrid crabapple with a wide-spreading crown of branches, and outstandingly prolific crops of bright scarlet edible fruits which last on the bare branches well into winter.

Pyracantha coccinea Lalandei is usually heavily laden with bright orange-red berries which last through the winter

Cotoneaster dammeri This prostrate Chinese shrub with trailing shoots makes an excellent evergreen ground cover, laden in autumn and winter with masses of brilliant scarlet berries.

Sorbus sargentiana A large Chinese rowan tree with a rigidly arranged crown of branches, noticeable in winter for their horse-chestnut-like sticky red buds, and for fine autumn foliage (see p94). Late to ripen, the individually quite small scarlet berries appear in large drooping clusters.

S. esserteauana This small open-crowned rowan from China produces tightly clustered, small scarlet berries which ripen and colour later than most related trees.

S. **Red Marbles** A small, stoutly twigged hybrid rowan, eye-catching in the autumn when laden with loose, heavy clusters of large, red, pink-spotted berries.

Berberis × *carminea* A group of vigorous, hybrid evergreen barberries with spreading branches, always well covered in the autumn with berries of variable colour, usually either pink, red or scarlet.

B. wilsoniae A small, densely branched Chinese barberry with good foliage colours (see p98), reliably covered in autumn with clusters of berries in a delicate shade of pale scarlet. The wild variety *B. wilsoniae guhtzunica* has berries which at first are translucent white, changing later to coral: and the taller *B. wilsoniae stapfiana*, which holds on to its glaucous sea-green foliage for at least most of the winter, has bright coral-red berries which stand out clearly against this pale background.

B. prattii A fairly large Chinese deciduous barberry with drooping branches, covered in autumn with bright coral-red berries.

B. **Bountiful** A small deciduous hybrid barberry with arching branches and spreading habit, heavily laden in the autumn with clusters of coral-red berries.

B. jamesiana A large deciduous Chinese barberry with upright stems, laden in autumn and early winter with drooping clusters of translucent coral-red berries of striking appearance when backed with autumn foliage tints (see p98).

B. koreana A fairly substantial deciduous Korean barberry which produces clusters of waxy-red berries, bright against the comparatively large, reddish-tawny autumn leaves.

Viburnum opulus, guelder rose The typical form of this large deciduous shrub with lobed, maple-like leaves is a familiar hedgerow plant in some areas of Europe and Britain, admired for its white flowers in early summer, and the autumn foliage tints which follow (see pp98–9). The translucent glossy red berries are produced in large and prolific clusters during the autumn, and persist on the branches as long as the birds allow them to remain.

Malus **Red Jade** This small hybrid crabapple usually takes the form of a weeping tree, though it is sometimes grown as an arching bush. Attractive throughout the year, the pink-and-white spring flowers are followed by small red apples which last on the bare branches well into winter.

Cotoneaster salicifolius floccosus A fairly large, gracefully slender evergreen shrub from China – a wild variety of the typical species – with a drooping, fan-like branch system and glossy, narrow leaves with white down on their undersides, consistently bearing masses of small red berries in the autumn.

Berberis aggregata A fairly large, densely crowned Chinese barberry whose bright-green leaves adopt rich colours before falling (see p98), when the bush is laden with masses of red berries.

B. polyantha A sizeable deciduous shrub, this Chinese barberry also displays vivid autumn foliage tints (see p100), and bears large drooping clusters of conspicuous oval red berries.

B. **Barbarossa** This fairly large hybrid deciduous barberry has upright branches which have to arch in autumn beneath the weight of numerous red berries.

Viburnum trilobum, cranberry bush This large eastern North American shrub is very similar to the European guelder rose, and bears large clusters of bright red berries which persist on the bare branches often throughout the winter.

Pyracantha crenatoserrata In its typical form, a vigorous Chinese firethorn with widely spreading branches and comparatively large, dark evergreen leaves, displaying prolific clusters of small bright red berries which often last until the spring.

Gaultheria procumbens, checkerberry or partridge berry This creeping evergreen shrub from North America is a heath-type plant which needs an acid soil. The dark green, purple-tinged foliage is dotted with bright red berries in the autumn.

Rhamnus alaterna A large evergreen buckthorn from southern Europe, useful in sun or semi-shade as a fast-growing screen of small, dark glossy leaves, and particularly suitable for use near the sea or in warm districts. In autumn it bears profuse clusters of bright red holly-like berries.

Rosa virginiana A suckering, thicket-forming shrub rose from eastern North America, noted for its autumn tints (see p98). The bright pink flowers produced during the summer give way to a profusion of little glossy red hips which persist well into the winter.

Sorbus alnifolia A small Japanese tree with a dense, rather wide-spreading crown of purplish-brown branches, very dark during the winter. The hornbeam-like leaves adopt bright autumn tints (see p95), and the small, bright red fruits hang conspicuously on the dark branches long after the leaves have fallen.

S. americana, American mountain ash A small tree with stiffly upright branches tipped during the winter with sticky red buds. The small, bright red berries are borne in large, dense clusters and, like those of the European mountain ash, are usually eaten by birds before the arrival of frosty weather.

S. scalaris A small, wide-spreading Chinese rowan tree with ferny leaves, dark glossy green above and grey-downed on their under-sides. In late summer it bears flattened clusters of small, glossy bright red berries which are usually eaten by birds before the magnificent autumn foliage tints appear (see p104).

Berberis yunnanensis A fairly large deciduous Chinese barberry with a neatly rounded crown silhouette, noted for its vivid autumn colours (see p107), and for the bright red berries which persist on the stout, red-tinged branches after the leaves have fallen.

B. morrisonensis, Mount Morrison barberry A small, compactly branched Taiwanese shrub, also noted for its striking autumn colours (see p93) and large bright red berries which are con-spicuous against the orange-tinted foliage.

B. diaphana A medium-sized deciduous Chinese barberry with stout yellowish branches, also noted for its autumn foliage (see p98) and its bright red berries.

Cotoneaster horizontalis This well-known Chinese shrub is useful for covering a bank or growing against a wall. The foliage turns red early in the autumn and soon falls, leaving the prolific bright red berries.

C. conspicuus **Decorus**   A low-growing and free-berrying form of a wild Tibetan shrub. Very useful as a ground cover or to clothe low walls and banks, this tiny-leaved evergreen becomes covered with strings of bright red berries which the birds leave alone for a long time, so that they often persist until the spring.

C. **Cornubia**   A tall tree-like hybrid cotoneaster, regularly laden during autumn and winter with heavy crops of bright red berries amongst comparatively large evergreen leaves.

C. salicifolius   A tall, graceful Chinese evergreen shrub, and parent of many hybrids and varieties. The prolific crops of small bright red berries last well into winter.

C. glaucophyllus vestitus   A large and vigorous Chinese evergreen bush with a neatly rounded crown silhouette. It is very late to come into flower, and correspondingly late to ripen its bright red berries, which colour around Christmas time and last through the winter.

C. **Hybridus Pendulus**   If grown on its own roots, this popular small evergreen hybrid cotoneaster makes a prostrate bush or low-mounding ground cover. Usually however it is trained or grafted on an upright stem to make a very attractive little weeping tree with glossy, dark green leaves. The long, trailing branches are well covered from late summer onwards with clustered red berries which often last throughout the winter.

C. **John Waterer**   A large semi-evergreen hybrid cotoneaster with long, spreading branches and prolific clusters of bright red berries.

C. bullatus   A sizeable Chinese shrub with large, attractive leaves of a dark metallic green, distinctively crinkle-veined. The long, arching branches are well covered with conspicuous red berries early in the autumn. The wild form *C. bullatus floribundus* has similar but more numerous berries, arranged in neat clusters.

C. adpressus   A dwarf Chinese deciduous cotoneaster with a spreading, prostrate habit, and small dull green leaves which adopt vivid autumn colours (see p99) before falling to leave a long-lasting display of bright red berries.

Skimmia japonica This small Japanese shrub forms neat mounds of leathery aromatic evergreen foliage. It is compact, shade-tolerant and slow-growing, with fragrant white flowers in the spring. There are several clones, some of which are exclusively male, others female, and it is desirable to include both sexes in a group to ensure that the female plants produce a good show of the bright red berries, which persist throughout the winter. Male plants, like the females, produce sweetly scented flowers in spring, and carry the added attraction of red buds during the winter.

Stranvaesia davidiana A vigorous Chinese shrub with erect branches and leathery, dark green foliage like a large evergreen cotoneaster. It is noted for its vivid changes of colour during autumn (see p100), and for clusters of bright red berries which cover the bush and last well into winter, usually ignored by birds.

Sambucus racemosa **Plumosa Aurea,** golden cut-leaved elder A beautiful golden-foliaged cultivar of the red-berried elder from Europe and Asia, slowly growing into a fairly large shrub, with clusters of creamy-white flowers in spring followed by large bunches of brilliant red berries which contrast strongly with the feathery yellow foliage. Unfortunately birds eat the berries greedily.

Ilex aquifolium, common holly A widespread native of Europe and western Asia, this little tree has been associated with Christmas traditions for many centuries. Besides the typical form, several cultivated varieties with variegated foliage are available – most of them excellent as hedges, screening shrubs, or small standard trees. Although these types often bear good crops of berries, the green forms usually provide the most eye-catching contrasts between leaf and berry, especially when used for indoor decoration. Gold and yellow variegations in particular tend to diminish the scarlet tone of the berries. The broad-leaved silver holly, *I. a.* Argentea Marginata, and the strongly pendulous Perry's silver weeping holly, *I. a.* Argentea Pendula, both have white-margined leaves and prolific berries, and both make marvellous small trees for the garden.

As hollies are single-sex plants, it is essential to select a female specimen if berries are required; and a female wild tree needs the proximity of a male holly to ensure a good crop. Most cultivated varieties are clones of either male or female plants. Some of the female clones will berry freely without the necessity for pollination; others need a male plant nearby. All-male clones such as the hedgehog holly, *I. a.* Ferox, and the silver hedgehog holly, *I. a.* Ferox Argentea, obviously will not berry. Some of the best green-leaved varieties of *I. aquifolium* are J. C. van Tol, which produces abundant crops of bright red berries amongst glossy dark green spineless leaves; Pendula, the weeping holly, a narrowly pendulous tree with spiny, dark glossy green leaves and copious berries; and Pyramidalis, a broadly conical plant, eventually a fairly large tree, with glossy bright green, barely spiny leaves, and very heavy crops of bright red berries.

I. × altaclarensis, hybrid holly or Highclere holly   A vigorous tree with comparatively large and not very prickly leaves. The hybrid holly also has several variegated forms, like the popular Golden King which, although beautiful, lacks the dramatic contrast between leaf and berry. The variety *I. × a.* Camelliifolia has spineless, almost camellia-like dark glossy green leaves, and produces a rather sparse display of very large bright red berries.

Sorbus aucuparia, British rowan or mountain ash   In its typical form, one of the most prolific berry-bearers of the genus, but the bright red berries are quickly eaten by birds.

S. × thuringiaca Fastigiata   A useful hybrid rowan which forms a symmetrically compact cone, very popular for street planting. It consistently produces large clusters of bright red, brown-speckled berries.

Arbutus unedo, strawberry tree   A small evergreen European tree with picturesquely shredding bark (see p155), white pitcher-shaped flowers (pink flowers in the case of variety Rubra), and round, dark red strawberry-like fruits, very attractively displayed beneath the dark glossy green foliage in late autumn.

A. × andrachnoides   A hybrid strawberry tree with attractively coloured bark (see p154) and dark red fruits which start to form whilst the white flowers are still on display during late autumn and early winter.

Malus **Red Sentinel**   A small hybrid crabapple with spreading branches and white spring blossom, valued particularly for its large clusters of dark red fruits which persist on the tree during winter.

Crataegus monogyna, European hawthorn   A familiar hedgerow plant in Britain, where it sometimes paints the landscape white with blossom in spring. As free-growing bushes or small, round-crowned trees, hawthorns are usually heavily laden in the autumn with dark red haws, but these are often quickly eaten by birds.

C. laevigata **(syn.** *C. oxyacantha***),** woodland hawthorn   A smaller tree, also native to Britain, and very similar both in blossom and berry.

Viburnum **Oneida**   This American hybrid between two Chinese viburnum species makes a fairly large, erect shrub with dark green deciduous leaves, late-summer flowers and clusters of glossy deep red berries which persist on the dark branches well into winter.

Crimson

Berberis **Buccaneer**   This hybrid deciduous barberry makes an upright bush noted for its autumn foliage colours, and well laden with clusters of large, crimson-red berries which last at least until Christmas.

B. georgei   A fair-sized deciduous Chinese barberry, very attractive in the autumn when large drooping clusters of crimson berries stand out against the tawny foliage.

Sorbus aria, whitebeam   A native British tree with a compactly rounded crown silhouette and attractively two-tone leaves, bright green above and vivid white on the undersides. The autumn foliage (see p87) displays the clusters of deep crimson berries most effectively.

Cotoneaster frigidus   A large, fast-growing Himalayan shrub with wide-spreading branches, sometimes trained as an attractive single-stemmed tree. This and several very similar hybrids bear clusters of heavy crimson berries which often hang on the branches long after the large leaves have fallen.

Rosa villosa, apple rose or downy rose   A fairly large and vigorous wild rose bush native to Britain and Europe, with downy, bluish-green leaves which are fragrant when crushed. The pink flowers of summer are followed early in the autumn by large, apple-shaped, crimson hips.

Skimmia reevesiana   An evergreen Chinese shrub which makes a low mound of dark green foliage, and is useful in partial shade. Unlike most skimmias, the white flowers embody both male and female characteristics and produce dull crimson berries which persist on the bushes through the winter.

Purple

Sorbus folgneri   A small Chinese tree with wide-spreading, grace-fully arching branches and contrastingly two-toned leaves, dark green above and white beneath. White flowers early in the summer are followed by drooping clusters of purplish-red berries, attractive amongst the unusually vivid foliage tints of autumn (see p96).

Gaultheria shallon, shallon or salal   A very vigorous evergreen shrub from North America. A thicket-former which spreads under-ground and sends up waist-high stems bearing broad, leathery, dark green leaves, and small pinkish-white flowers in late spring, followed by clusters of dark purple berries in the autumn.

Viburnum henryi   A fairly large Chinese evergreen shrub with a compact crown of stiffly erect branches and glossy, leathery leaves. The white summer flowers are followed by masses of red berries which darken progressively as autumn advances until there are red, purple and glossy black berries on display simultaneously.

Black

Cotoneaster lucidus   A fairly large Asian shrub which adopts bright autumn leaf colours (see p101), and is unusual among cotoneasters in producing glossy black berries which contrast boldly with the foliage.

Rosa pimpinellifolia (syn. *R. spinosissima*), Scotch briar or burnet rose   This small, densely suckering, thicket-forming shrub rose is often used to make an impenetrable hedge, and has been much hybridised. The abundant white or pink flowers are followed in the autumn by small glossy black hips.

Rhamnus cathartica, common buckthorn A large British and European shrub with glossy dark green deciduous leaves and spiny branches, laden in autumn with masses of glistening black fruits.

R. davurica, Dahurian buckthorn A small Asian tree with glossy deciduous foliage and black berries in the autumn.

R. frangula (syn. Frangula alnus), alder buckthorn A native of Britain and Europe, this large shrub has glossy green deciduous leaves, and berries which are red in late summer, ripening to black for the autumn.

Berberis gagnepainii This small evergreen Chinese barberry forms a dense thicket of erect leafy stems and makes a useful dog-proof hedge, conspicuous in the autumn with clustered black berries, bloomed bluish like a grape.

Blue

Decaisnea fargesii A fairly large deciduous Chinese shrub, its long stems topped with whorled pinnate leaves. The drooping clusters of greenish-yellow flowers in early summer are followed by a great profusion of broad bean-shaped pods of a beautiful gun-metal blue, vivid against the light green foliage and yellow leaf-stalks. The pods ripen late in the autumn and remain on display long after the leaves have fallen.

Symplocos paniculata A twiggy Asian shrub, sometimes becoming a small bushy-crowned tree, with rounded, conspicuously veined deciduous leaves, and clusters of fragrant white flowers in the spring, followed as a rule by a great profusion of berries. Green when they form in late summer, these start turning blue in September and are a vivid shade of blue by mid-October. If the weather is mild they persist after leaf-fall until the New Year, or until the birds eat them.

Clerodendrum trichotomum fargesii A fairly large deciduous Chinese shrub which produces fragrant white flowers in late summer and early autumn, followed by a spectacular display of bright blue berries, each set in a crimson star-like calyx – a very striking combination of colours.

Viburnum davidii A small evergreen mound-forming Chinese shrub, wide spreading and very useful *en masse* for use as ground cover (see p198), with large, narrowly oval, conspicuously veined leaves of a leathery, glossy green. It is a single-sex plant, and one or two males should be included with a group of females to ensure pollination. The bright blue berries on their red stalks make an effective contrast with the dark green foliage, and last well through the winter.

Callicarpa bodinieri A fairly large deciduous Chinese shrub noted for its autumn foliage tints (see p109), and heavily laden at that season with bunches of tiny lilac-purple berries – but more than one bush is needed for effective pollination.

C. bodinieri giraldii A wild regional Chinese form similar in appearance to the type, but usually a somewhat larger shrub, covered with masses of pale lilac berries when planted in groups.

C. japonica, murasaki A small, compact Japanese shrub, with violet-coloured berries which blend beautifully with the pinkish autumn leaves.

Pink

Euonymus europaeus, spindle tree Several varieties of this shapely little European tree are cultivated, but the typical wild form has pink capsules which split in the autumn to reveal orange-scarlet seeds, attractive against the green stems of early winter.

E. yedoensis A large Chinese spindle bush with good autumn foliage colour (see p80), and purplish-pink seed-cases which make an eye-catching combination. The fruits contain bright orange seeds which are partially revealed, though not as conspicuously as with some other spindle species.

Symphoricarpos × ***chenaultii*** **Hancock** A dwarf hybrid snowberry which makes a dense, low thicket, useful beneath trees, and colourful in the autumn when covered with clusters of unusual purplish-lilac berries.

S. orbiculatus, coral berry or Indian currant   This fairly large, densely bushy shrub from the eastern USA bears thick and very prolific clusters of purplish-pink berries.

S. × *doorenbosii* **Erect**   A hybrid Dutch snowberry which grows into a small, compactly upright shrub, and makes an excellent hedge plant; covered in late summer and autumn with clusters of pinkish-lilac berries.

S. × *doorenbosii* **Magic Berry**   A small, compactly spreading cultivar of this hybrid snowberry, heavily laden in autumn with clustered rose-pink berries.

Sorbus poteriifolia   A small Chinese rowan tree with an erect crown of purplish-brown branches, and deep rose-pink berries in large loose clusters which stand out well against the dark green foliage, and remain on display through leaf-fall.

S. **Rose Queen**   This small hybrid rowan tree is partly derived from *S. poteriifolia*, and bears similar but larger bunches of bright pink berries during the autumn.

S. insignis   A small Asian rowan tree with distinctively stout, stiffly upright branches of a dark purplish-brown, conspicuous in the winter when decorated with large clusters of small pink berries, which often persist on the bare branches until spring.

S. vilmorinii   A small Chinese rowan, often a large bushy shrub. It is sometimes seen as an elegantly spreading little tree, its long branches weighed down in autumn and early winter by large drooping clusters of rose-red berries which fade as they ripen to a pale shade of pink.

S. **Pearly King**   This small hybrid rowan tree is partly derived from *S. vilmorinii*, and has similarly slender, spreading branches, made to droop in autumn by large clusters of pale berries, rose-pink at first, ripening to pearly-white tinged with a pink blush.

S. hupehensis   A small Chinese rowan tree with vigorously upright branches – particularly ornamental in the autumn with its bluish-green foliage backing large, loosely drooping clusters of pale pink and white berries in a subtle combination of colours.

Disliked by most birds, the berries often remain on the bare branches well into winter, contrasting strongly with the puce-coloured bark.

White

***Symphoricarpos × doorenbosii* Mother of Pearl**   A small, densely foliaged hybrid snowberry which produces very heavy crops of pearly-white berries charmingly flushed with rose-pink.

Gaultheria miqueliana   A dwarf Japanese evergreen shrub, with glossy bright green leaves and conspicuous white heath-type flowers in midsummer, followed by pale pink or white berries.

G. cuneata   A dwarf Chinese evergreen shrub with aromatic, dark green foliage, white flowers in summer and large white berries in autumn. Like others of the genus, both these plants enjoy a partially shaded site with an acid, peaty soil.

Sorbus prattii   A Chinese rowan (see p101) which usually takes the form of a large shrub with long, slender branches, heavily laden in the autumn with drooping clusters of small pearly-white berries.

S. koehneana   Another small shrubby Chinese rowan, which also bears pearly-white berries in drooping clusters.

S. cashmiriana   This small rowan tree from Kashmir (see p86) is unusual in producing pink flowers in spring, followed by gleaming white berries in loosely drooping clusters, disliked by birds and often persisting on the bare branches throughout the winter.

***Symphoricarpos × doorenbosii* White Hedge**   This cultivar of the Dutch hybrid snowberry makes a very useful dwarf hedge, vigorous and compact, and decorated in late summer and autumn with erect clusters of very prolific small white berries.

***S. rivularis,* common snowberry**   A fairly large thicket-forming shrub from western North America, naturalised in Britain, and often seen in shady woodlands and game coverts. The dense clusters of large, glossy white berries are often ignored by birds, and usually last well through the winter.

Viscum album, mistletoe   This shrub grows as a parasite, usually on apple trees, sometimes on poplar, willow, lime, hawthorn, maple, mountain ash or pear, and occasionally on oak. Rearing mistletoe entails smearing the pulp of crushed berries containing ripe seed on the bark of young shoots on the intended host. Mistletoe berries do not ripen properly until spring, and cut sprays brought into the house for Christmas are rarely suitable for propagation. For this purpose, the berries should be left intact on the tree until March before picking. The pearly-white berries are not popular with birds, and often pass the winter unscathed unless the weather is harsh. A young female mistletoe plant takes four or five years to become properly established on its new host and commence bearing.

9

Winter Ground Cover

Perhaps the best-known ground-covering plants to be seen in the countryside, next to the grasses, are the heathers and heaths which keep a protective mantle of evergreen foliage over the open, windswept acid upland soil. In Britain the true heather, *Calluna vulgaris*, grows wild over extensive tracts of upland moor and lowland heath, which it tints purple with its flowers at the end of summer. More or less all the garden varieties of *Calluna* heathers produce their splendid flowers at this same time, in a concerted display ranging from white through shades of pink to deep purple, but most have beauty throughout the winter too, and several with coloured foliage are outstanding. All like a moist soil, dark with peat, and though they will certainly survive in a modicum of shade, both the heathers and the heaths grow leggy and unattractive if there are tree branches overhead; and fallen autumn leaves allowed to lie on their foliage will soon rot them and cause ugly gaps in the carpet.

Some of the best cultivars of *Calluna vulgaris* with coloured foliage are: Arran Gold, about 45cm (18in) high, the foliage a glowing reddish-gold throughout the year; Aurea, about 30cm (12in) high, with bronzy-gold foliage during the winter; Blazeaway, a very vigorous 45cm (18in) high, the foliage green in summer, glowing dark red in winter; Coccinea, about 23cm (9in) high, an unusual shade of pale greyish-green during summer and winter; Cuprea, about 30cm (12in) high, a yellowish-copper in summer darkening to a bronzy-orange for the winter; Golden Feather, about 45cm (18in) high, golden-yellow in summer and golden-orange in winter; Gold Haze, about 50cm (20in) high, with golden-yellow foliage summer and winter; Inshriach Bronze, about 30cm (12in) high, pale yellow in summer, darkening to bronze in winter; John F. Letts, about 30cm (12in) high, with foliage brightly tinted a pale amber throughout the year; Joy Vanstone, about 40cm (16in) high, with pale yellow foliage in summer, changing to dark orange for the winter; Orange Queen, about 50cm (20in) high, with yellow foliage in summer darkening to orange in winter; Robert Chapman, about

35cm (14in) high, the young foliage pale golden-yellow, darkening to orange and deep red in winter; Silver Queen, about 60cm (2ft) high, with silvery-grey foliage summer and winter; Sir John Charrington, about 40cm (16in) high, gold in summer and tinted crimson in winter; Spitfire, about 25cm (10in) high, with golden-yellow foliage in summer, darkening to bronzy-orange in winter; and Sunset, about 25cm (10in) high, with foliage variegated in shades of green, cream, yellow and orange, appearing golden-yellow from a distance, and ideally sited at the forefront of a design where it can be admired in close-up.

In gardens, heathers and heaths are often accompanied by conifers; they associate so naturally that it is comparatively easy to achieve impressive results when designing layouts for them on a sunny site. Most of the true heathers, however, are too vigorous to associate directly with dwarf or slow-growing conifers. In such mixed arrangements, it will be found that the erica heaths are less likely than calluna to swamp and spoil the vulnerable lower foliage

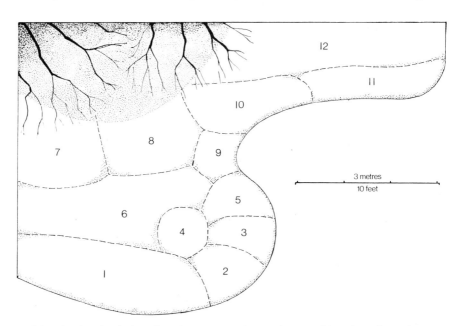

A heather border designed to cheat perspective, and to provide colour throughout the year:

1 *Calluna vulgaris* Joy Vanstone;
2 *Erica cinerea* Apricot Charm;
3 *Erica herbacea* Springwood White;
4 *Erica cinerea* Golden Hue;
5 *Erica herbacea* Winter Beauty;
6 *Calluna vulgaris* Gold Haze;
7 *Erica erigena* Brightness;
8 *Erica erigena* W. T. Rackliff;
9 *Calluna vulgaris* Silver Queen;
10 *Calluna vulgaris* Golden Feather;
11 *Calluna vulgaris* Inshriach Bronze;
12 *Calluna vulgaris* Blazeaway

of these little trees. The numerous ericas available for the garden can provide, between them, virtually a year-round flowering season, and there are several varieties which are acclaimed for their colourful foliage. Most of the winter-flowering heaths belong to the species *Erica herbacea* (syn. *E. carnea*), the mountain heath – a European Alpine native which forms a spreading carpet usually not more than 25cm (10in) high, and is able to grow on alkaline as well as acid soils. Some of the best mid and late winter flowering cultivars of the mountain heath are: Alan Coates, pale pink; Cecilia M. Beale, white; Eileen Porter, carmine-red; Loughrigg, purple; Praecox Rubra, pink; Queen Mary, rose-red; Snow Queen, white; Springwood Pink, pink; Springwood White, white – probably the best-known and most vigorously spreading variety; Startler, pale pink; Vivellii, deep carmine-red; Winter Beauty, bright pink. Other cultivars of *E. herbacea*, usually selected as much for their unusually fine foliage, brightly coloured during the winter, as for their flowers, include Aurea, which has yellow foliage throughout the year; Foxhollow, with yellow foliage in summer darkening in winter to an orangy shade which harmonises very dramatically with the pale pink flowers; Ruby Glow, with foliage of a dark bronze; and Vivellii, already noted for its carmine-red flowers during the winter, which has dark bronzy-red foliage.

The bell-heather, *Erica cinerea*, a native of Europe and Britain, is not so enthusiastic a coloniser as either the mountain heath or the common heather, and usually forms isolated clumps on the drier, sandier parts of the heather moor. But although the soil of its natural habitat may lack acid humus, it shuns the slightest trace of lime. Most of the bell-heather cultivars flower in late summer, but several have unusually fine foliage which is highly coloured during the winter months. These include Golden Drop, about 15cm (6in) high, an excellent, spreading clump-former for hot, dry situations, with coppery-gold foliage in summer, turning tawny-orange in winter; Golden Hue, about 40cm (16in) high, with golden-yellow foliage in summer becoming amber-red in winter; and Apricot Charm, about 15cm (6in) high, the foliage yellow in summer, darkening to a warm apricot for the winter.

Erica erigena (syn. *E. mediterranea*), is a tall native heath of Spain and Portugal, able to grow in limy soils. The best winter-flowering cultivars of the species are: Brightness, usually about 75cm (30in) high, an excellent performer in dry, alkaline soils, with dark purple flowers covering the bush from February onwards through the spring; W. T. Rackliff, about 1m (3ft) high, a vigorous clump-former bearing white flowers which stand out clearly against the dark green foliage; and Golden Dome, a similarly sized sport of W. T. Rackliff, which bears white flowers during winter on foliage that remains a clear golden-yellow throughout the year.

Erica vagans, the Cornish heath, native to south-western Europe, is also to be found on acid heaths in the south-western corner of England. The flowering season is late summer and autumn, but one cultivar which stands out in winter because of its striking colour is Valerie Proudley, about 45cm (18in) high, its foliage a bright yellow which mellows in summer to a pale lime-green.

The cassinias are moderately hardy evergreen shrubs which, at first glance, bear some resemblance to the heathers and heaths. They need a completely unshaded site which need not necessarily have an acid soil, and are better adapted at building up tall, isolated clumps than forming an even carpet. *Cassinia fulvida*, with tiny, crowded, yellowish leaves, is known in its native New Zealand as the golden heather. The so-called silver heather is *C. vauvilliersii albida*, also from New Zealand, at about 1.5m (5ft) high somewhat taller than the golden heather, with hoary-white stems and leaves that bestow a silvery appearance. The tiny flowers, produced in dense clusters during summer, show clearly that these plants are not related to the true heathers and heaths.

More heath-like in appearance, with their fine evergreen foliage, and belonging to the same family, the South American pernettyas create first-class ground cover on sunny, acid sites, and display a mass of coloured berries during the winter (see p169).

Less particular about the soil they grow in, thriving even in difficult chalky types, and needing only a site fully open to the sun, the evergreen shrubby veronicas or hebes make useful front-markers for delineating the edges of a border, and act quite naturally as neutral buffer zones to separate or isolate vigorous spreaders, small herbaceous plants and annual summer bedders. With their interesting foliage texture, they are always valuable during winter. *Hebe* Carl Teschner has closely compact foliage but spreads quite rapidly, forming even mounds of small, bright green leaves, covered in summer with globular clusters of violet flowers; *H. colensoi* Glauca is similarly densely foliaged, in an eye-catching shade of glaucous blue; *H. × franciscana* Blue Gem is one of the hardiest hybrid shrubby veronicas, excellent as a close ground cover in winter, forming neat domes of dull green foliage laden in summer with beautiful blue flowers; *H. pinguifolia* Pagei makes wide-spreading mats of tiny grey leaves, covered with clusters of white flowers in the spring; *H. rakaensis* makes dense and compactly spreading mounds of tiny pale green leaves, first-class as a winter ground cover, with the bonus of numerous small white flowers in summer.

Also suited to a sunny border, but able to grow in partial shade, is *Lonicera pileata*. More typically shrub-like than the hebes, with a foliage cover still dense enough to eliminate weeds, its arching foliage to about 1m (3ft) makes an unusual clump to clothe the gappy stems of tall shrubs. It covers the ground well with tiny leaves, evergreen except in the coldest winters, bright green in spring and summer and dark green in winter. Though one of the honeysuckle genus, the flowers are inconsequential, but it often produces interesting purple berries during late summer.

A more colourful shrubby ground cover could be provided by some of the hybrid firethorns, particularly *Pyracantha* Soleil d'Or, which forms a 1m (3ft) high sprawling thicket of small, dark evergreen leaves on arching, rambling stems. The orange-yellow berries are brighter and more numerous in sun than in shade, although the foliage luxuriates whether shaded or not.

Many of the cotoneasters similarly make ornamental, colourful thickets, though the drawback to this type of ground cover is that perennial weeds tend to be harboured rather than suppressed beneath the rather thin foliage. To be efficient, shrubby ground coverers need to form a light-excluding canopy over the soil, such as might be provided by the prostrate junipers; or conversely to produce short stems so closely crowded together, or rising from a root system so tightly matted, that weeds have no chance to become established.

The Oregon grape, *Mahonia aquifolium*, is a useful multi-purpose plant (see p115) and wiry enough to tolerate hoeing amongst its stems. Less commonly seen in British gardens is the closely related but dwarfer western North American *Mahonia nervosa*, which suckers and spreads vigorously to make a thicket about 35cm (14in) high; it has a handsome, fern-like appearance, with leathery, spine-toothed leaves of a green so dark that they appear almost black. It is particularly effective in the garden when sited in front of contrasting grey or olive-green foliage. It needs a moderately fertile, moist soil, and will not tolerate prolonged periods of drought. The site needs to be lightly shaded, at least in the summer, and a high cover of deciduous branches amid surrounding shelter against cold winter winds would be ideal. If it likes the site it makes an excellent ground cover, producing its clusters of lemon-yellow flowers slightly later in the spring than *M. aquifolium*.

Intermediate between the two classes of ground cover, the Chinese *Viburnum davidii* makes low, spreading mounds of deeply grooved evergreen leaves, with a glossy metallic darkness about them in the winter, when they are often decorated with bright blue berries (see p189). This is a useful dwarf shrub to run between taller evergreen shrubs and small trees, and link them smoothly with the front of the border.

Amongst ground-covering herbaceous perennials, the bergenias, in their way, are every bit as versatile as suckering and spreading shrubs. Most of them are evergreen, many colouring brightly during the winter in shades of red and pink. They always look their best when allowed to form extensive groups or drifts and, to the garden designer, rank amongst the most useful of plants, their rounded leaves ideally suited for delineating and smoothing sharply jutting corners. Angularity on the ground has its equivalent in the profile of certain types of foliage, and shrubs with elongated or pointed leaves are foiled or contrasted very tellingly by bergenias at their feet. The latter have a shape and texture that seems to satisfy the eye, and particularly beautiful effects can be created when the larger-leaved types are used as water plants to edge a pond or stream. The red tints of winter are usually brighter when the leaves are exposed to all available sunlight, and though bergenias will usually grow and spread well beneath the cover of large trees, their spring flowers as well as the foliage tints are comparatively poor in the shade.

Bergenia roots are very near the surface, and provide little competition for the deeper roots of the shrubs around which they grow; but for the same reason they are easily disturbed by surface cultivation and seldom take kindly to hoeing or forking. The best maintenance treatment, apart from spot weeding as required, is a top dressing of bonemeal applied during winter. Some bergenias are hardier than others, one of the best for its winter performance being the Chinese species, *Bergenia delavayi*, with beautiful 23cm (9in) crimson leaves. The Siberian *B. cordifolia* is also hardy and very vigorous. A proportion of its leaves colour well in autumn and winter, and it makes a close, thick ground cover 30cm (12in) or more high. The naturally occurring pink-flowered variety *B. cordifolia purpurea* is similar in leaf, and *B. cordifolia minor*, small and neat at 20cm (8in), is one of the best for leaf colour in autumn and winter. The Himalayan *B. purpurascens* makes an excellent thick cover of

The evergreen bergenias look their best when allowed to form extensive drifts. Their leaves have a very pleasing shape when contrasted with other plants

foliage, 23cm (9in) high, turning a rich bronze in autumn. Also from the Himalayas, *B. schmidtii* spreads vigorously in summer and makes a good 30cm (12in) ground cover; but heavy frosts cut the leaves back, though the plant recovers in the spring. Bergenia hybrids include: Abendglut (Evening Glow), less spreading than most bergenias, with 30cm (12in) rounded leaves which become copper coloured in winter; Ballawley Hybrid, with very hefty 35cm (14in) leaves that turn bronze in the winter; Bressingham Bountiful, which has vigorous, dark green, somewhat pointed 30cm (12in) leaves, subject to cutting back by frost; Distinction, with vigorous 30cm (12in) rounded leaves bronzing slightly in winter; Margery Fish, better known for its spring flowers than for its foliage; Pugsley's Purple, a hardy bergenia that spreads vigorously in full sunlight but does less well in the shade, with 38cm (15in) dark green leaves; and Silberlicht (Silver Light), a vigorous 27cm (11in) plant.

Another spreading herb – a native of eastern North America suitable for acid, peaty soils – *Galax urceolata* makes a light, ankle-deep cover of glossy evergreen leaves, rounded or heart-shaped, often margined with a metallic tawny border which spreads into an overall bronze during winter. It grows well in heavy shade, but the attractive bronze tint is usually more pronounced on open sites. In summer it produces a drift of white flowers like lilies-of-the-valley.

With their looping, trailing shoots, rooting as they spread, the periwinkles make a good close cover of foliage in sunlight or shade. The greater periwinkle, *Vinca major*, at first covers the ground rather sparsely with its glossy, dark evergreen leaves, thickening as it becomes more firmly established. The variegated form *V. major* Variegata is as vigorous as the green type, and eventually makes a fairly close shin-high cover of very attractive foliage. The lesser periwinkle, *V. minor*, makes a fairly dense but much lower evergreen cover of interlacing stems and bright-green leaves. It has several variegated forms, including Aureovariegata with yellow-blotched leaves, and Variegata with creamy-white blotched leaves; and both these and the green types of the greater and lesser periwinkles produce violet-blue or white flowers in spring and summer. Both are widely distributed native plants of Eurasia, which also grow wild or have been long-naturalised in Britain. As woodland plants they are excellent, and their trailing habit suits them for carpeting large areas of semi-woodland garden rather than more formal plots.

A similarly useful but somewhat coarse subject for carpeting beneath trees is *Pachysandra terminalis*, a native of Japan. An evergreen shrubby herb with pale green leaves clustered in rosettes at the tips of 30cm (12in) shoots, it is interesting in February when it produces spikes of greenish-white flowers. The variegated form *P. t.* Variegata is more ornamental, with conspicuous white markings on the leaves, but it does not form so dense a cover.

Euonymus fortunei radicans, an evergreen creeping shrub which typically has dark green leathery leaves, is more usually seen in one of its several variegated forms – chiefly Variegatus, or the particularly brightly coloured cultivar Silver Queen. The leaves of both are mottled in shades of green and creamy-yellow, bordered with cream and often tinged with pink. They make excellent ground coverers (or wall-climbers, if encouraged), and rank amongst the finest of prostrate plants for siting in front of dark yews, thriving on the edge of deep shade and in full sunlight. The plain, dark green type grows more vigorously in heavy shade and makes a thick, weed-excluding cover. A Far Eastern native creeper, it is seldom obtainable from nurseries, but the very common variegated forms tend to revert here and there, and these green shoots can be taken as cuttings, which root very readily.

With their bonus of sweetly scented winter flowers (see pp23, 41), the Christmas boxes, *Sarcococca* species, make an excellent dark, glossy ground cover of willowy evergreen leaves and, like the non-variegated trailing euonymus, are able to tolerate heavy shade. *Sarcococca hookerana digyna*, or *S. h.* Purple Stem, are the most ornamental for the front of a border.

Another prostrate creeping shrub, which makes a particularly attractive dark green carpet of little rounded leaves on trailing shoots, is *Gaultheria procumbens*, the North American partridge berry, also known as the creeping wintergreen. Particularly useful in partially shaded situations on acid, peaty soils beneath trees, it will grow well in more exposed sites too, and the leaves often become tinted bronzy-red in the sunlight. It has the added attraction of bright red berries which are usually on display during autumn and winter. The North American *Mitchella repens* is also sometimes called the partridge berry, and this makes a similar evergreen ground cover for lime-free soil in a shaded site, with wide-spreading mats of tiny, glossy dark green leaves, decorated in autumn with scarlet berries.

The ivies often make first-class ground cover, but they tend to trail rather sparingly instead of thickening into a weed-proof cover and sometimes climb where they are not wanted, smothering the foliage of choice shrubs (see p159). A hybrid between ivy and *Fatsia japonica*, ×*Fatshedera lizei* makes a popular houseplant, often

The hard shield fern, *Polystichum aculeatus* (*opposite*), remains green through the winter and the ruffled variety of the hart's tongue fern, *Asplenium scolopendrium* Crispum (*above*), is one of the most ornamental clump-formers for a deeply shaded site

known as fat-headed Lizzy. This hardy evergreen shrub with large, glossy, leathery, ivy-like lobed leaves, makes a loosely piled mantle of foliage in sunlight or shade, with globular clusters of tiny creamy-white flowers as a bonus in the autumn. It can prove one of the most useful gap-fillers for difficult corners, as it will thrive in the most unpromising sites.

With their happy gift of mixing easily with all types of plant, some of the hardy evergreen ferns make indispensable additions to the shaded garden, and several ferns native to Britain – also to be found wild over much of the world – can be used. Polypody, *Polypodium vulgare*, is amongst the most useful, retaining its vivid green, deeply lobed fronds in the winter, reaching a convenient 30cm (12in), completely hardy and particularly ornamental when rimed with frost. The rhizomes of polypody run just beneath the surface soil, and sometimes spread up the stems of trees, rocks and walls, to create something of a ferny grotto in the garden. The hard shield fern, *Polystichum aculeatum*, also remains green through the winter before opening its new foliage in the spring – a really typical clump-forming fern, with its wide-spreading glossy green fronds. The hart's tongue fern, *Asplenium* (syn. *Phyllitis*) *scolopendrium*, completes a trio of contrasting ferns, for it has leathery strap-like leaves in dark glossy green. It is one of the most ornamental clump-formers for a deeply shaded site. Its ruffled variety, *A. s.* Crispum, is one of the most unusual, and of unique beauty when allowed to arch over a miniature outcrop of rock. Large woodland gardens can often support great banks and drifts of ground-covering ferns in a wide variety; even the smallest garden can take a carefully chosen clump or two, adding something of the atmosphere of wild mountain forest to the domestic winter scene.

10
Autumn and Winter Vistas

In the countryside, the most striking plant associations have usually
happened by chance; and this can happen in the garden too. For
instance, a wild sycamore seedling has been establishing itself
between the stones of a low retaining wall in my garden for the past
couple of years, defying extraction without dislodging the stones; it
has been clipped off to the stump every time somebody with a pair of
secateurs has happened to pass by. In response to this drastic
treatment, the stump has thickened while new shoots have coppiced
repeatedly, until its metabolism has been so disturbed that in early
autumn the final crop of miniaturised leaves is quite unlike the
typical greens and autumnal browns and yellows of its free-growing
parents; the little plant presents a bold splash of vivid orange and
crimson whilst most of the surrounding vegetation is still green. It is
a small patch of colour that many would overlook, but seen from the
windows it is in perfect harmony with the yellowish-grey stones.

Beyond the retaining wall, rather more by design than fortune, a
stag's-horn sumach, *Rhus typhina*, has been planted near a hybrid
laburnum, *Laburnum × watereri* Vossii, and even as early as September the leaves of these two small trees are demonstrating how
harmoniously they co-operate. On the laburnum, little clusters of
leaves at the branch-tips have already started to turn a warm yellow,
bright enough to give the fleeting impression that it is in bloom for a
second time – like the autumn-flowering *Laburnum anagyroides*
Autumnale. Along the undersides of the sturdy sumach branches the
drooping, pointed leaves have already turned orange in anticipation
of the brilliant scarlet-orange motley to come. The immediate visual
effect is the traditional match of orange and lemon – a theme which
can be repeated over and over in a large garden, with numerous
subtle variations of colour to prevent any possibility of monotony.

At ground-level, the herbaceous *Sedum spectabile* in rose-pink
and the taller *S.* Autumn Joy in crimson are arranged behind the
autumn crocus *Colchicum speciosum* – a perfect colour-blend, and
not only of flowers, for the naked white stem of the colchicum

reiterates the smooth glaucous fleshiness of the sedum leaves and stems. This is a corner intended almost exclusively for autumn viewing; in spring and early summer it presents little more than a weed-excluding thicket of greenery which will look after itself whilst one's attention is drawn elsewhere.

Summer runs into autumn with a colourful display from several shrubs such as the hardy late-flowering broom, *Cytisus nigricans*, a waist-high bush of erect, downy stems, unusual in a largely spring-flowering genus for producing its long clusters of yellow flowers so late. The yellow of its flowers is intensified into a dramatic focal point if planted in front of the purple smoke tree, *Cotinus coggygria* Royal Purple, trained as a low-foliaged bush, its leaves daily turning a lighter shade of crimson before finally falling for the winter.

The visual effect of any association will depend to a large extent on the habit and growth-style of the plants, and on the texture of their foliage as well as the colour of their flowers. Yellow and blue make a classic colour-blend, but the final effect varies greatly with different plants even when the flower colour is the same. *Potentilla fruticosa* and the related hybrid potentillas must rank amongst the longest-flowering of shrubs, their yellow buttercup-sized flowers often on display from spring until November; with their soft greyish-green, finely textured foliage spreading into smooth mounds, they manage to give a very mellow overall impression. The primrose-yellow hybrid *Potentilla* Elizabeth looks all the more beautiful when the late-flowering and easily grown Chinese gentian *Gentiana sino-ornata* has been arranged in a drift at its base to form a miniature thicket of vivid-blue trumpets rising from a dark carpet of little bright green pointed leaves. For an utterly different but equally charming effect in the autumn, the vigorous Chinese clematis *Clematis rehderana* can be trained on a fence or trellis-frame at the back of a narrow border, fronted with a bed of the herbaceous leadwort, *Ceratostigma plumbaginoides*. The latter creeps with thin, wiry black stems into the lowest trails of the clematis foliage, and the clear blue flowers near ground-level harmonise perfectly with the long-stalked clusters of sweetly scented yellow bells.

Earlier, at the first inkling of autumn, a similar association of colours is to be seen where a lavender cotton, *Santolina chamaecyparissus*, is fronted by a group of *Crocus speciosus* Aitchisonii. Here the blend is balanced differently, the crocus a pale, pastel shade of blue, the santolina flowers a bright lemon-yellow – the combination made more interesting by the feathery silver-grey foliage of this southern European shrub. Used in a different way the lavender cotton, like all grey- and silver-foliaged plants, associates very happily with pink flowers. It is an association more appropriate to spring and summer than autumn or winter; but in this case it can involve the autumn-flowering cyclamens, *Cyclamen europaeum* and *C. hederifolium*. Yellow sometimes clashes with pink, and the association is improved by clipping the lavender cotton as soon as flower-buds appear, both to save the plant's energy and to thicken the foliage into an evenly dense, silvery mound.

Planning to use autumn leaves as a colour-foil for seasonal flowers is a chancy arrangement, as foliage tints are transient and the timing never sure; but some of the more reliable autumn-colouring shrubs can be used in this way. *Lindera benzoin*, the North American spice bush, for example, infallibly turns a warm amber-yellow over a prolonged season, and this coloured phase can be matched with a drift of autumn-flowering crocuses such as *Crocus salzmannii*, which has large, yellow-throated flowers of a clear lilac-purple.

Still on the theme of yellow and blue, the autumn-flowering *Clematis tangutica* combines its bright yellow nodding lanterns perfectly with blue flowers, and its follow-up, the wholly companionable fluffy seedheads, lend an interesting textural quality to any group. Michaelmas daisies can be associated with this clematis, the many different varieties of varying heights and hues carrying the flowering season through until November. With a shrubby thicket that includes small-leaved evergreen cotoneasters and pyracanthas, *C. tangutica* can be planted so as to intermingle naturally. In a sunny border the resultant profusion of yellow and blue flowers, silky seedheads and dark evergreen foliage with masses of red and orange berries will be an arresting sight.

The Chinese and Japanese callicarpas are known to flower and fruit best when three or four are grouped together, when their massed purple berries make a memorable display against the bright autumn-foliage tints of purple and mauve. The effect is intensified and prolonged if elements of silver, or grey, and orange are added to the scheme. The wide-spreading branches of *Elaeagnus umbellata*, which has soft-green foliage backed with silver, are heavily laden at this season with orange berries; the sea buckthorn, *Hippophae rhamnoides*, which loses its silvery-grey foliage without colouring, also becomes laden in the autumn with masses of orange-yellow berries. Both these large shrubs are excellent associates for the callicarpas. The sea buckthorn blends well with several other shrubs which colour brightly in the autumn, notably the winged spindle tree *Euonymus alatus* – an association to be seen in a sunny glade at

Westonbirt Arboretum, where the silver and orange-yellow of the former combines with the intense mauve and pink of the spindle tree to make a memorable scene.

The most vivid autumn-foliage plants, such as *Acer nikoense* and *Parrotia persica*, sometimes seem too distinctive of colour to associate satisfactorily, for their brilliance outdoes that of most others. But some of the vines, though spectacular, are very well suited for a partnership with less colourful trees. The large-leaved *Vitis coignetiae*, or *V. wilsonae* which has comparatively small, woolly leaves, both turn a deep, glowing red at this season and provide a fascinating combination with silver birches. It is not always easy to establish climbers on trees because competition at ground-level is fierce, and birch roots tend in any case to be matted near the surface. In the past this problem has been overcome by using an open-topped planting container, a simple wooden box, which will assist the vine to develop roots until it is strong enough to compete on equal terms, and will safely rot away after a year or two in the soil. The vine leaves tend to persist into early winter, hugging the white stems long after the yellow birch leaves have fallen, and give the impression of unseasonal maypoles draped with crimson ribbon.

The blue cedar, *Cedrus atlantica glauca*, is always easy to place in a garden as it associates happily with most colours and textures. But it comes into its own most tellingly when a yellow-foliaged tree is nearby, whether this colour is a permanent, evergreen feature, a summer variegation, or a fleeting phase of autumn. The witch hazels make excellent escorts for the blue cedar, both in their warm yellow autumn foliage and when decked with winter flowers, and several of the maples also associate well in the autumn, particularly the yellow-leaved *Acer rufinerve*, *A. saccharum* and *A. platanoides*. In winter, birches always look good near a blue cedar, and the European silver birch is generally used. But more striking, though less often seen, is a partnership with the North American yellow birch, *Betula lutea*, its glossy amber-yellow stems intensifying the warm blueness of the cedar foliage.

Silver birches always look right when accompanying plants similar to those of their native heath – though they may have originated many thousands of miles apart. The European heathers and heaths are always well partnered by a grove of these trees, and so are the South American pernettyas, their colourful berries matching the winter flowers and coloured foliage of the heaths, and complementing the blank pallor of the birch bark.

One of the most versatile of the heather family is the mountain heath *Erica herbacea*, and the popular varieties Springwood White and Springwood Pink can be used in numerous beautiful arrangements designed to be seen from close at hand. Springwood White associates particularly well with orange and buff stems, and makes a perfect carpet to front the flaking paperbark maple *Acer griseum* – a combination which can be seen at the Royal Horticultural Society's gardens at Wisley. Springwood Pink combines charmingly with a collection of winter-flowering hellebores, the greenish yellow and mauve shades of their flowers matching the pale pink and dark green of the heath. Both cultivars perform efficiently as a carpet beneath small trees, provided the shade cover is not too heavy in summer, and fallen autumn leaves are removed quickly before any damage is done. Springwood Pink in particular will foil some of the witch hazels admirably, and the colour combination is outstanding in the case of the orange-flowered *Hamamelis × intermedia* Jelena. Darker-flowered varieties of *Erica herbacea* such as *E. h.* Vivellii which has dark carmine flowers and bronzy-red foliage, make a wonderful carpet to front the pale yellow flowered *Hamamelis mollis* Pallida. *H. japonica flavopurpurascens* is a wild variety of the Japanese witch hazel, seldom used in living plant arrangements; but its flowers glow wine-red when touched by winter sunshine, and make the perfect accompaniment to a drift of the tall, yellow-foliaged heather, *Calluna vulgaris* Gold Haze.

Witch hazels display their flowers most clearly against a dark background, but they themselves flower best and have a better shape when there is no shade overhead. These large shrubs adopt a spreading, high-arching habit, and their ideal site is to the forefront of taller deciduous trees which have dark evergreens such as yews and hollies planted beneath their canopy. The foreground needs to remain clear and sunny – a place for ground-covering plants, where the witch hazels can spread their flowering twigs. On a south-facing site both they and the ground coverers at their feet will then be open to the maximum of light and warmth.

There are, of course, several flowers which associate marvellously with witch hazels, including all the winter-flowering crocuses; and a drift of bright yellow winter aconites beneath a grove of *Hamamelis mollis* is a simple scene, but one hard to beat. A spectacular arrangement often seen in large gardens and arboreta consists of a clump of the winter-flowering *Rhododendron mucronulatum* sited often directly beneath the witch hazels. It is a combination of colours too intense during its comparatively brief season of glory to differentiate clearly between the distinctive varieties of witch hazel, but it is truly outstanding while the rhododendron flowers last.

Garrya elliptica is a single-sexed plant, the male being noteworthy as a winter evergreen, with leathery greyish-green leaves and numerous long, slender, grey-green catkins on display in January and February – a very unusual colour and texture that lends itself to a variety of effects by siting other plants of complementary or contrasting colour and shape nearby. In cold districts, garrya is sometimes planted in the angle of a warm wall, and here it may be fronted with the purple *Iris unguicularis* to give a sunny, lavender-like effect. But one of the most dramatic arrangements seen recently in a large garden near the English south coast included the tall, purple cabbage tree from New Zealand, *Cordyline australis* Atro-purpurea, with two or three garryas grouped closely against the stem, and a clump of the red-variegated New Zealand flax, *Phormium tenax* Dazzler, planted at the front. A somewhat similar colour scheme, suitable for less mild districts and giving a quite different cold-temperate rather than sub-tropical effect, can be obtained by fronting *Garrya elliptica* James Roof or the hybrid Pat Ballard with a drift of crimson-leaved bergenias emerging from overhead shade – a sunny arrangement backed by a dark corner or a large group of tall shrubs.

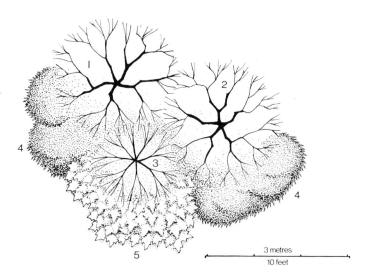

3 metres
10 feet

A very effective combination of pink and white winter flowers, thicketing stems and variegated foliage:

1 *Prunus subhirtella* Autumnalis;
2 *Prunus subhirtella* Autumnalis Rosea;
3 *Viburnum farreri*;
4 *Sarcococca hookerana digyna* Purple Stem;
5 *Hedera colchica* Dentata Variegata

The autumn cherry, *Prunus subhirtella* Autumnalis, flowers over winter whenever the weather permits, often showing colour for a full four months; and a simple but very effective combination can be made by planting the white and the pink forms together. The pink-budded, fragrant white flowers of *Viburnum farreri* have a similar habit, opening as the weather permits at any time through the winter months, and this deciduous shrub makes an excellent companion for the trees. An impressive arrangement has been made in this way by adding a ground cover of the Chinese Christmas box *Sarcococca hookerana digyna* Purple Stem, the whole group fronted with the ornamental large-leaved ivy *Hedera colchica* Dentata Variegata.

The pink form of Father David's peach, *Prunus davidiana* Rubra, opens its blush-pink flowers in January and February, and this little tree is greatly enhanced if given a ground-planting of winter crocuses – *Crocus sieberi* interspersed amongst a wide-spreading drift of *C. tomasinianus*, the latter to include both the typical species and the darker and later-flowered variety, *C. t.* Whitewell Purple. *Daphne mezereum*, the European mezereon with fragrant madder-pink flowers, though tricky in some gardens, is one of the best winter-flowering shrubs to associate with bulbous plants. It, too, looks marvellous amid a drift of *Crocus tomasinianus*, or when surrounded by a group of the deep-blue *Iris histrioides* and the rather later-flowered *I. reticulata*.

The theme of pink and purple is as valuable in the garden as the combination of yellow and blue, and it can sometimes be repro-duced to subtle effect in shades of evergreen foliage. A sheltered, unshaded bank, or a heather garden which features coloured foliage, is made more interesting in winter with the addition of a small clump of *Cleyera japonica*, or a single specimen of the rather hardier *C. fortunei*, their wide-spreading leathery foliage being tinged with shades of pink and red. Ideally they would be fronted by *Berberis × stenophylla* Pink Pearl, which has arching branches with small leaves mottled pink and cream; an outstanding combination when sited next to a drift of the purple-flowered *Erica herbacea* Loughrigg.

Of more transient beauty, the Glastonbury thorn of legend – *Crataegus monogyna* Biflora, a variety of the common British hawthorn – often comes into flower in January, and its clusters of fragrant little white flowers, especially if the lower branches sweep near to the ground, can be framed with pinkish-purple if a generous planting of the early-flowering primulas *Primula juliae* and *P.* Wanda is made beneath and beyond the canopy. These dainty carpet-forming primulas will thrive in light shade, and the thorn bush is best trained as a low semi-standard or a short-stemmed bush.

The coloured-bark willows and dogwoods are easily satisfied as to soil provided their site is open to the sun, and they do particularly well in moist, water-side gardens. Coppiced, almost any of them makes a perfect background for a bank of heathers or heaths, and the effect on a sunny winter day can be as colourful as any lavish floral vista of spring and summer. Particularly useful near heathers, the scarlet and the golden willows, *Salix alba* Chermesina and *S. a.* Vitellina, and the violet willow *S. daphnoides* with its purple-white bloom, all need to be cut to within 20–25cm (8–10in) of the ground in March or April to maintain a regular display of compact, vividly coloured stems. In the case of dogwoods, the bright red of the Westonbirt dogwood, *Cornus alba* Sibirica, makes a bold splash when combined with the pale greenish-yellow of the yellow dogwood, *C. stolonifera* Flaviramea, and these similarly need coppicing annually wherever they are intended to retain a symmetrical silhouette. In wild surroundings, a stooling on alternate years is usually sufficient, or an annual thinning to maintain a succession of colourful shoots. When yellow and red dogwoods are associated in a group, the yellow forms quickly outgrow the red, so more of the latter should be planted to hold the balance. To provide a little extra summer colour in a group of dogwoods, variegated forms such as the yellow-splashed *C. alba* Spaethii, or the white-mottled *C. a.* Elegantissima, can be interspersed without loss of winter effect, for both have conspicuous plum-crimson bark; but their coppicing in the spring should be less severe.

The very popular golden weeping willow, *Salix* × *chrysocoma*, is frequently planted as a central feature in its own right; often in gardens too small for it, where regular curtailing is necessary to keep it within bounds. In rather roomier plots its beauty is enhanced if given a background of evergreens and silver birches: one of the most telling of tree groups planted in a fairly large garden included the golden weeping willow with a clump of three silver birches and a solitary blue evergreen. In this case it was *Chamaecyparis lawsoniana* Pembury Blue, but any blue-foliaged conifer of comparable size, such as *Cedrus atlantica glauca*, would contribute equally to a magnificent visual effect.

One of the most memorable willow-planting schemes on a patch of rough ground includes a group of coppiced scarlet willows, *Salix alba* Chermesina, interplanted with the two violet willows, *S. irrorata* and *S. daphnoides*, the stools underplanted with a drift of the very early spring-flowering Siberian squill, *Scilla sibirica*. The bright bluish-purple of the flowers brings out the purple tints of the white-bloomed violet willows and accentuates their orange catkins; but the job of stooling has to be postponed until late April to derive the full effect and see the squill flowers through.

An unusual combination in the theme of crimson and pink involves two deciduous shrubs – *Lonicera setifera*, a deciduous Chinese bush honeysuckle which bears clusters of sweetly fragrant pink-and-white trumpet flowers in the winter, and a Chinese shrub rose, *Rosa omeiensis pteracantha*. The latter loses its hips early, with the leaves, but it has strangely large, translucent, flat triangular thorns which glow crimson as the winter sun filters through them. Planted closely together, these two shrubs make a thicket which can be clipped to shape in the spring rather than pruned. Thus one achieves an unusual patch of prickly foliage in the summer, covered with large cross-shaped white roses in May and June, followed by very decorative red and yellow hips in the autumn, and a fascinating winter display.

The winter jasmine, *Jasminum nudiflorum*, is perhaps the best-known winter-flowering shrub, finding a valued place in numerous gardens. With its long flowering season, it manages to associate equally well with the last of the autumn- and the earliest of the spring-flowering crocuses. Trained on a south or west-facing wall with crocuses, or *Iris unguicularis*, planted at its feet, the winter jasmine will repeat the familiar combination of yellow and blue to good effect; but when grown as a scrambling, thicket-forming shrub to be clipped back in the spring, it can be allowed to intermingle with *Mahonia aquifolium* to make an unusual all-yellow and dark green display. A range of yellow shades on their own can be effective when viewed against a dull winter background, and the tiny massed flowers of the Cornelian cherry, *Cornus mas*, will be enlivened if they overlook a carpet of winter aconites or, in a wilder garden, a drift of celandines – an impressive late winter or early spring scene that will flourish most brightly beneath a cover of deciduous tree branches high overhead.

A succession of subtle colour can be provided with a group of unusual shrubs which will be happiest when backed by a warm wall. To the rear of the group, taking advantage of the sheltering wall, *Abeliophyllum distichum* opens its sweetly scented pinkish-white forsythia-like flowers in the New Year, closely followed by its neighbour, *Correa backhousiana*, which produces clusters of lime-green bells on interestingly two-toned evergreen foliage. *Stachyurus praecox*, a fairly large shrub, bears slender clusters of tiny, pale-yellow bells to carry the succession of unusual flowers into spring. Adjacent shrubs include two forsythias – the very early *Forsythia giraldiana*, which has pale yellow flowers displayed on buff twigs, and *F. suspensa* Nymans, with large primrose-yellow flowers on purplish twigs. The whole group is interspersed and fronted with a broad drift of *Anemone blanda* in one of its deep blue varieties, such as *A. b. atrocoerulea*. As an alternative to the blue anemones, bergenias could be used, for instance the purple-leaved *Bergenia delavayi* or *B. cordifolia minor* or, if the vista is wide, the very large-leaved *B.* Ballawley Hybrid to add a touch of bronze to the scene. The flowering season will be prolonged until summer with their pink and purple flowers.

The planting plan opposite was designed for a sandy loam rich in humus, and mildly acid at pH6. It is important not to add lime, as many of the plants included in the design will not tolerate it.

Autumn and winter vistas in a small garden:
  1 *Malus* Golden Hornet;
  2 *Betula albo-sinensis septentrionalis*;
  3 *Prunus serrula*;
  4 *Acer palmatum* Senkaki;
  5 *Prunus pseudocerasus* Cantabrigiensis;
  6 *Yucca flaccida* Golden Sword;
  7 *Orixa japonica*;
  8 *Disanthus cercidifolius*;
  9 *Lindera benzoin*;
10 *Salix alba* Vitellina;
11 *Cornus alba* Sibirica;
12 *Pernettya mucronata* Pink Pearl and White Pearl;
13 *Rhododendron*, spring and summer flowering evergreen hybrids;
14 *Rhododendron dauricum* Midwinter;
15 *Ceanothus* Autumnal Blue;
16 *Rhododendron*, spring-flowering deciduous azalea hybrids;
17 *Ceratostigma willmottianum*;
18 *Potentilla* Elizabeth;
19 *Cyrilla racemiflora*;
20 *Eucryphia glutinosa*;
21 *Chaenomeles × superba* Crimson and Gold;
22 *Hydrangea serrata* Preziosa;
23 *Viburnum × burkwoodii*;
24 *Hydrangea serrata* Bluebird;
25 *Abeliophyllum distichum*;
26 *Camellia × williamsii*;
27 *Rhododendron mucronulatum*;
  a *Crocus speciosus, C. elwesii, C. kotschyanus*, and *Gentiana sino-ornata*;
  b *Hosta* species and varieties;
  c *Crocus tomasinianus, C. biflorus*, and *Galanthus* species and varieties;
  d Herbaceous perennials;
  e Ferns;
  f *Crocus imperati*, and *Eranthis hyemalis*;
  g Annuals

13

15

14

3

4

2

16

c

20

17

b

18

19

11

21

12

22

10

d

9

23

24

1

5

a

e

25

27

8

f

g

26

7

Kitchen herbs

6

N

a

3 metres

10 feet

Although this garden is quite tiny, the plan draws its inspiration from features belonging naturally to a woodland glade, and makes full use of broad-leaved, largely deciduous plants to provide a green and restful place throughout spring and summer, enlivened now and again with a bold splash of colour. On this basis it contains elements one might expect to find in far larger gardens: in particular it makes use of interacting vegetational layers – the crowns of small trees partially covering the bushes, small shrubs, bulbs and herbs which are able to flourish in light summer shade – and provides for the inclusion of colour and interest during autumn and winter. These factors add up to a labour-saving garden, in which there should be time to relax during the summer, and a place of beauty designed to be admired through the house windows and enjoyed for the constantly changing succession of colours and forms which appear throughout the year. There is room for temporary planting while the trees and shrubs are growing to their full size.

As autumn arrives the garden is still well furnished with flowers, apart from the beds which have been set aside for annuals and herbaceous perennials. Here, the dwarf varieties of Michaelmas daisy and other asters could well play an important part and, of course, in making use of a basic design such as this there will usually be odd pockets which can also be filled with flowering plants. The glorious flowers of the eucryphia, like white cups filled with golden stamens, are still lavishly displayed on their tall, bushy spire, and the evergreen hybrid Californian lilac, *Ceanothus* Autumnal Blue, is spectacular with profuse clusters of magnificent deep blue flowers. Both shrubs have been in bloom almost since midsummer, but there is often a gap between early and late flowerers. With this woodland style of planting scheme, particularly in moist climatic regions and where the soil is peaty and acid, discriminating gardeners sometimes like to establish the perennial flame nasturtium, or Scotch creeper, here and there at the back of the border. By doing this they extend the early flowering season, for example of the azaleas, by allowing the nasturtium to scramble over them – which it will do without causing harm – or creep amongst such shrubs as orixa and disanthus, which are not noted for their flowers, and give them a splash of bright scarlet during high summer.

Bounding the lawn at the far end, the shrubby leadwort is still flowering in dark sky-blue, the colour blending beautifully with the primrose-yellow flowers of *Potentilla* Elizabeth nearby. The foliage of these two shrubs also relates well, the softly bristling outline and rather metallic texture of the former combining harmoniously with the soft sage green of the latter. The association of yellow and blue is a theme repeated here and there several times through the seasons. Half-sheltered by the crabapple, *Disanthus cercidifolius* has started to change colour already, its foliage taking on a golden-yellow glow as the opening scene of a show that should last throughout autumn. Both this shrub and the yellow-striped *Yucca flaccida* Golden Sword have the autumn-flowering *Gentiana sino-ornata* planted in front and around them to form a dazzling patch in the foreground of almost kingfisher-blue. This easily grown gentian could also be introduced to the company of the potentilla if space is available, for their colours would complement each other perfectly at this season.

Along the shadier boundary of the garden, by the pathside, the hydrangeas are in full flower, twin varieties of *Hydrangea serrata* at their best now in the early autumn. With the dark, glossy evergreen foliage of the viburnum between them to give the appearance of stability, the two cultivars balance one another perfectly in vigour, size and colour. Preziosa, with purplish-red stems (an attractive feature later on when the leaves have fallen), has prolific flowers of bright pink which slowly turn in the autumn to a dusky red-purple; Bluebird, amongst the bluest of hydrangeas, in this acid type of soil produces dark-blue flowers without any hint of the mildly artificial effect that characterises some of the hortensia cultivars; and if grown on alkaline soils the flowers will be purple. In the case of both varieties the flowers last well into autumn, and remain ornamental even when they finally fade.

Following the lead of disanthus, the leaves of shrubs and trees start to change colour in sequence. Near the window viewpoint, a few of the rounded, aromatic leaves of the orixa are amongst the earliest, turning a pale primrose or lemon-yellow which seems to intensify the vivid blue of the autumn-flowering gentians now reaching their peak, and a colour that also sets off the blue, lilac and pale purple tones of the first autumn-flowering crocuses. These are not to be confused with colchicums, the 'autumn crocuses' which flower naked in the autumn and produce their somewhat ungainly leaves in the spring. *Crocus speciosus* is the darkest, a rich violet-blue; the fragrant *C. elwesii* is lilac-blue with a dark purple stripe on the petals; *C. kotschyanus* is a paler shade of lilac, each petal marked at the base with bright orange.

By October the inconspicuously tiny purple flowers of the disanthus are out, and the yellowing leaves of this relative of the witch hazels are now well stained and splashed with crimson. The two prunus trees have started to change colour too, their foliage losing chlorophyll here and there – the small Chinese cherry *Prunus serrula* the brighter of the two, with a few leaves tinted orange and scarlet amongst the yellows and browns. The birch foliage too has yellowed, especially at the branch-tips, where leaves of near cadmium-yellow are conspicuous amongst the light green; and more noticeably the coral-bark maple has a pronounced cast of golden-yellow evenly developed over its bronze-green foliage, with a brighter flush of daffodil on the uppermost parts bathed by the sun. *Malus* Golden Hornet has not yet changed colour, but the small clustered crabapples have been ripe for some time, and are bright golden-yellow now amongst the dark green leaves.

At ground-level, the foliage of the shrubby leadwort has started to redden at the tips as the blue flowers fade – a combination of two colours which do not really complement one another, for their association darkens them, and the blue element is lost. The group of *Pernettya mucronata* fronting the dogwood is as dark-foliaged as ever, but these hardy South American heaths are well covered with colourful berries in luminous pink and white. Attractive in spring when laden with white heather-like flowers, now in the autumn they are even more conspicuous, and make a very bright display. Cultivation, as already mentioned, must take into account the fact that they are one-sex plants.

Strong colour is still to be seen on the right flank of the garden too, beyond the dark green camellia where the similarly dark and glossy evergreen viburnum acts as a central focal point for its neighbouring hydrangeas; Bluebird is as clear a blue as ever, and the bright pink of Preziosa is only now darkening to a glowing reddish-purple, well in keeping with the other seasonal flowers.

As autumn foliage colours develop more strongly with the approach of November, it becomes evident that the trees selected for this garden, though they are not native British species, exemplify a typically British autumn with the subtlety of their hues. In a small garden such as this, to choose trees for their autumnal brilliance might well overdo the effect. A large garden can accommodate bright colours at tree-top level, but here, like the woodland glade on which this design is modelled, the dominant tone of the uppermost canopy is most effectively a tawny russet and yellow, illuminated from below with a splash of brilliance in the underbrush. The beauty of these small trees can be greatly enhanced by their surroundings: the Golden Hornet crabapple is an unassuming little tree on its own, save for its white spring blossom and spectacular crop of golden apples, but the warm rusty-brown of its autumn foliage associates

Malus Golden Hornet mounts an autumn display of bright golden yellow crabapples amongst dark green leaves

perfectly with the dark chrome-yellow of the taller birch tree to the rear. The Cambridge cherry in the foreground is typical of its genus in autumn coloration, displaying a rusty tawny-orange, laced with streaks and splashes of scarlet and yellow. Now in mid-autumn it stands over a small island of greenery, for though the winter-flowering rhododendrons beneath are deciduous, at present they are still in leaf, as bright a green as their accompanying ferns. The first really cold spell of early winter will cause most of these rhododendron leaves to fall, bringing the evergreen ferns more fully into view.

Besides the birch, the willowy leaves of the graceful little Chinese cherry, *Prunus serrula*, have finally turned a clear tawny-orange, almost identical in colour to its glistening, peeling stem, forming a dark combination of orange and lemon reflected palely by the birch bark contrasted strongly now against the dark evergreen background of rhododendrons.

Now that the last of the ceanothus flowers have faded, the rounded, glossy leaves of this evergreen Californian lilac form an attractively two-toned background. Flanking the ceanothus, the broad dome of the coral-bark maple is a pure shade of pale daffodil-yellow – a warm colour strengthened by glimpses of the pink twigs beneath the leaves. To the right of this striking feature, as though to frame and emphasise it, the eucryphia rises in a narrow column of flaming orange-red, and at its feet the twin waist-high evergreen cyrillas have turned dusky crimson – a colour reflected darkly by the shrubby plumbagos nearby. Beyond them, and partly beneath the maple, the deciduous azaleas have adopted a motley of yellows and reds to link the group harmoniously: brick-red, scarlet and crimson tones uppermost where the sun can reach the foliage, cool yellow and pale orange in the shade beneath.

To the forefront of the garden, at the left, the orixa bush has blanched completely to the palest shade of lemon-yellow, one of the lightest of autumn leaf colours, and itself an interesting focal point. In close-up it is accentuated rather than contrasted by the Golden Sword yucca with its subtly blending green and yellow stripes, and it takes the rich violet-blue of a drift of *Crocus speciosus* at their feet really to bring these quiet colours to life. The citrine leaves of the orixa, however, are almost exactly similar in size and shape to those of the disanthus immediately behind it, coloured now a bright crimson, so that as seen from the window the whole clump of bushes seems to be changing colour, with crimson tints glowing through the topmost pale leaves. This is an effect sometimes admired in spring when a drift of crimson 'Welsh' primroses runs through a bank of the common sort, but the colour rises in this case from ground-level to intermingle with the russet foliage of the crabapple, where a tinge of crimson touches the lowest golden-yellow fruits. A continuation of this pot-pourri effect occurs beyond the crabapple stem, where the warm golden-amber of the spice bush strikes exactly the right note to blend the group into harmony.

The spice bush itself is an outstandingly effective companion at this season to the two coppiced shrubs beyond – the Westonbirt dogwood and the partially concealed golden willow – for their leaf colours blend perfectly. The golden willow – silvery lemon-yellow, visible now through the lowest crown branches of the crab and backed directly by the dark evergreen foliage of the spring- and summer-flowering rhododendrons – and the dogwood – light purple, tinged with a greenish shade of crimson, its topmost sprays reaching into the chrome-yellow of the birch crown – intermingle in a colour blend that would please the eye of an artist.

At the lawn edge, fronting the birch and the little Chinese cherry tree, the hosta leaves now form a drift of rich cadmium-yellow, as though the spice bush and the birch had combined to spread the colours of their foliage along the ground. Together, the bright yellow leaves frame a fascinating area of comparative darkness beneath the foliage canopy against the dark green backing of rhododendrons, though the intensity of shade beyond the hostas is not in fact great, and birches in general have unusually light canopies.

The amount of light reaching the ground through overhead leaves is a matter calling for careful management where standard trees overshadow shrubs and small plants in the garden. The main trees within this layout – crabapple, small Chinese cherry, Cambridge cherry, Chinese birch and coral-bark maple – should all be full standards, preferably already trained at the time of planting, with 1.5–2m (5–6ft) clear length of stem below the lowest branches. Although usually sold in bush form or as a young feathered tree, the coral-bark maple in particular needs to be standard-trained so that the lowest crown branches give clearance enough for the shed, and allow the path to pass beneath; the slender branches may, however, be allowed to sweep down at the front if they show a tendency to do so, forming a curtain of attractive twigs and foliage.

A garden shed is sometimes an eyesore, and in a design such as this, if the tree foliage is too sparse or high to camouflage it, interesting effects can be obtained by planting one of the creepers or vines against the wall, or on a conveniently placed section of trellis. Several suitable climbers are renowned for their magnificent autumn tints, and any one of them would glow very warmly from beneath the clear yellow foliage of the maple. Some consideration, however, should be given to the size of leaf, depending on the visual effect required. A particularly large-leaved vine such as *Vitis coignetiae*, while magnificent in every other respect, and easy to keep within reasonably compact bounds by periodically pinching out the growth buds, would by the sheer size of its leaves tend to create a false perspective and make a normal-sized shed seem to dwindle to the scale of a doll's house. For this reason, the small-leaved Virginia creeper would be a suitable choice, and preferable to the larger-leaved Boston ivy: it would help perpetuate the illusion of distance which the elongated curves of the lawn edge and the planned gradation of shrubs are intended to convey.

Amongst the other standard trees in the garden, *Prunus serrula*, although small, and positioned as it is partially beneath the crown of the taller birch, needs early standard treatment to at least a clear 1.5m (5ft), both to allow the full beauty of its winter bark to develop and to give fair latitude to the fine, willowy foliage. On many trees, low branches can be left for several years before being removed in easy stages, but on *P. serrula* this method tends to produce large, dark, warty calluses which mar the clarity of smoothly gleaming orange-mahogany bark that should be revealed at leaf-fall. The standard stem-height offers a great advantage in the spring, too, allowing the white flowers to hang in long clusters from the spreading branches, and later forms a drapery of drooping, willowy foliage framing the late spring- and summer-flowering rhododendrons.

Early training of standard trees in any case lessens the eventual need for heavy pruning, although within a small garden such as this it will certainly be necessary to remove a few branches sooner or later. Whole-branch pruning is by far the most appropriate method of keeping the ground-level shade light enough for the subsidiary shrubs and herbs to thrive. Nothing looks more out of place in a garden of informal design than brutally shortened branches and clipped twigs; they spoil the natural appearance of the vista as a whole, and rob each tree of its individual grace, besides originating dead stumps and dangerous fungal infection. Should the shade beneath a tree become too dense for its associate plants, or its crown too widespread, one or more whole branches can be selected for removal, making a careful choice based on inspection from all angles.

Shrubs, of course, may need pruning back in the traditional manner, and this can often be done without marring their natural appearance; but even here the removal of an entire branch is often preferable to clipping. Most shrubs grown for their foliage lend themselves to the technique of pinching out the growing buds occasionally so that each shoot either forks or checks, growth slows, and the density of the crown thickens. The overall tendency thus is to thin the upper canopy and thicken the lower one, creating by degrees a healthy, well-balanced, weed-free garden community.

Most of the shrubs planted here against the eastern boundary can be kept within bounds by pinching out the growth buds periodically in spring and summer, as can the orixa, the disanthus and the lindera. The eucryphia will certainly need curtailing from time to time to keep it within bounds, to prevent the shapely columnar silhouette giving way to middle-aged spread, and to keep the pathway clear. This can be achieved by encouraging new shoots to grow upwards rather than outwards, pruning if necessary to an appropriately positioned bud, and removing any branch that threatens to protrude at right angles and so spoil the symmetry of this beautiful little shrubby tree.

As the leaves fall and are collected to make the rich leaf mould that this type of garden appreciates – there is room for a wire-netting frame beneath the maple, or behind the rhododendrons – the scene is scarcely less colourful than it was during the growing season. The early winter sunshine slanting through the crown twigs of the Cambridge cherry strikes the huge yellow berries clustered on the crabtree and, although some of these are falling, the main display should last another month or more. Beyond are the smaller but equally eye-catching berries of the pernettya, in pearly-white and milky-pink, thickly clustered on their low evergreen bushes. A few crimson leaves still linger on the disanthus; otherwise the foliage has fallen from this group of shrubs, and through the loose tracery of their dark twigs comes a glimpse of vivid colour from the coppiced shoots beyond. The sun's rays intensify the egg-yolk yellow of the golden willow shading into the brilliant crimson-red of the Westonbirt dogwood, but their glowing tones are filtered by the twigs, so that the effect is refined and unobtrusive. This bright spot in the garden will be even brighter when snow lies on the ground, but now it is the dark backing of evergreen rhododendron foliage that brings the colours into high relief. Coppicing of these two shrubs should be carried out in March as the first buds of spring are beginning to break, removing the old stems almost to the tree-like stumps which develop over the years. This treatment, so unlike the normal pruning of shrubs, will produce the vigorous young shoots needed to provide the following winter's display, and incidentally clear a way for the earliest spring-flowering rhododendrons to be seen unobscured. At present the dark, almost black-green of these background evergreens also serves to highlight the bark of the Chinese birch, pale but glowing beneath its dark tracery of twigs – a warm orange, bloomed with grey and tinged with copper and pink in thinly layered, peeling patterns.

There are many birches with beautiful, light-toned bark, and several of these would suit this situation. *Betula albo-sinensis septentrionalis* is one of the finest foreign birches; some of the American species would be equally beautiful; and there are few to match the British silver birch *Betula pendula*. A tree which forks low down, or a small multi-stemmed group – perhaps two or three planted closely together, if space allows – will augment the atmosphere of a woodland glade, provided all the stems have been trained as clean standards, and not allowed to develop feathered side-branches. The dark mass of slender, reddish-black birch twigs contrasts strongly with the bold, sweeping lines of the neighbouring cherry, its stem and limbs glowing in buff and orange, the spreading branches carrying the eye towards the domed coral-bark maple.

When the upper crown of the coral-bark maple is bathed in winter sunshine, the inspiration for its popular name becomes very clear, for every twig is alight and glowing with a colour not often seen in the plant world – an exquisite coral-pink – within a dark frame formed by the evergreen Californian lilac, the dense column of the eucryphia, and the crimson-green foliage of the cyrilla bushes positioned at its foot.

The hosta leaves which formed a rich yellow base to the dark hollow beneath birch and cherry soon disappear, barely leaving the tips of their dormant buds visible above ground. A carelessly wielded hoe could cause them great harm at this time, and if they need moving they can be difficult to find but, like some bulbous plants, hostas have no objection to being transplanted whilst in full leaf during late summer. The great advantage of their deciduous habit is to clear the way and open a vista for winter-flowering bulbs, especially the snowdrops which are now in full bloom beneath the birch, in company with the delicate-looking but perfectly hardy winter-flowering crocuses – *Crocus tomasinianus* in pale lavender and silvery-grey making a strangely luminous colour scheme, or its variety Whitewell Purple, which is deep crimson-purple; also the much rarer and consequently more expensive *C. biflorus*, a dark glossy purple, or some of its white varieties which are more commonly seen and cheaper to buy. They and the snowdrops benefit from the dark background of rhododendron leaves which allows them to stand out brightly even on dull days, especially if they are arranged in pure groups and drifts, closely planted rather than scattered, so that their colours can be clearly seen even at a distance.

Immediately beyond the snowdrops, January sees the first of the rhododendrons breaking into flower. This is *Rhododendron daur-*

icum Midwinter, which has bright phlox-purple flowers in ones and twos, or small clusters, their colour forming an interesting link between the purple, silver and white of the small flowers covering the ground, the pale orange-buff of the birch stem, and the bright orange-brown of the Chinese cherry. This winter-flowering rhododendron is sometimes deciduous when grown in the open, but here it is so well sheltered by the surrounding plants that it retains its dark green leaves in all but the very coldest weather.

As the season advances, though still gripped by winter, there is always something new and colourful to be seen in the garden, with flowers appearing now on the right-hand side of the lawn as though to balance the bulbs and sunlit stems on the left. In the foreground the Cambridge cherry opens its buds in a charming display of pink flowers, their fragrance filling the air on still February days. And beneath its picturesquely rugged stem, *Rhododendron mucronulatum* has formed a double column of luminous mauve flowers, less bright a shade of purple than the other winter-flowering rhododendron, Midwinter, which by now has almost finished its display, but lustrous and irresistibly eye-catching in its unusual setting. To the front of this twin mound of flowers lies a drift of sheer harmony: a bank of *Crocus imperati* in pale purple and buff is nearing the completion of its display as the winter aconites emerge fully in their bright buttercup-yellow, to remain on show until the spring. These small bulbs are eminently suitable for planting beneath deciduous trees and shrubs to provide a winter display, because their habit of growth is exactly adapted to that situation, and they will shed their leaves and lapse into dormancy as soon as the tree foliage develops and the overhead shade increases in the spring.

Seen through the lower branches of the Cambridge cherry and beyond the flowering rhododendron, the chaenomeles opens its first scattered blooms of the season with a splash of crimson; whilst the evergreen hybrid viburnum half-way along the pathside – its foliage still a dark, glossy green – is already covered with the sweetly fragrant white flowers which will remain on show with the 'japonica', until spring is almost through. Sheltered and half hidden behind the dark evergreen camellia, the deciduous *Abeliophyllum distichum* has also opened its scented flowers, strung along naked twigs like a white forsythia, flushed overall with a pale creamy-pink. *Camellia* Anticipation flowers intermittently at any time between November and May – a strangely exotic sight when snow lies on the ground, or caps the camellia bush itself above the huge deep pink flowers and contrastingly dark glossy leaves.

Index